NONAVERSIVE INTERVENTION
FOR BEHAVIOR PROBLEMS

NONAVERSIVE INTERVENTION FOR BEHAVIOR PROBLEMS
A Manual for
Home and Community

by

LUANNA H. MEYER, Ph.D.
Professor
Division of Special Education and Rehabilitation
Syracuse University

and

IAN M. EVANS, Ph.D.
Professor
Department of Psychology
State University of New York, Binghamton

·P·A·U·L·H·
BROOKES
PUBLISHING Cº

Baltimore • London • Toronto • Sydney

Paul H. Brookes Publishing Co.
Post Office Box 10624
Baltimore, Maryland 21285-0624

Typeset by Brushwood Graphics, Baltimore, Maryland.
Manufactured in the United States of America by
Thomson-Shore, Inc., Dexter, Michigan.

Library of Congress Cataloging-in-Publication Data
Meyer, Luanna H.
   Nonaversive intervention for behavior problems.

   Bibliography: p.
   Includes index.
   1. Mentally handicapped—Care—United States. 2. Mentally
handicapped—Rehabilitation—United States. 3. Behavior
modification I. Evans, Ian M. II. Title.
HV3006.A4M49 1989   362.3'8'0973   88-34151
ISBN 1-55766-018-2

CONTENTS

PREFACE

Several years ago, we published a manual that is in many ways quite similar to this one. Our book *An Educative Approach to Behavior Problems: A Practical Decision Model for Interventions with Severely Handicapped Learners* (Evans & Meyer, 1985) represented the cumulative knowledge of our respective professional careers as we had been challenged to assist schools attempting to provide good educational services to children and youth who had developmental disabilities and behavior problems as well. In our efforts to frame an *educative* approach to the difficulties faced by these students and their schools, we emphasized the importance of more neutral terms such as *excess behavior* rather than *behavior problems*, along with a recognition that such behaviors were, above all, purposeful for the individuals in almost all cases.

We also argued that, for the most part, the presence of such behaviors reflected needs to acquire other, more appropriate and socially acceptable skills and access to new activities, and that it was illogical to approach these *needs* by continuing to try to decrease and eliminate behavior. In contrast to a model that assumes the client already has positive alternatives and needs only to be motivated to use them, we assumed that people with developmental disabilities did not already have more positive options in their repertoires. First, they needed to learn such alternatives, then, as these were acquired and becoming effective for the student, we could expect that student's "behavior problems" to decline proportionately. Schools and educational systems provide perhaps the ideal environment and context for such an approach, both because they are fundamentally educative in purpose and because legislation has established a prior framework of program quality within which these ideas could function.

The material in this manual represents both a further application and an extension of our earlier work. Obviously, challenging behaviors are not confined to school settings, nor are they confined to the school years. Services for persons with severe developmental disabilities should and do exist in nonschool settings and across the life span, and to some extent there are requirements for individualized programming in work and other settings for adults that parallel the school's Individualized Education Program (IEP) structure. Thus, if there is both a similar need (excess behavior) and an opportunity to meet that need systematically (service systems and individualized program planning), a manual written for nonschool settings and perhaps focusing primarily on adults might have adopted a structure very similar to our book for schools. We have deliberately chosen not to write this manual in that way.

This guide is not focused on writing intervention programs for people as much as it attempts to apply the principles and practices of learning and behavior theory to daily living at home, work, and in the community. Just as it would be a mistake, we think, to imagine that families would be improved by the training of typical parents to write IEPs for their children or collect and analyze data to decide how much nurturance each child should receive on any given day, it would be both incorrect and probably futile to expect natural environments for people with disabilities to similarly professionalize daily life and relationships. In fact, we have come to believe that many of our problems in "service delivery" emanate from our continued inability to provide services and support to people that do not compromise their rights to a reasonable way of life in the process. Similarly, professional and paraprofessional staff cannot and should not relate to adults—no matter how severe their disabilities—in the same manner as teachers might relate to their students. Services and supports to adults (and children as well) must reflect recognition of those individuals' rights to self-determination. Our own experiences with families, consumer groups such as People First, and individual discussions with people with disabilities have perhaps taught us the most. We want to emphasize this because the differences between this manual and our earlier one represent an important progression in our thinking as well as the obvious need to design something that would be useful for slightly different purposes. The major theme of this manual is the design of behavioral programs that do not compromise the individual's lifestyle and dignity.

We are indebted to many individuals for the ideas and materials included here. The suggestions and strategies are based as much as possible on empirical data, and we have cited the published sources for these in a representative way. The systematic research of these colleagues provides the building blocks for an integrated, more systems-oriented approach. The specific examples and descriptions of individuals exhibiting challenging behaviors are all based on our personal clinical experience—learning is always a reciprocal encounter, and we are grateful to these individuals for such opportunities. As the basis for a training manual, each chapter and component of this book has been used dozens of times in various statewide and regional training efforts. We are grateful to those experienced and thoughtful service personnel who have planned and attended those workshops and validated our strategies.

Dedicated with love and admiration to
our parents,
Jean and Robert Evans and Betty and George Meyer,
for raising their children with
affection, acceptance, kindness, a sense of fairness,
and, always, respect.

NONAVERSIVE INTERVENTION
FOR BEHAVIOR PROBLEMS

Introduction

This manual is about nonaversive intervention strategies for dealing with problem behavior in home and community environments. It has been written primarily for use by professional and paraprofessional staff working with persons with developmental disabilities in residences, employment and employment training settings, community recreation programs, and other general community environments.

Full implementation of the concepts and practices described in the manual would require that persons with disabilities and severe behavior problems have access to family-scale community living, supported work, normalized leisure lifestyles, meaningful social interactions with family and friends, and participate fully in the variety of community experiences taken for granted by persons who do not have disabilities. For such access to occur, of course, the existing service delivery system would need to be redefined as *services* and *supports* for enabling community participation. This would be quite different from the predominant contemporary pattern whereby such services and supports invariably are tied to increasingly restrictive and atypical placements. The authors do not consider full community participation an unrealistic goal and can, in fact, point to entire regions and states across the United States where persons with even the most severe disabilities receive the kinds of services and supports that are needed to make this goal a reality. Until then, in many other parts of the United States where services have not yet evolved into networks of support for community integration, various

components of the approach described in this manual nevertheless can be implemented. Therefore, this manual must be equally useful to personnel working in group homes, sheltered workshops, day treatment programs, and even developmental centers. In fact, if used as intended, the approaches described here should provide concrete examples of how agencies can begin to update services and increase options for clients regardless of the various fiscal and administrative obstacles that might otherwise be viewed as insurmountable.

The manual is directed to meeting the needs of persons who exhibit problematic behavior and represent a range of developmental disabilities, including levels of mental retardation from mild to profound, physical disabilities, sensory impairments, autism, and so forth. It also is intended to address the life span, with particular attention to adults in all environments and children in nonschool environments. The manual is not primarily designed for use by professional educators in educational programs, and use of the companion volume, *An Educative Approach to Behavior Problems* (Evans & Meyer, 1985), is recommended to address the needs of children and youth with severe behavior problems in school settings. That volume is specifically designed to incorporate school-specific processes such as educational service delivery patterns and requirements such as the individualized education program (IEP). This manual does not assume, nor does it emphasize, an initial focus on an individualized intervention plan, but instead concentrates on approaches to address individualized needs in a variety of formal and informal circumstances. Agencies that require formal individualized program plans for adults should find it easy to blend these approaches with those requirements, but the manual also emphasizes generic environmental and situational modifications that can and should be made affecting entire programs and possibly the experiences of all clients. Throughout the guide, however, the emphasis is on the individual who displays serious and perhaps long-standing behavior problems that are a challenge to their environments, programs, and the people with whom they interact.

HOW TO USE THE MANUAL

This manual has been written so that it can be used by an instructor to guide training of other professionals or paraprofessional direct service staff. It can also be available to staff for reviewing information and practicing particular procedures on an ongoing basis. Thus, paraprofessional assistants in a group home or job coaches providing training and support in employment situations should be able to read and use the various sections to address particular needs they might have. The authors' recommendation is that the material here be presented initially through a systematic staff training effort, combining both knowledge level and direct experience training. Thus, the most critical concepts and specific strategies are described in detail sufficient for a staff person to acquire at least a conceptual understanding of the issues and the approach.

Knowledge level training might begin with a series of short meetings held with direct service staff to cover the material contained in each unit, and such meetings could be scheduled to coordinate with an agency's pattern of in-service training. For example, one agency might arrange for a block of in-service training days for new

employees, so that it would be possible to include much of the material in the manual at the outset of employment. Another agency might arrange briefer time periods on a periodic basis for in-service training, so that the material in the manual would have to be covered in a larger number of shorter sessions. This is likely to be a useful training agenda when the agency utilizes a set schedule of in-service units or time periods for training of a mixed group of employees, including those newly hired and others with varying amounts of time in their jobs. In fact, because much of the material in this manual will be new even to most professional staff, flexibility is encouraged in the delivery of training to meet the needs of various agencies and staff in those agencies. Throughout training, the manual itself should be readily available to staff, with the expectation that each staff member individually review the material included in any in-service presentations.

In addition to the knowledge level training implied by in-service sessions and individual study of the manual, the authors believe that *direct experience training* involving supervised practice of specific processes and procedures is essential. This includes at least two types of experiences. First, the decision process outlined in this approach assumes that direct service staff will become involved and play an important role in reviewing, analyzing, and planning programs. Since they are most likely to know the individual best, they have invaluable information to contribute to this process. Thus, initial training should include actual team planning meetings (Chapter 5, this volume) and problem-solving sessions on behalf of specific clients. Second, staff will need to have various strategies demonstrated for them, be given opportunities to practice those strategies and receive immediate feedback on their performance, and will appreciate having specific examples pointed out in the relevant environment. Supervisory psychological personnel must seek to provide practice opportunities as follow-up to any information presented initially in a workshop format.

WHAT THE APPROACH IN THIS MANUAL REPRESENTS

The principles and practices presented in this manual represent both a broad range of lifestyle issues as well as specific instructional and behavioral strategies for addressing excess behavior. Most readers will know that the predominant approach to remediate behavior problems has been behavior modification, involving the systematic application of laws of behavior, principles of learning, and the individualized modification of contingencies to reduce and, it is hoped, eliminate undesirable behavior. Behavior modification techniques are widely known and are both described in many textbooks and incorporated as core components of graduate training in fields such as school psychology, clinical psychology, and special education and rehabilitation. Similarly, approaches to the design of active treatment plans for persons with disabilities across the life span have involved knowledge of instructional strategies from disciplines such as special education, communication science, and vocational rehabilitation to remediate skill deficits in adaptive behavior, communication, and vocational performance.

Nevertheless, this manual has been written so that basic concepts and practices from behavior therapy and special education, for example, are explained sufficiently for the reader so that prior knowledge in these areas is not necessary for successful use of a nonaversive approach to behavior problems. This is for two reasons. First, many of the staff working in the kinds of settings for which this manual is designed are not graduates of professional training programs and thus are unlikely to

have prior formal training in behavior modification, communication training, and so forth. The authors do build on the personal knowledge that people generally have about the lawfulness of behavior and how people learn but do not assume familiarity with more complicated applications of such principles. Second, the approach described here represents a broader, more systems-oriented perspective toward addressing the needs of persons with serious behavior problems than would be the case from any of these disciplinary or theoretical perspectives alone. Attention to creating the circumstances that support a meaningful lifestyle and encourage normalized patterns of social experiences goes beyond the specific manipulations of antecedents and consequences that have become the focus of behavior modification efforts, for example. This means that the authors have attempted to integrate both behavior therapy and educative principles and practices into the context of appropriate lifestyles and community integration concerns. Thus, this book is not about the design of isolated behavioral interventions to address specific target behaviors. Instead, this manual refers to both clinical strategies and social values that influence the design of environments and influence clinical decision-making—not just techniques that emphasize behavioral control.

Nonaversive approaches to addressing excess behaviors are, in a very real sense, a product of both the professional developments and social values of the 1980s. They represent a synthesis of advances in technological and clinical sophistication—knowledge regarding effective practices—and the dignity and respect that should be accorded persons with disabilities as reflected in social attitudes. Programs should foster and enhance the opportunities available to persons with disabilities, rather than being available at the expense of normalized living and the chance to participate fully in society. Thus, this manual is about techniques—but it is also about lifestyles.

WHY NONAVERSIVE BEHAVIOR INTERVENTIONS ARE A GOOD IDEA

In essence, the authors believe that the reasons for using nonaversive approaches reflect attention to both empirical validity and social validity. There is a great deal of evidence that nonaversive approaches have equal or greater empirical validity than the alternatives. They are more likely to result in significant and lasting behavior changes that are reflective of worthwhile outcomes. Also, nonaversive interventions are more acceptable and feasible than the alternatives. They have greater social validity than aversive techniques. These broad issues of validity can be broken down further into at least six specific reasons why there is a critical need to develop and implement nonaversive behavior intervention strategies to remediate behavior problems:

1. Nonaversive strategies are *humane*. The nonaversive approach is values-based, and the authors believe that service delivery systems must strive continuously to incorporate critical quality-of-life components into programs. The approach outlined in this manual is consistent with the rights of individuals to both effective treatment and freedom from harm. It is supportive of the kind of lifestyle to which citizens with disabilities are entitled.

2. Nonaversive strategies are *effective*. The authors maintain that there are effective nonaversive strategies available to address even the most severe behavior problems and that limitations in using them are far more likely to reflect limitations in organizing resources in certain ways than actual limitations in the knowledge base. In fact, if the criterion of effectiveness encompasses

long-term behavior change that is maintained in a variety of normalized and integrated community environments, educative approaches are by definition more effective than aversive ones.

3. Nonaversive strategies are *socially valid*. It has been and will become increasingly difficult to utilize aversive strategies—which are not acceptable for use on nondisabled people—with people who have disabilities. Both the professional community (e.g., the American Association on Mental Retardation [AAMR], the Association for Retarded Citizens/United States [ARC/US], the National Association of School Psychologists [NASP], The Association for Persons with Severe Handicaps [TASH]) and the public have questioned the social acceptability of certain procedures; this has included placing legislative restrictions on their use. If persons with disabilities are indeed part of society, their rights should be and will become appropriately parallel to those of others to preclude the use of procedures that society would judge to be bizarre, cruel, and unduly harsh.

4. Nonaversive strategies are *legal*. Corporal punishment has long been barred from use in many public school environments (typically by state statute) and, as mentioned under number 3, certain procedures are restricted by both legislation and regulation in various settings. Nonaversive strategies, which are educative, are obviously legal.

5. Nonaversive strategies are *practical*. Certain punishment strategies and aversives reported in the literature clearly are not applicable for use in typical settings. Regardless of the level of training and supervision of staff, the use of such procedures clearly presents a risk to both the person with a

behavior problem and staff using the procedures. In contrast, educative and nonaversive approaches would be reflected in the overall program of an agency on a day-to-day basis. Many involve rearrangements of environmental conditions and most do not require complex behavior management programs. As persons with disabilities rightfully move from restrictive and specialized segregated environments into the community, the strategies must be practical in those environments.

6. Nonaversive strategies will contribute to *positive attitudes* toward persons with disabilities. Whenever bizarre things are done to persons with disabilities that would simply be unacceptable for use with others, something is communicated to the general public. Rather than there being an emphasis on the similarities (including equal protections) between persons with disabilities and nondisabled persons, the message is that someone is so deviant that the practices used for them must be equally deviant. Each time persons are treated differently, the notion that they are indeed different is reinforced.

THE CRITICAL COMPONENTS OF A NONAVERSIVE APPROACH

Following is a brief summary pointing out several features that are essential for a nonaversive, educative approach to work most effectively.

1. The approach involves *decision-making*, not a potpourri of techniques from which staff pick and choose, matching intervention with behavior. Behaviors and interventions may differ greatly across individuals, which is tied in to the second point.

2. The approach is *individualized* and is *accountable* to the individual. Efforts are focused on using personal information to tailor the intervention to meet the individual's needs, and then to design an intervention process so that someone on staff will be accountable for its integrity.

3. The approach is *values-based.* An educative approach will not work in a purely custodial environment where there is neither evidence of habilitative programming and active treatment, nor consideration for normalized lifestyles and the dignity of the individual. The approach is built on a foundation of appropriate environments, habilitative programming, and respect for persons with disabilities.

4. The approach emphasizes *active treatment goals* for the individual as a strategy to address behavior problems, rather than deceleration goals to decrease behavior problems. Behavioral repertoires should be increased through an educative approach, and the authors believe that a behavior will diminish to the extent that the individual has another behavior to take its place.

5. The approach emphasizes *quality-of-life.* Sometimes people exhibit behavior problems because of the absence of certain important aspects in their lives. These include friendships and other personal relationships, novel and interesting environments, intrinsically enjoyable activities and tasks, and self-determination through meaningful personal goals and choices. People probably would not exhibit certain problems if their lives contained those experiences. Thus, evaluation of successful outcomes must include evidence of participation in meaningful lifestyles.

6. The approach emphasizes *local expertise and problem-solving.* The authors feel that given certain fundamental principles and practices, agency staff can successfully address nearly all individual needs. Rather than believing

in the existence of techniques that are so specialized that only a few highly qualified experts know them, one can argue that, in fact, there are good problem-solvers in any agency and region. To utilize local expertise effectively requires that staff be given more flexibility to develop the necessary skills, particularly through group problem-solving experiences. An educative, nonaversive approach can be implemented without being dependent on outside expertise that may not always be available.

LOOKING AT RELEVANT ADMINISTRATIVE ISSUES

Finally, there are certain components of a nonaversive approach that will have an impact on administrative policies and practices for the agency. These include at least the following:

1. *Team problem-solving* Staff must have the opportunity to problem-solve as a group. This requires meeting times for staff who invariably work different shifts and would otherwise be unable to share ideas and information.
2. *Accountability* Regardless of staffing ratios, one professional must be identified in a case manager type of role for a manageable number of client programs. This is different from the more typical designation of a supervisory professional (e.g., the chief psychologist) as the person responsible for all programs, which often involves signing off on dozens of plans and programs.
3. *Program and environmental flexibility* Programs written for individual clients may require that the client experience some novelty in his or her daily schedule and purposefulness in activities and tasks. Something as ap-

parently simple as going out for a walk can become enormously complex under certain agency circumstances. Staff will need to negotiate some degree of program flexibility for clients.
4. *Relationships* Persons with disabilities must have experiences in meaningful relationships with other individuals. As a minimal step toward this goal, agency staff should strive to identify two direct service workers who will assume a more personal interest in each client. There should be someone who likes the client and communicates that caring to him or her on a daily basis.
5. *Control* Clients need to have more control over their lives and the decisions that traditionally have been made *for* them. These include relatively straightforward decisions such as what to wear, what time to go to bed at night, or when to get up on a Saturday morning, as well as more complicated decisions such as choice of a roommate. These decisions are seldom made by clients, though they could and should be. To allow this to happen and to teach clients to make such decisions, agencies will have to incorporate client choice into the delivery of services.
6. *Resources* Unfortunately, the service system often does not make resources available until after something else has failed. The availability of special help, staffing, and services may be tied to segregated and restrictive environments and even a request to utilize aversives. Instead, resources need to become available early on as a behavior problem emerges, not after it has reached crisis proportions. While prevention does impose more immediate use of resources, it also reduces the need for far more expensive and restrictive services over the long term.

7. *Heterogeneous groupings* Agencies are only beginning to experiment with grouping clients differently. Clients should be grouped with people they like and in a manner that complements their abilities and disabilities. The creation of behavior management groups and nonambulatory units prevents staff from providing habilitative conditions to the persons in such environments. Heterogeneous groups allow staff far greater flexibility in designing positive environments and activities.

SUMMARY

It is hoped that this brief overview of the principles and practices involved in non-aversive interventions for behavior problems provides a clear and honest picture of the intent and purposes of this manual. The actual content of the manual represents a bringing together of some of the best ideas and most promising practices that have been developed by many professionals from various disciplines, so the authors want to emphasize that these ideas and practices are not somehow our own. At the same time, we claim full responsibility for our own personal and professional biases that inevitably influence the nature of the approaches and strategies recommended here, and these biases are stated explicitly throughout. This does not mean that the authors claim credit for having originated attention to such important considerations as normalized lifestyles, community integration, and behavioral interventions which are both effective and consistent with respect for the dignity of the individual. These are, of course, long overdue, increasingly emphasized goals that should appropriately guide the design of services and supports for persons with disabilities. The authors do intend, however, that this manual be a serious effort to integrate at-tention to such issues into any effort to remediate the behavior problems of individuals. It is, therefore, both conceptual and, we hope, practical.

The chapters that follow present information and procedures relevant to each of the components of the nonaversive approach to meeting the needs of persons with challenging behaviors. Chapter 1 elaborates on the advantages and disadvantages of particular perspectives on remediating behavior problems. This chapter also argues the values base for a nonaversive approach, with a detailed rationale to support the use of procedures that have been proven effective as well as socially valid.

Chapter 2 provides a brief summary of the literature on behavior problems in persons with developmental disabilities and identifies intervention research efforts that reflect attention to the kinds of variables that influence behavior. These include contingencies, the responses available to the individual (i.e., what skills and behaviors already exist in his or her repertoire), cognitions about environmental events, and the extent to which a person's lifestyle and environmental opportunities support clinically significant behavior change. This chapter is not a comprehensive review, nor do the authors regard its content as essential material for either an initial training workshop or prerequisite reading. In fact, it is recommended that the chapter be regarded as a background for those who are interested in or wish to have more information regarding the empirical evidence supporting the validity of a nonaversive perspective.

Chapter 3 describes a lifestyle perspective that should be the starting point for both the overall design of service delivery systems and the development of individualized treatment plans. Concepts such as normalization, integration, and even quality-of-life are not helpful as guiding principles unless they can be operationalized.

The most difficult challenge is to operationalize such principles without at the same time involving professionals in every aspect of the lives of people with disabilities so that any degree of autonomy or the right to be a person becomes impossible.

Chapters 4–9 detail the specific steps and procedures for designing effective and nonaversive interventions for problematic behavior. In Chapter 4, a team process for decision-making to identify individual intervention priorities is described. Assessment procedures also are detailed to provide the information needed for designing interventions most likely to be effective. Chapter 5 presents an overview of an intervention planning process, including format and procedures to guide the preparation of the treatment plan and the evaluation of its effects. The planning process represents a synthesis of recommended best practices in lifestyle planning, teaming, instructional strategies, behavioral change techniques, and monitoring and evaluation procedures. Chapters 6–9 deal with general and specific intervention strategies to allow meaningful behavior change, including ecological modifications (Chapter 6); teaching specific replacement skills as alternatives to problem behavior (Chapter 7); and both environmental and client-focused mechanisms to support behavior that is adaptive, appropriate, and contributes to a client's ability to exercise self-control under conditions and in response to expectations that are reasonable and fair (Chapter 8).

Chapter 9 provides a framework for evaluation, where the emphasis is not only on change in referral behavior but also the documentation of multiple outcomes reflecting the environmental and social relevance of behavior change. At the back of the manual is an appendix with blank copies of all the forms utilized in examples throughout the manual. Readers may duplicate these forms for use in their own programs.

The intent throughout this manual is to reinforce some new directions for behavior management in adult community services. The authors believe that a new generation of behavior therapy, special education, vocational rehabilitation, and other content specialties and disciplines must merge with one another conceptually and integrate practices into service delivery systems as well as normalized lifestyle support networks. The historically narrow focus in research on the behavior of one individual must give way to an expanded consideration of effective formal systems change strategies and more invisible clinical and professional contributions to informal social support networks for people with disabilities. Just as children must synthesize their separate experiences in reading, math, social studies, health, recreation, and so forth into the career, leisure and social lifestyle, and home and family of adults, so the various disciplines and professionals should be ready by now to work together to narrow the gap between what is known to be possible and what actually now exists for people with disabilities.

chapter

1

The Educative Approach to Behavior Problems

OVERVIEW

This chapter introduces the challenges presented by behavior problems and describes alternative approaches to meeting the needs of persons with developmental disabilities who display such excess behaviors. First, the traditional eliminative approach is described, and arguments are presented regarding the validity and practicality of this approach. An alternative educative approach—the focus of the manual—is then introduced and four assumptions behind this model are summarized.

The purpose of this chapter is to present a rationale for a nonaversive and educative approach to addressing excess behaviors. The authors believe that it is critical to begin training with an open and candid presentation of a values-based perspective that is both effective and consistent with contemporary positive programming. This chapter would thus provide the content for the initial training session.

TRAINEE OBJECTIVES

At the completion of this unit, participant trainees will be able to:

1. Give several examples of problem behavior typical of nondisabled persons, including examples of self-injurious behavior, aggression, disruption, and stereotypic behavior.
2. Recognize examples of the eliminative approach to behavior problems and describe the disadvantages of that approach.
3. Describe the components of an educative approach to behavior problems, including four assumptions behind the model.
4. Critique the accuracy of images presented to the general public through media coverage of behavior problems in persons with disabilities.
5. Summarize the positions taken by various major advocacy organizations

in the United States regarding the use of aversives with persons who have disabilities.

INTRODUCTION

This manual is about making decisions concerning behavior problems displayed by persons with developmental disabilities in various community and residential settings. The presence of behavior problems in these individuals causes considerable demands to be made on any environment. A person's behavior problems such as aggression toward other persons—others with disabilities as well as toward staff and family members—can seriously interfere with attempts to include the person in activities and environments on a daily basis. Aggression can also, of course, be dangerous to others. Disruptive behavior such as tantrums, yelling, clothes ripping, and throwing objects are difficult to handle in any situation. Behaviors that might be regarded as passively disruptive such as refusal to move, noncompliance, or failure to follow rules or obey instructions also are problematic. Even relatively less serious actions such as wandering away from the group and leaving the area can interfere with programming and have serious consequences for the safety of the individual. Self-injurious behaviors such as head banging, hitting oneself, biting oneself, vomiting, pica, and so forth are dangerous to the individual's health and sometimes place his or her life in jeopardy. These behaviors are even more difficult to deal with for caregivers and staff because they can be frightening to others, so that the usual calmness of staff and their usual careful use of well-specified procedures can be interrupted if others react with panic. Social/emotional behavior disorders such as stealing, exposing oneself, and swearing may occur. Stereotypic behavior such as finger flicking, body rocking, mouthing objects, tooth grinding, arm flapping, and other sometimes very complex rituals repeated many times by the individual seem to be extremely common in persons with developmental disabilities. These behaviors look unusual to the observer, so that a trip to the community grocery store might be met with stares from other shoppers and might contribute to the negative attitudes toward persons with disabilities held by those who do not understand such behaviors.

UNDERSTANDING BEHAVIOR PROBLEMS, AND INDICATED INTERVENTIONS

While all of these behaviors are problematic to caregivers, staff, programs, and environments, it is important to recognize certain facts about behavior problems:

1. It is helpful to realize that no matter how deviant or unusual or extreme behavior problems may be, *similar types of behavior occur in almost everyone.* Persons with disabilities engage in stereotypic behavior, but so do nondisabled persons. The reason this principle is important is that it points out that all people do these things under certain circumstances and at certain times. There might be some situations in which the behaviors can easily be tolerated by others, are fairly typical, and are not a priority for change.

2. It seems that even the most extreme behaviors are not bizarre or purposeless or, as they often are called, maladaptive. Nearly all behavior problems actually *serve a purpose for the individual.* Most behavior problems are an effective strategy to accomplish something that the individual needs or wants. This is particularly likely to be the case for individuals with severe disabilities who initially may lack the skills to accomplish something in a more agreeable, constructive manner.

Thus, in most cases, behavior problems are *adaptive* for the individual, that is, they represent the person's most successful strategy to achieve some purpose. This is an important point, because the individual has to acquire a more powerful strategy that will bring what he or she needs or wants for the behavior problem to be truly solved.

3. Precisely because the behavior problems are really adaptive for the individual, *not all behaviors will respond to the same intervention techniques.* Different behaviors have different purposes. This is true for different individuals, but it is also true for the same individual at different times and in different situations. Knowing only the form of a behavior problem—for example, hitting others—is not particularly helpful for the design of an intervention. What is the person trying to accomplish when he or she hits others? A careful analysis of the purpose or function of the behavior problem is essential as the basis for designing a strategy to intervene with that behavior.

AN EXERCISE

List some examples of typical stereotypic behaviors that might be displayed by anyone:

a. Leg swinging (When would someone be likely to do this?)
b. Finger and pencil tapping (situations?)
c.

List some examples of self-injurious behaviors that can be found in nondisabled adults:

a. Nail biting
b. Picking skin
c. (What about smoking and alcohol abuse?)

Under what circumstances might an otherwise well-behaved adult become aggressive?

a. Traffic jams or being cut off on the road
b. Family arguments
c. (are there milder forms of aggression that people sometimes use at work?)

Think of some minor instances of inattentive and disruptive behavior that the reader used lately:

a. Leaving a workshop to get a drink of water
b. Making up an excuse to avoid talking with an acquaintance met in a store
c.

For each of the above examples (and those the reader has added), which seem to be examples of normal deviance that one would not want to or be willing to change? Is it important to change these behaviors? When would it be important to change them and how did the reader make these decisions? Next, even though all of the above examples are things that nondisabled people might do, which of the behaviors are problematic and should be changed? Why?

Summary

Behavior problems do occur in persons with disabilities and present a challenge to efforts to provide meaningful and productive environments and activities for these individuals. At least some of these behaviors also occur in persons who do not have disabilities. In nearly all cases, there appear to be reasons for the behavior; that is, the behaviors are not random or purposeless but seem clearly motivated to accomplish some goal for the individual.

If the behavior serves a purpose for the individual, that purpose must be identified in order for the need to be addressed and the behavior effectively changed. The next two sections describe two approaches to addressing the behavioral needs of persons with disabilities and present information regarding the kinds of purposes or functions that certain behavior problems seem to have for these individuals.

THE ELIMINATIVE APPROACH TO BEHAVIOR PROBLEMS

The eliminative approach views behavior problems as maladaptive or interfering actions that make it impossible or difficult for children or adults with disabilities to function as efficient learners.

Description of Eliminative Approach

The goal of the eliminative approach is to decrease and eliminate those behaviors judged by trainers, parents, employers, and others to be maladaptive, inappropriate, interfering, and so forth. According to the eliminative approach, the following kinds of behaviors might be eliminated:

Noncompliance

Stereotypic mannerisms

Aggression

Self-injurious behavior

Tantrums

Getting out of seat, running away, and so forth

The traditional intervention rule using an eliminative approach is that these undesirable behaviors must be eliminated before new, adaptive responses can be targeted and acquired by the individual. (Alternatives to this rule will be suggested.)

According to this view of behavior problems, negative behaviors are regarded as high priority intervention goals. Such behaviors are seen as being displayed by the individual at such high levels of frequency, intensity, and duration that no other sensory input and/or learning is possible for the individual while the behavior is taking place. At the very least, even if the behavior is not technically interfering with learning, it is interfering with efforts by caregivers to teach the individual, and it disrupts the otherwise smooth functioning of the environment.

When a child or adult has significant behavior problems, it is not unusual to find an entire Individualized Education Program (IEP) or Individualized Program Plan (IPP) devoted to deceleration targets, that is, plans to decrease behavior problems rather than plans to teach new skills. This is because, according to an eliminative perspective, the behaviors are regarded as directly preventing adaptive behavior from occurring. The individual must be ready to learn before positive programming can begin. Behavior problems that interfere with learning must be reduced before the person is able and ready to learn. According to the eliminative perspective, skill instruction and more positive programming are distant goals, to be addressed at some time in the future when the individual has become a compliant and attending learner —and the behavior problems are solved.

Finally, when behavior becomes particularly problematic, specially trained staff might be needed, and the individual might be placed in a specialized behavior management unit. Thus, according to this approach, a person with severe behavior problems often is grouped with others who exhibit behavior problems in a specialized environment. The person may leave that environment and return to the community only *after* behavior problems are eliminated. The eliminative model thus assumes that homogenous groupings of persons with problem behavior are an appropriate and constructive setting for both reductions in those behaviors and the acquisition of positive alternative behaviors. It also assumes that successful adjustment to a special behavior management environment facilitates successful adjustment to the original and/or future community environment.

EXAMPLES OF BEING READY TO LEARN

John spends nearly all of his time rocking in his seat, finger flicking, and paying no attention to staff or other residents. A deceleration goal for John that will be included in his IPP is that, "John will sit quietly, without rocking and without finger flicking, for up to 10 minutes during breaks in structured activity." Another is that, "John will refrain from body rocking and finger flicking while completing prevocational benchwork assembly tasks for 1/2 hour periods of time."

Jenny is 7 years old and is diagnosed as autistic. Jenny does not establish eye contact with others, and is described as being non-compliant. When asked to sit in her chair or do any task, Jenny typically refuses to participate by avoiding eye contact, trying to run away, falling limp on the floor, and whining or crying. A deceleration goal for Jenny's IEP is that, "When presented with the verbal cue, 'Look at me,' Jenny will make eye contact with the trainer for 2 seconds." Another is that, "When presented with simple one-step commands such as, 'Sit down,' and, 'Come here,' Jenny will comply within 30 seconds."

Kevin is 43 years old and can be both aggressive and disruptive at times. During his day treatment program, Kevin very often yells loudly and may throw materials. He occasionally hits staff members and other adults seated close by when he is asked to do things. Kevin has several deceleration goals on his IPP, to be carried out both in the group home where he lives and at the day treatment program. Two of them are, "Kevin will sit quietly without yelling or throwing objects for 1/2 hour during group activities," and, "Kevin will decrease incidents of hitting others to fewer than 2 attempts weekly from the present rate of 5 incidents and 10–15 attempts weekly."

In each case, the behaviors are considered serious enough that John, Jenny, and Kevin are regarded as not being ready to learn or actively participate in activities and environments. In fact, Jenny is being considered for placement in another program designed specifically for children with autism who have similar problems, and Kevin is about to be transferred to a day program for adults with behavior problems.

Problems with the Eliminative Approach

There are a number of problems with this approach. First, does it really work well? There is considerable evidence that some behaviors can be decreased under certain circumstances, particularly when the trainer is present. Sometimes these behaviors can be changed quite quickly with only a few days of systematic efforts to change them. But there is also a great deal of evidence that: 1) the behaviors tend to

reappear when the program is ended; 2) the behaviors will continue to occur in other environments, particularly when the trainer is not present; and 3) over time, the behaviors may reappear and even escalate so that the program has to be reintroduced repeatedly to eliminate them.

There is also evidence that in certain cases where a behavior has been changed successfully, something even more serious might take its place, most likely in response to the negative aspects of the intervention plan. For example, a few years ago a client of the authors' was placed on a response-cost program for making obscene gestures to his supervisors in a vocational training program. He subsequently made every effort to avoid the program, such as refusing to leave for the program in the mornings and, once there, leaving the building without permission.

This kind of result occurs often enough that we now know that the fact that something works in the classroom or in the day treatment program is no guarantee that the behavior problem has been improved in other environments. Thus, the program must be extended to these other environments, and everyone who interacts with the individual might be expected to apply it when the behavior occurs. Even then, the behavior might reappear whenever staff fail to be vigilant, and/or equally serious behavior problems might suddenly increase just as the original problem seems to be solved.

A second issue is whether something else might have worked better. Particularly when initial progress is followed by a return of the problem behavior or the replacement of that behavior by other challenging behaviors, staff need to ask whether another approach might have resulted in more lasting and meaningful behavior change. Third, whenever positive programming and participation in various experiences and activities are postponed until a person's behavior problems are solved, there might be serious delays in teaching the person new skills. This could create future difficulties. Sometimes children and adults will have IEPs and IPPs dominated by deceleration goals year after year, with no goals to be taught new skills until they are ready, which could take years. In the meantime, valuable learning time is lost and individuals are being deprived of participation in activities and experiences. This seems particularly serious considering that these individuals might need the most instructional time to learn new things and are at greatest risk for being deprived of nearly all positive environments and activities unless they acquire certain skills. They could wait for their entire school careers and adult program time and never quite be judged ready to learn.

Six problems argue against the rigid application of an eliminative approach to treatment:

1. The behavior problem is a functional means used by the individual to control his or her environment. To eliminate it, the individual must have another functional means to accomplish the intended purposes. Suppressing the behavior does not eliminate the intentions.
2. Even if the behavior problem is improved in one setting and in the presence of trainers, this does not necessarily mean that the improvement will generalize to other environments and persons.
3. Decelerative techniques typically involve negative and/or punitive interactions between caregiving staff and the individual with a disability. These interactions sometimes produce even worse problem behaviors. They require that staff administer techniques that the client does not like, so that a negative interaction is encouraged. The treatment generates its own problems.

4. Homogeneous groupings or placements designed specifically for persons with behavior problems create a new environment that is not conducive to positive adaptive behaviors likely to be useful in the community. First, all models in such a situation are negative and clients may even provoke each other. Second, precisely because the setting is designed specifically to deal with behavior problems, it is generally quite different from the referral or future community placements. The client may be learning adaptations of little use in the real world.
5. Once the behavior change program is phased out, the behavior problem seems to return or other behaviors may take its place. The individual may be locked in a cycle of temporary improvements and eventual setbacks.
6. In some cases, treatment is not successful in eliminating problematic behavior, and the individual may wait for years without positive programming and environmental experiences. He or she may even be restricted and isolated and at risk for chemical or physical restraint.

THE EDUCATIVE APPROACH TO BEHAVIOR PROBLEMS

The alternative approach to solving problems begins with four assumptions:

First, *the major purpose of habilitative services is to encourage adaptive behavior and to promote maximum participation by the individual in meaningful daily experiences.* Thus, instruction and participation would not be delayed until after behavior problems were eliminated or even reduced. Instruction and participation would be the major focus of an individualized program plan. Deceleration programs are supplemental at best and need not subtract from active treatment goals and access to certain essential and positive experiences.

Second, *not all behavior problems are equal priority targets for behavior change.* In some situations modifying an excess behavior would be a priority, but there are other situations in which this would not be a priority. In general, altering behavior problems should be a priority only when unavoidable. Criteria can be applied to identify the cases in which behavior problems must be addressed and cases in which they need not be, at least at a particular time.

Third, *even when a behavior problem is a priority, the most effective strategy to reduce it is to replace it with a skill that accomplishes its function for the individual.* This means, again, that the IPP would focus primarily on building adaptive behavior and teaching new skills, even when there is complete agreement that a behavior problem is serious and must be reduced and eliminated. At the very least, if lasting behavior change is to occur, the individual must learn that an adaptive skill will accomplish the intended purpose while the problem behavior will not. As the treatment goal is to change behavior rather than simply control it, the individual must have a positive alternative or replacement skill in his or her repertoire.

Fourth, *even when a behavior problem is a priority and there will be a decelerative program to change it, interventions to do this must be normalized.* Interventions and management programs that are bizarre, that themselves threaten the safety, health, and well-being of the individual, that are painful and/or stressful, and that deny the dignity of the individual because they would not be acceptable for use with nondisabled persons, must be replaced by habilitative and nonaversive procedures. Effective (perhaps even more effective) nonaversive interventions are available to address behavior problems, even those

that are most serious. In addition, these more normalized procedures can be used with far less risk to the individual and conflict for staff, caregivers, agencies, and the community. Finally, it is becoming increasingly important that alternative nonaversive procedures be developed and implemented as the public and professional community continue to express serious misgivings about the appropriateness of aversives and sometimes even legislate restrictions on their use.

PROFESSIONAL RESPONSIBILITY

In the 1980s, several major professional organizations passed or reaffirmed new resolutions and policy statements regarding the use of aversives and corporal punishment with persons with disabilities. These include The Association for Retarded Citizens/US (ARC/US), the American Association on Mental Retardation (AAMR), The Association for Persons with Severe Handicaps (TASH), the Canadian Association for Community Living (CACL), the National Association of Private Residential Resources, the National Association of Developmental Disabilities Councils, and the National Association of School Psychologists (NASP). The statements speak out against the continued use of aversive procedures with persons who have disabilities. They also call for the development and dissemination of nonaversive alternatives that are both effective and respectful of the dignity of the individual. Tables 1.1–1.4 show reprints of some of these statements.

ACTIVITY

In a special feature on a network television newsmagazine in 1987, a prominent television journalist introduced a story about the controversy surrounding the use of aversives by stating, "Last summer in our report, 'When all else fails,' we told of a controversial treatment for the most extreme cases of autism—a brain disorder that can send some children into vio-

Table 1.1.   TASH Resolution on the Cessation of Intrusive Interventions (November, 1986)

In order to realize the goals and objectives of the Association for Persons with Severe Handicaps, including the right of each person with a severe handicap to grow, develop, and enjoy life in integrated and normalized community environments, the following resolution is adopted:

Educational and other habilitative services must employ instructional and management strategies which are consistent with the right of each individual with severe handicaps to an effective treatment which does not compromise the equally important right to freedom from harm. This requires educational and habilitative procedures free from chemical restraint, aversive stimuli, environmental deprivation or exclusion from services;

Therefore, TASH calls for the cessation of the use of any treatment option which exhibits some or all of the following characteristics: (1) obvious signs of physical pain experienced by the individual; (2) potential or actual side effects such as tissue damage, physical illness, severe physical or emotional stress and/or death that would properly require the involvement of medical personnel; (3) dehumanization of persons with severe handicaps because the procedures are normally unacceptable for persons without handicaps in community environments; (4) extreme ambivalence and discomfort by family, staff and/or caregivers regarding the necessity of such extreme strategies or their own involvement in such interventions; and (5) obvious repulsion and/or stress felt by peers who have no handicaps and community members who cannot reconcile extreme procedures with acceptable standard practice;

It is further resolved that The Association for Persons with Severe Handicaps' resources and expertise be dedicated to the development, implementation, evaluation, dissemination, and advocacy of educational and management practices which are appropriate for use in integrated environments and which are consistent with the commitment to a high quality of life for individuals with severe handicaps.

An earlier version of this resolution was passed by the TASH Executive Board in October 1981.

Table 1.2.   NASP Resolution on Corporal Punishment

As the purpose of the National Association of School Psychologists is to serve the mental health and educational needs of children and youth; and

The use of corporal punishment as a disciplinary procedure in the schools negatively affects the social, educational, and psychological development of students; and

The use of corporal punishment by educators reinforces the misconception that hitting is an appropriate and effective technique to discipline children; and

Corporal punishment as a disciplinary technique can be easily abused and thereby contribute to the cycle of child abuse; and

School psychologists are legally and ethically bound to protect the students they serve; and

Research indicates that punishment is ineffective in teaching new behaviors, that a variety of positive and effective alternatives are available to maintain school discipline, and that children learn more appropriate problem solving behaviors when provided with the necessary models;

Therefore it is resolved that the National Association of School Psychologists joins other organizations in opposing the use of corporal punishment in the schools and in other institutions where children are cared for or educated;

And will work actively with other organizations to influence public opinion and legislative bodies in recognizing the consequences of corporal punishment, in understanding and researching alternatives to corporal punishment, and in prohibiting the continued use of corporal punishment;

And will encourage state affiliate organizations and individual members to adopt positions opposing corporal punishment, to promote understanding of and research on alternatives to corporal punishment including preventive initiatives, and to support abolition of corporal punishment at state and local levels.

This resolution was adopted on April 19, 1986, in Hollywood, Florida, by The National Association of School Psychologists.

A position paper supporting this position statement is available from the National Association of School Psychologists.

Table 1.3.   ARC/US Resolution on Use of Aversives

WHEREAS, it is in the tradition of this Association to challenge current practices that are inhumane and depersonalizing; and

WHEREAS, research does not support the long term efficacy of aversive behavioral intervention; and

WHEREAS, the use of aversives raises disturbing legal and ethical issues; and

WHEREAS, the use of aversives may diminish the dignity of the administrator and does diminish the dignity of the recipient;

NOW THEREFORE BE IT RESOLVED that the ARC/United States calls for a halt to those aversive practices that 1) deprive food, 2) inflict pain, 3) use chemical restraint in lieu of programming; and

BE IT FURTHER RESOLVED that ARC/United States communicate this resolution to the entire membership, advocacy, parent and consumer groups, the media and legislative bodies; and

BE IT FURTHER RESOLVED that ARC/United States promote the use of positive non-aversive techniques and training in these techniques; and

BE IT FURTHER RESOLVED that ARC/United States review those aversive practices listed above and other related practices, revise its policy statement on behavior management in conformance with this resolution, and present the revision to the delegate body at its 1986 annual convention.

Adopted by the Delegate Body, ARC/United States, November 23, 1985, Reno, Nevada.

Table 1.4.   AAMR Position Statement on Aversive Therapy

Some persons who have mental retardation or developmental disabilities continue to be subjected to inhumane forms of aversive therapy techniques as a means of behavior modification.

The American Association on Mental Retardation (AAMR) condemns such practices and urges their immediate elimination. The aversive practices to be eliminated include some or all of the following characteristics:

1. Obvious signs of physical pain experienced by the individual;
2. Potential or actual physical side-effects, including tissue damage, physical illness, severe stress, and/or death; and
3. Dehumanization of the individual, through means such as social degradation, social isolation, verbal abuse, techniques inappropriate for the individual's age and treatment out of proportion to the target behavior, because the procedures are normally unacceptable for nonhandicapped individuals.

The AAMR urges continuing research into humane methods of behavior management and support of existing programs and environments that successfully habilitate individuals with complex behaviors.

This position statement was passed by the AAMR Board of Directors in December, 1986.

lent, almost uncontrollable fits of self-destruction" (Walters, 1987).

Similarly, a printed story described autism as, ". . . an incurable mental disorder that usually strikes in early childhood and is characterized by extreme withdrawal and sometimes dangerously aggressive behavior" (Salholz & Hutchinson, 1986).

And, in the *New York Times*, in an article about the use of aversives such as pinching, slapping, food deprivation, cold showers, mechanical restraint, ammonia and water spray, and a white noise visual screen helmet: "The parents asserted that the method, combining punishments with rewards, has been the only way to control their children, who suffer from the brain disorder that leads to speech defects and aggressive or self-abusive behavior" (*New York Times*, January 10, 1987).

Finally, the *Newsweek* article also stated: ". . . they have learned the hard way that their only choice is aversive therapy—or some forgotten ward in a state institution. 'Oh, there are alternatives all right,' says Bill Martin. . . . 'There are rubber rooms, straitjackets and drugs.' " (Salholz & Hutchinson, 1986).

In a small group, discuss reactions to the following issues and questions:

a. What images of persons with disabilities and persons with autism in particular are portrayed in these media presentations?

Example:

". . . a brain disorder that can send some children into violent, almost uncontrollable fits of self-destruction;" "autism [is] an incurable mental disorder."

b. Do these reports provide an accurate description of the kinds of programs and services available today to persons with disabilities?

Example:

"Oh, there are alternatives all right. There are rubber rooms, straitjackets and drugs."

c. If the reader knew nothing more about persons with autism or the kinds of programs that should be available to these individuals other than what is included in these reports, would the reader be influenced to believe that such treatments as spankings, pinches, and ammonia were acceptable?

d. If the reader knew nothing about persons with autism and other disabilities other than the information provided here, how would the reader react if a group home for adults with autism were proposed for his or her neighborhood, of if his or her son or daughter came home from school and said that a new classmate had autism?

chapter

2

The Nature of Excess Behavior

OVERVIEW

This chapter provides an overview of the major categories of excess behavior that might be exhibited by persons with developmental disabilities. This is not intended to be a comprehensive review of the causes and treatment of problem behavior but does provide a summary of various explanations offered for different behaviors, along with selective examples of evidence to support the various interpretations. Finally, the treatment implications that can be derived from the different perspectives are introduced.

It is not recommended that training begin with an inservice session dealing with problem behavior in any detail. Instead, the trainers should present only the major categories of excess behavior and have the group discuss a few examples of clients familiar to them who have similar problems. This chapter also can be used as background reading after a training segment based on Chapter 1 and before the next training session focused on the content of Chapter 3. Finally, the activity provided should be used in a group discussion to illustrate why different behaviors have different treatment implications.

TRAINEE OBJECTIVES

At the completion of this unit, participant trainees will be able to:

1. Give an example of a stereotypic behavior that might indicate the absence of play skills.
2. Give an example of how a stereotypic behavior might be used to self-regulate.
3. Describe at least two different causes for self-injurious behavior, and suggest how each cause might affect efforts to change such behavior.
4. Differentiate aggression that is an emotional reaction to fear or anger from acts that seem intended to manipulate others.
5. Explain why socially inappropriate behavior can sometimes interfere with community integration, and differentiate situations in which the client should change from situations in which others should change instead.

INTRODUCTION

Many individuals with developmental disabilities display challenging behavior (Barrett, 1986). The prevalence of such behavior appears to be especially high in individuals who have been diagnosed as autistic, although inappropriate behavior is also a diagnostic criterion for autism. Moderate to severe mental retardation also is associated with a high rate of excess behavior, although this probably reflects a shifting distribution in types of problems in that any undesirable behaviors of more mildly handicapped persons are more generally identified as either social/emotional problems or criminal offenses similar to the problems of nondisabled individuals. Behavior problems within this wide spectrum have been variously labelled bizarre, inappropriate, maladaptive, and disordered, yet there seems to be some advantage in using the more neutral term *excess behavior* (Meyer & Evans, 1986). This is because there is a great deal of evidence to suggest that such behaviors in persons with developmental disabilities are not random or purposeless as much as they reveal information about the person's needs. Such behaviors often have a function; even though their form is judged to be undesirable by others, such behaviors may be somewhat effective for the individual who has no other fluent strategy available to meet his or her needs.

Suggesting a more neutral terminology is not an attempt to diminish the seriousness of excess behavior. In addition to the harmful direct effects to the individuals themselves, it is now well recognized that excess behaviors create special problems for families, caregivers, and supervisors. Parents have indicated that expert assistance with behavior management is a top priority for maintaining children with severe disabilities at home (Cole & Meyer, in press). Problem behaviors can strain marital relationships, may interfere with time otherwise available for family activities, create real or perceived adjustment difficulties for siblings, and decrease the amount of assistance families can expect from relatives and the community (e.g.,

making it impossible to find sitters). Similarly, teachers (Kerr & Nelson, 1983), direct care providers (Reid & Schepis, 1986), and vocational educators (Hanley-Maxwell, Rusch, Chadsey-Rusch, & Renzaglia, 1986) report special difficulties working with persons with severe behavior disorders.

EXPLANATIONS AND INTERPRETATIONS OF EXCESS BEHAVIOR BY CATEGORY

Because excess behaviors are so varied, there have been many attempts to classify them (e.g., Forehand & Baumeister, 1976). Typically the categories proposed have focused on the presumed functions of the behavior (e.g., manipulation versus self-stimulation), on causes or etiological factors (e.g., seizure disorders or Lesch-Nyhan syndrome), on response topography (e.g., hand and finger mannerisms), or on presumed sources of behavioral control (e.g., respondents versus operants). So far, the field has not agreed on any nosology based on a unitary principle. However, there is reasonable consensus that the categories described below are convenient, pragmatic, and help to identify some of the central issues that are relevant to the design of prevention or proactive treatment. The categories that seem to best cover serious excess behavior are *stereotypy, self-injury, aggression, inappropriate social behavior, disorders of physical regulation,* and *specific emotional disturbance.* Following are brief summaries of the conceptual issues surrounding each category, in addition to summaries of the implications that are common to all of them.

Stereotypic Behavior

Repetitive cycles of behavior that persist for long periods of time, such as body rocking, finger flicking, hand flapping, tapping objects, and so forth, have been referred to as stereotypic because of the consistency in form of each cycle of the response. These behaviors have been formally investigated in considerable detail, using both operant behavioral methodologies (e.g., Hollis, 1978) and ethological/biological concepts (e.g., Berkson, 1967). Comprehensive reviews of these studies have been provided by Baumeister (1978) and Romanczyk, Kistner, and Plienis (1982). Stereotypic behavior is also often described and categorized as *self-stimulation*. Some authors have objected to this as a descriptive term since it implies that the function of the behavior is known. To say that a behavior is self-stimulatory suggests that it is indeed reinforced or maintained by its sensory consequences, including proprioceptive feedback from receptors in the muscles, tendons, and joints.

While it may well be that not all stereotypic behavior serves a self-stimulatory function, the evidence that many such behaviors do have this function is quite convincing. The most direct support comes from the work of Rincover and Devany (Rincover & Devany, 1982). Their studies demonstrated that stereotypic behavior decreased when its sensory consequences were limited through physical manipulations, such as padding hard surfaces to prevent noise from occurring that was presumably reinforcing. More circumstantial evidence comes from the large number of studies showing that stereotypic behavior tends to decrease when the stimulation level of the environment is increased (see Romanczyk, Kistner, & Plienis, 1982). As some of these studies enriched the environment by providing play materials and activities, several authors have argued that teaching leisure/recreational skills (e.g., Voeltz, Wuerch, & Wilcox, 1982) would serve to reduce excess behavior. Favell (1973) published one of the first demonstrations of this effect. In fact, this early study emphasized the importance of teaching persons who had few appropriate alternative skills such leisure alternatives, be-

cause it appeared that depending solely on reinforcing the existing repertoire was not sufficient to maintain the improvements in behavior. Thus, Meyer, Evans, Wuerch, and Brennan (1985) taught leisure skills as a curriculum priority (rather than just an isolated intervention) and were able to show a concomitant reduction in self-stimulation for a number of teenagers with severe disabilities during free time with leisure materials.

A slightly more elaborate version of this perspective on self-stimulation is the notion that stereotypic behavior serves a *self-regulatory* function. In situations where the individual has limited stimulation or lacks the skills to initiate more elaborate and acceptable forms of leisure activity, stereotypic behavior might serve to increase stimulation and arousal. Conversely, in situations where the individual is overexcited or bombarded with stimulus input, stereotypic behavior may serve to reduce arousal, much as repetitive rocking, sucking, or hugging a security blanket is seen to modulate arousal in young children. Appealing as this idea is, the direct evidence is limited (Sroufe, Steucher, & Stutzer, 1973).

It is important to recognize, however, that the literature clearly indicates that stereotypic behavior is sometimes increased, sometimes decreased, and sometimes uninfluenced by stimulating surroundings and the availability of leisure/play materials (e.g., Frankel, Freeman, Ritvo, & Pardo, 1978). This finding emphasizes the importance of individual assessment, understanding the relationships among behaviors, and not assuming that all topographically similar actions belong to a single response class (Voeltz & Evans, 1982).

The hypothesis that stereotypic behavior may be self-regulatory or be a form of entertainment during down time obliges acknowledgement that such behavior can serve an adaptive function for the individual. Even so, its predominance in the person's repertoire is clearly deleterious. One major reason for being concerned about stereotypic behavior is that it may interfere with learning and productive behavior (Koegel & Covert, 1972; Koegel, Firestone, Kramme, & Dunlap, 1974). At the same time, however, there are other indications that the interfering effect is not always pronounced. For example, in detailed observational studies, Evans and Voeltz (1982) repeatedly recorded instances of a behavioral category labeled *appropriate on-task behavior plus self-stimulation*. Watching students taking an exam or teenage children doing homework shows that much self-stimulatory behavior often accompanies effective cognitive activity.

The actual degree of interference seems to relate to the degree to which the behavior monopolizes the individual's attention relative to the interest level of the task and the materials (attentional interference), and the degree to which the stereotypic behavior actually interferes physically with performance of the required task (Chock & Glahn, 1983). For instance, a worker with severe disabilities who is doing a manual job task will experience less interference from repetitive vocalizing than from a repetitive hand or finger mannerism. Of course, the negative consequences of the vocal behavior might be the social impact on the attitudes of coworkers, supervisors, or any others about that individual. These consequences are not trivial, but they are not significant enough to suggest that first the stereotypic behavior must be reduced, and only afterward can instructions, productive work, or learning occur. And, in some cases, it may be quite simple for attitudes to change so that others are more comfortable with the individual's behavior, in which case it may not be a priority to change the behavior. The rather widely assumed professional rule that the clients must change first has often had negative consequences, such as the individual being assigned to a behavior

management program rather than to an educational and habilitative program endowed with attention-getting, interesting, relevant curricula and activities.

One additional factor that must be considered when judging the seriousness of stereotypic behavior is that it is possible for certain of these behaviors to develop into more harmful activities. Behaviors like tooth grinding (bruxism), eye poking, picking skin, and tapping at oneself can increase in intensity and duration until they are severely injurious. If done often enough, other stereotypic behaviors— such as finger or hand mouthing—can cause secondary harm to the skin, such as callouses, open sores, and infections.

Self-Injurious Behavior

Responses that inflict direct harm on the behaving individual generally have been categorized as self-injurious. Logically this category might include behaviors that could be called indirectly harmful, such as abusing drugs, but in practice this is done rarely. Nevertheless, an expanded definition helps emphasize that behaviors that self-inflict harm are not unique to persons with disabilities. In other psychiatric disorders, they might even be viewed as parasuicidal behavior. In all cases, however, the puzzling feature is why behavior that produces immediate painful consequences would not rapidly terminate. One possibility is that when a painful stimulus regularly precedes a positive stimulus, the aversive conditioned stimulus can come to elicit positive emotional behavior. Pavlov demonstrated this in early classical conditioning studies, and the phenomenon has been used to explain many instances of masochistic behavior. In experimental psychopathology, there are numerous demonstrations showing that when a painful stimulus increases gradually, concomitant positive reinforcement contingencies can be established that will induce animals to self-administer painful stimuli (Fowler,

1971). Neuropsychological hypotheses have considered that the individual who is self-injurious may have heightened pain tolerance (i.e., can tolerate more and more pain over time) or that the self-initiation of pain provides a natural opiate through the production of endorphins in the central nervous system (Cataldo & Harris, 1982). Behaviors that would be consistent with the latter interpretation include pinching oneself during a painful medical or dental procedure (e.g., when receiving an injection or having a cavity filled). While there is little hard evidence for these positions, such ideas are worthy of systematic study.

Self-injurious behavior undoubtedly is one of the most dramatic categories of excess behavior in persons with disabilities. Seeing clients striking themselves with their fists, pounding their heads against solid objects, or biting their own extremities is a devastating experience for any care provider, professional or not. One feels compelled to intervene physically and do whatever is possible to prevent further harm. Unfortunately, the severity of the possible injuries that some individuals may self-inflict can give rise to horror stories, that is, accounts and anecdotes that emphasize the physiological damage. While in no way wishing to underestimate the seriousness of a few self-injurious behaviors, the authors believe that inflammatory and lurid accounts appearing in the media are designed to justify extreme methods of punishment that ultimately are used with other, less serious behaviors and cases as well. The dignity of persons with disabilities also is substantially compromised by such negative images, which thus generate and continue to promote negative attitudes toward persons who have developmental disabilities.

Prevalence estimates of self-injurious behavior are influenced by the age range involved in the statistics, the service setting, and the criteria used to judge the severity of the injury. Using the general criterion of behavior that results in "physical harm or tissue damage," Baumeister and Rollings (1976) reported a prevalence of self-injurious behavior of between 10% and 17% in persons with mental retardation living in institutions. Schroeder, Schroeder, Smith, and Dalldorf (1978) provided some interesting data based on a repeated survey of one institution. Overall prevalence for self-injurious behavior was 10%, with the more severe behaviors associated with increased levels of mental retardation and longer histories of the behavior. The connection between degree of disability and self-injury has also been noted by Maisto, Baumeister, and Maisto (1977) in their factor analysis study. They found that self-injurious behavior was associated with more profound mental retardation, specific indications of neurological impairment, and higher rates of stereotypic behavior.

The emotional effect of self-injurious behavior on caregivers provides one possible clue to its maintaining factors. Carr (1977), in an important theoretical analysis, suggested that self-injurious behavior could be reinforced by social reward (positive and negative attention) or could serve to reduce demands from caregivers and thus be negatively reinforced. He also considered that some self-injurious behavior might be an extension of self-stimulatory behavior (as discussed in the previous section) and raised the possibility that self-injurious behavior is organic in origin (as revealed, for example, in the Lesch-Nyhan syndrome).

The authors propose that organic and social/environmental influences inevitably interact, and thus the four hypotheses reviewed by Carr (1977) would not be mutually exclusive. For different clients, there may be very different explanations for the behavior, and even within one individual, there could be more than one influence responsible for its emergence and maintenance. These multiple explanations are further supported by the range of treatment approaches that are reported to be successful in reducing self-injurious behavior. As is well known, the success of a treatment does not automatically indicate the causes or controlling factors of a behavior problem. However, the variety of supposedly successful interventions lends credence to the assumption that self-injurious behaviors are multiply determined. Among the strategies reported to have reduced the frequency of self-injurious behavior are contingent aversive stimuli (e.g., Tate & Baroff, 1966), time-out (e.g., Solnick, Rincover, & Peterson, 1977), overcorrection (e.g., Harris & Romanczyk, 1976), and differential reinforcement of incompatible behavior (e.g., Tarpley & Schroeder, 1979).

Schroeder, Mulick, and Rojahn (1980) have reviewed much of the literature concerning self-injurious behavior. Some of their synopses seem particularly significant for the development of comprehensive treatment strategies and can be summarized as follows: self-injurious behaviors rarely occur as unitary responses. The individual may have a variety of harmful behaviors and also exhibit other excess behaviors. The harmfulness of self-injurious behavior is only one of many important features; individuals with severe handicaps may exhibit other physically harmful behaviors (e.g., vomiting, pica, inserting foreign objects into bodily orifices, food refusal) that have etiologies quite different from, say, head pounding. Regardless of the intervention strategy, long-term successful outcomes are not commonly reported. For example, in their large scale study, Schroeder et al. (1978) found only 2 out of 52 clients had maintained treatment reductions in self-injurious behavior at a 2-year follow up.

Aggression

In the authors' studies of decision-making in the design of interventions with excess behaviors, the most highly rated reason for needing to intervene with a behavior was that it represented a danger to the client *or*

to others (Voeltz, Evans, Derer, & Hanashiro, 1983). Thus aggression, like self-injury, is an excess behavior that has a special impact on the peers, family members, caregivers, and instructors of persons with disabilities. Physical aggression does not need an elaborate definition since the reference here is mostly to acts of physical violence perpetrated against other individuals. However, scholars do make a crucial functional distinction between two types of aggression: There is fear motivated aggression, in which to some extent the physical attack on another person is incidental to attempts to escape a fearful situation, and angry aggression, in which the aggressive behavior is triggered by frustration and anger (Blanchard & Blanchard, 1986). A third function of aggression involves the deliberate manipulation of other people in order to coerce them into conforming to one's wishes, for example, threatening or bullying types of behavior (Evans & Scheuer, 1987); such aggressive acts would be quite different from those that are outcomes of strong emotional reactions such as anger and fear.

Although all three types of aggression may be seen in persons with developmental disabilities, there is a slightly greater tendency for manipulative aggression to be seen in higher functioning individuals, who might be classified as having conduct disorders or emotional disabilities even though they may have IQ scores in the mental retardation range. Similarly, violent behavior elaborated into criminal acts such as assault, rape, armed robbery, or murder, can be perpetrated by persons with developmental disabilities and/or known brain injuries. Well-defined delinquent and criminal behavior, however, has its own special properties and dimensions that would go beyond the scope of this manual. However, the educative approaches espoused here have an interesting parallel in the similar emphasis on a skills development model even for aggressive youth who do not evidence developmental delay or cognitive deficits in general (Glick & Goldstein, 1987).

Aggressive behavior—especially angry aggression—often occurs as part of a more general tantrum, that is, a combination of such behaviors as crying or screaming, thrashing out, attacking others, and damaging property. Thus, the aggression category might be expanded to include such disruptive outbursts and destructiveness (Whitman, Scibak, & Reid, 1983). Aggression and tantruming have been functionally analyzed, with some studies indicating that this pattern of behavior is elicited by demand situations (Carr, Newsom, & Binkoff, 1980; Weeks & Gaylord-Ross, 1981) or a task that is complex (Sailor, Guess, Rutherford, & Baer, 1968). Thus, demands may serve as a discriminative stimulus for aggression, which may then be negatively reinforced through termination of demands. Martin and Foxx (1973) demonstrated that aggressive behaviors were eliminated by a strict extinction procedure in which the victim simply ignored all instances of aggression. As a general strategy, however, the needed level of ignoring would be impractical, since ignoring to that degree is so difficult to do. One of the secondary problems with aggressive behavior is that because peers and caregivers become wary of the aggressive client, avoidance behavior occurs that could further restrict opportunities for positive social interaction.

Passive-aggressive, disruptive, resistive, and noncompliant behavior can also be regarded as part of the aggression category when they represent attempts to counter-control. Refusing reasonable requests, running off instead of coming when called, becoming limp and dropping to the floor, resisting transitions and demands for physical movement (e.g., hanging onto the door handle of a van instead of exiting properly), and not performing chores or duties when required, all are quite common exam-

ples of behaviors often interpreted as efforts to control others. As will be emphasized later, assertion, claiming independence, and exercising control over one's own activities are highly desirable social skills. To some extent, the severity of power struggles can actually be the direct result of failure of families or direct care staff to allow persons with disabilities the right to express their preferences and exert some control over their everyday lives. In a very real sense, then, such behaviors may reflect the need to develop better social/communicative skills to use in social interactions by the individual. They also reflect the need for some very important changes in the social environment to allow those skills to be used reasonably and appropriately.

Inappropriate Social Behavior

There is a collection of behaviors in people with mental retardation sometimes referred to as antisocial behaviors that really seem to reflect failure to have learned more appropriate skills and rules rather than being a deliberate challenge to social convention per se. Examples of such behaviors are stripping off clothes, showing affection to strangers, stealing or hoarding possessions, lying, masturbating in public, and swearing/shouting obscenities. Behaviors of this kind can acquire special significance in integrated and community environments (Mulick & Schroeder, 1980). With important exceptions (e.g., Hill & Bruininks, 1984), almost all of the epidemiological data on excess behavior has been collected in institutional settings where the behavior is either more tolerated or has fewer opportunities to emerge. In employment training sites, group homes, and similar community based programs, inappropriate social behaviors are repeatedly raised as matters of concern. The authors have dealt with problems such as a group home resident wandering across to a neighbor's party, a young man with autism in a vocational program pestering his superior with redundant and irrelevant questions, and a moderately mentally retarded teenager wearing inappropriately revealing clothes during dancing lessons with nondisabled peers.

With the goals of achieving the greater social integration and full community participation that are characteristic of current trends in the field has come a special awareness of sexual problems in adolescents and young adults with severe disabilities. Foxx, Bittle, Bechtel, and Livesay (1986) have provided a comprehensive review of inappropriate sexual behavior in persons with mental retardation. The most commonly treated problems have been exhibitionism, pedophilia, public masturbation, and promiscuity, with aversive treatment strategies predominating until the more recent work being done by, for example, Dorothy Griffiths and her colleagues in Toronto. Despite investigators' willingness to use contingent electric shock, lemon juice, and facial screening, the older studies were inadequately designed and executed, with little proper outcome data being gathered. It may also be deceptive to assign psychiatric labels to inappropriate sexual behavior. For example, pedophilia as a clinical disorder implies erotic sexual preferences for children, whereas clients with developmental disabilities are more likely to have responded sexually to children on an indiscriminate basis. In any case, since society is especially intolerant of deviant sexual behavior, its occurrence in community settings can have very damaging consequences for developmentally disabled perpetrators, including arrest and imprisonment. It is interesting to note that Foxx et al. (1986) ended their review with a call for better assessment of the client's social and sexual skill level prior to treatment, and for better and more extensive sex education, including direct instruction in sexual behavior (Foxx, McMarrow, Storley, & Rogers, 1984).

Disorders of Physical Regulation

This category represents a range of excess behaviors resulting from limited physical control due to a failure to acquire (or a loss of) self-regulation over bodily functions. Examples from this category would be encopresis, enuresis, drooling, and tongue thrusting. Despite the general assumption that these become excess behaviors largely because of a failure to train the individual, punishment procedures have been used with all of them (see DiLorenzo & Ollendick, 1986). Various other deregulation of physical functions (breath holding, hyperventilation, playing with or eating feces, rumination, and vomiting) can be mentioned in this connection, although often these behaviors are predominantly ritualistic or even self-injurious. Another important set of behaviors in this group is eating disorders, such as overeating and food refusal.

Clearly, some of these behaviors represent serious problems for the individual and perhaps for the environment as well. But it is important to remember that other behaviors in this category simply are not under good voluntary control by the individual—drooling, for example. Where it is known that the person has little control over drooling, the intervention might more profitably focus on the design of certain adaptations that make it less noticeable (e.g., having the individual wear a fashionable print scarf) and/or teaching the individual to keep a handkerchief handy to wipe his or her face often rather than attempting to stop the drooling altogether. And in many cases, the attitudes of those in the environment could be expected to change and become more tolerant. For example, a child with cerebral palsy who is learning to eat independently should not have to worry about offending others by the way he or she eats. Table manners and other conventions of etiquette should not be allowed to become insurmountable obstacles to integration and used to justify a lack of tolerance. Children and adults can adjust their expectations regarding conformity with standards so unnecessarily restrictive that they lead to prejudice or even exclusion and segregation.

Specific Emotional Disturbance

The final category of behavior, specific emotional disturbance, recognizes that persons who have developmental disabilities may also exhibit the range of problems of emotional development and psychological adjustment that can be seen in nondisabled individuals. It is difficult to draw clear boundaries between excess behaviors of the kind described thus far, and a specific psychiatric disorder. At one level it is clearly necessary to consider emotional disturbance as a causal variable. For instance, a developmentally disabled client with acrophobia (fear of heights) who refuses to work near the window of the fifth floor of a worksite is as much at risk for job termination as a client whose self-stimulation interferes with productivity. So too, a group home resident who abuses alcohol or is addicted to illegal drugs, will have difficulty learning to be independent in the local community. Therefore, it is crucial to include in our range of causal hypothesis for excess behavior the possibility that the behavior is related to such emotional problems as phobia, depression, social anxiety, addiction, and so forth. This recognition makes relevant for people with disabilities a rich set of positive therapeutic strategies, particularly those that teach personal and interpersonal skills like self-control, problem-solving, assertiveness, and social competence.

Conclusions

As can be seen from the preceding discussion, the excess behaviors that interfere with social integration, employment, family living, and normalized and integrated community participation of individuals with developmental disabilities run the gamut from the discrete motor responses involving self-injury and stereotypic acts, to complex social and emotional problems. Despite the diversity of these problems, there are certain common themes that emerge when the total spectrum is considered:

1. The first theme has become so widely recognized that it may become a cliché in the field: Excess behaviors generally seem to serve important functions for the individual, even though their forms may be inappropriate and their consequences for the individual may be deleterious in the long run.

2. If excess behaviors have a function, it is possible that, for each one exhibited, there is an alternative form that is, if not more adaptive, at least more socially acceptable, or more closely resembling the behavior of a nondisabled individual and so more clearly interpretable in the community. Thus, it follows that excess behavior reflects both an important need and a crucial skills deficit, that is, the lack of a more appropriate alternative behavior or skill.

3. While the absence of functional, socially appropriate alternatives is an important explanation for behavior and suggests a major direction for proactive treatment plans, it does not seem sufficiently explanatory for the development of all excess behavior. Excess behaviors appear to be multiply determined.

4. Regardless of cause or etiology, excess behaviors are socially defined. They do vary in terms of their negative consequences for the individual, such as effects on health, physical well-being, and learning. But the social consequences, and with them quality-of-life and opportunity, are largely a func-

tion of social judgment and tolerance, so that some behaviors can lead to particularly negative outcomes.

5. If social consequences influence excess behaviors, as they often appear to, and if social judgments about the behavior influence placement, caregiving, and treatment decisions, it would appear that the person with developmental disabilities exhibiting serious excess behaviors is enmeshed in a social system, regardless of the original etiology of the behavior.

6. Although excess behaviors may be classified for convenience, for individual clients there is likely to be a variety of different excess behaviors, all serving quite different functions. A given topography of excess behavior may have more than one function, either at the same time or at different times over the course of development.

7. Both the appropriate and inappropriate behaviors in an individual's repertoire form a complex interactive system that must be considered in the attempt to understand individual behaviors. Thus, behaviors might have functions that are part of a response repertoire or the biological system—not all excess behaviors have social functions or serve as operants. Some inappropriate behaviors are the most salient aspect of reactive behavior patterns, elicited by environmental as well as physiological events.

8. Finally, both the nature of excess behaviors and their impacts on the individual determine whether any particular behavior is indeed a treatment priority.

A CONCEPTUAL MODEL OF VARIABLES AFFECTING BEHAVIOR

In Table 2.1, the authors have organized the various theoretical models that have guided interventions with the kinds of be-

havior problems discussed in this manual. Thus, in the column to the left is listed the focus of a particular model, then, across the row, the table shows the intervention strategies most likely to be used, the assumptions of the model regarding behavior, and one or more references that represent and elaborate on the perspective involved. Earlier, it was noted that one possible advantage of the recognition of emotional problems would be the availability of psychological treatments that may well work but have not been used with persons who have mental retardation. One possible disadvantage of the "dual diagnosis" category, however, could be an increased emphasis on medication for any emotional disturbance that has been treated this way in persons without retardation. It is a well known fact that persons with mental retardation already are at great risk for being overmedicated over long periods of time with infrequent monitoring of dosage levels and side effects. A diagnosis that includes depression or schizophrenia—syndromes that may be considered to have organic causes and for which medications are commonly used—could lead directly to the prescription of additional medications for the client. Alternatively, a focus on the importance of social roles as causes for excess behavior may lead to principles and practices that entail long-overdue social justice for persons with disabilities but could also lead to a tendency to devalue clinical efforts to help individual citizens with disabilities who do have serious problem behaviors that restrict their participation in meaningful interactions with others in society.

In the authors' view, no one of these perspectives is sufficient either as a theory to explain problem behavior or as a guide to the design of effective interventions for problem behavior. In Figure 2.1, the authors have attempted to illustrate how the various perspectives might be viewed as complementary and integrated with one

Table 2.1. Theoretical models for intervening with behavior problems

Focus	Intervention strategies	Assumptions	References
Organic etiology and affective illness	Pharmacology/ medical	Behavior generated by internal stimuli (e.g., dysfunction of central nervous system)	Aman and Singh (1983) Bruening, Davis, and Poling (1982)
Behavior and its consequences	Punishment and/or reinforcement of specific target behaviors	A particular behavioral response is encouraged or discouraged by consistent application of consequences	LaVigna and Donnellan (1986) Matson (1985)
S^D-R-S^R	Functional analysis of behavior to identify relevant stimuli and consequences	Systematic behavioral chains can be predicted by knowledge of stimuli and affected by manipulation of consequences	Carr and Durand (1985) Evans and Meyer (1985) LaVigna and Donnellan (1986)
Individual's repertoire	Educative approach to build positive repertoire of necessary skills	Existing behavior is adaptive for the individual (i.e., has a function); behavior that does occur is dependent on stimuli and consequences but also restricted by skill repertoire of individual	Evans and Meyer (1985) Meyer and Evans (1986)
Individual's repertoire and self-efficacy	Cognitive behavior therapy and skill-streaming	Cognition, affect, and learning history affect individual's ability and motivation to acquire and use positive adaptive behavior	Goldstein (1981) Meyer and Evans (1987)
Individual and the environment	Eco-behavioral and personal futures planning	Climate and context for positive social interactions and behavior is broadly affected by personal environmental experiences and opportunities	Jones, Lattimore, Ulicny, and Risley (1986) Meyer and Evans (1987) O'Brien (1987)
Social roles	Social and personal values and attitudes toward disability	Societal judgments about the value of the individual restrict or support individual development and participation	Wolfensberger (1983)

another. For example, the behavioral perspective tends to emphasize the lawful relationships between behavior (particularly learned responses) and the antecedent stimuli and consequences that predict the occurrence of such behavior. Alternatively, the ecological perspective emphasizes the fit of the person into his or her environ-

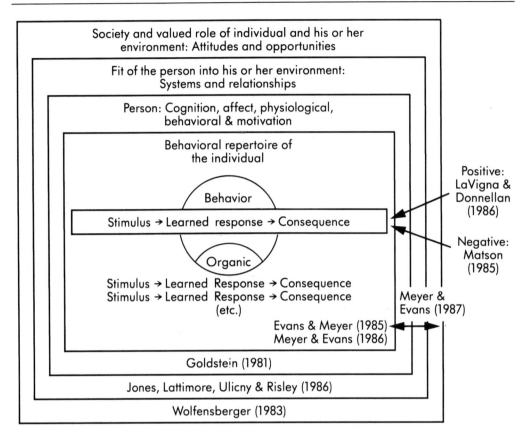

FIGURE 2.1.   Variables affecting behavior.

ment, suggesting that behavior is viewed as problematic or normal as a function of how well the person's behavior matches the expectations, tolerance, and preferences of the people and situations around him or her. The authors do not believe that it is sufficient to tackle behavior problems by rearranging specific stimuli and consequences (behavioral perspective) or by finding environments that are tolerant of such problems (ecological perspective). Similarly, aggression motivated by fear or anger will not be completely remediated by cognitive training to perceive events more objectively. The individual will need to learn some positive problem-solving or coping strategies as behavioral alternatives to acts such as hitting and tantruming.

The approach represented in this man-ual incorporates attention to each of these variables potentially affecting behavior, and details strategies to address each level of behavioral influence in the design of interventions to remediate excess behavior. Thus, the model extends beyond simply being nonaversive or even educative. In addition to incorporating attention to the educational and training contexts of the intervention, the model incorporates the human and personal needs of the individual with disabilities in all environments and situations, including work, home, and community.

Clearly, the obligation is to identify treatments to address serious behavior problems to meet the needs of individual clients. However, attention must also be given to the social environment as well as to individual needs. Training persons to better adapt to deficit or aberrant environments is not only disrespectful of the rights and needs of those individuals, it is also a futile enterprise. Ultimately, staff will need to accept responsibility to evaluate and, where necessary, alter the social environment to accommodate the individual. Attending to the characteristics of the physical and social environments in which persons with disabilities are expected to live, work, and recreate is critical if efforts to meet their individual needs are to be made in such a way that their full participation in society is ensured rather than restricted. This task is analogous to architecture accessibility for persons with physical disabilities. Society has come to accept responsibility not to impose unnecessary obstacles that prevent full participation by persons with motor and sensory impairments through the design of buildings, facilities, vehicles, and public areas in the community. Society must now also accept the responsibility to remove the far more pervasive and devastating restrictions in quality-of-life that confront persons with intellectual impairments and behavior problems.

The theoretical models described in Table 2.1 and organized together in Figure 2.1 reflect these concerns, ranging from variables controlling individual target behaviors to societal judgments that affect opportunities available to persons with disabilities and challenging behaviors. This manual will guide the design, implementation, and evaluation of behavioral interventions that address each of these multiple levels affecting the individual rather than relying on a single approach to deal with what are clearly complex needs requiring an integrated systems model.

ACTIVITY: A CASE EXAMPLE

Tom

Tom is 16 years old and has several behavior problems. He frequently hits himself on the head with his fist, and sometimes does this so hard that his skin becomes red and even bruised. He also pushes at the side of his eyeball with a finger, but does not do this very hard and does not seem to be causing any harm. Tom very much likes his new job training experience stamping freshness dates on milk cartons at a grocery store, and sometimes when he seems pleased with himself he bursts into excited hand flapping for about 10 seconds, then stops. Finally, he has a very awkward gait that may reflect some very mild cerebral palsy.

Discussion Questions

1. Suggest a purpose or cause for each of Tom's behaviors.
2. Which of Tom's behaviors sounds the most serious? Why?
3. Which of Tom's behaviors sounds as if it could become serious, even though it is not really a problem at the moment?
4. Suppose some customers in the grocery store where Tom is learning to work stare at him, particularly when he is walking and when he flaps his hands. What should be done?
5. In designing a program to improve Tom's behaviors, which behaviors should staff try to change? Why? Which behaviors should staff leave alone for now? Why? Are there any behaviors that might involve change by others? Which ones?

chapter

3

Lifestyle Perspectives

OVERVIEW

This chapter addresses lifestyles in terms of the extent to which a person's daily lifestyle reflects a quality-of-life that would be considered personally meaningful and socially valued. Issues of opportunity, roles, choice and control, social relationships, and affection and approval will be discussed as they apply to the daily life and life-span experiences of individuals with disabilities who exhibit excess behavior.

TRAINEE OBJECTIVES

At the completion of this unit, participant trainees will be able to:

1. List and describe the people, things, and activities they most enjoy in their own daily lives.
2. List and describe the people, things, and activities enjoyed by a client who has disabilities and exhibits severe behavior problems.
3. Discuss discrepancies between the daily lifestyle of a nondisabled individual and someone with disabilities and behavior problems, and make some general suggestions to reduce those discrepancies.

4. List at least four of ten daily choices that could be made available to a particular client and give specific examples for each choice.
5. Describe two major lifestyle choices —where to work and with whom to live—that persons value and suggest ways in which a person with severe disabilities could be involved in such lifestyle choices.
6. Identify social relationships that are or could be both personally valued and the source of a network of social support for a particular client.
7. Give an example from one's everyday experiences of how a family member or friend is a source of affection and approval, and explain how this differs from the idea of positive reinforcement for good behavior or punishment for bad behavior.
8. Identify aspects of valued social roles and activities in the four domains of home, work, recreation, and community, and recognize examples from the life of a person with disabilities that do and do not reflect those values.

ACTIVITY

John O'Brien and his colleagues have done work on lifestyle planning (e.g., O'Brien, 1987). The following activity is based on that work:

Arrange for a meeting that includes at least all team members to be responsible for the design of an intervention plan for a client who has severe behavior problems. Using a chalk board or a flip chart, draw the shape of a house at the center of a large space, leaving around the house at least one half the area available (this space will be used later). Next, identify three columns in the house, labeling them *People*, *Things*, and *Activities*. In the attic space of the figure, write the word *Choices* with a star at the beginning of this word. The figure of a house should look something like Figure 3.1.

People

Begin the group discussion by explaining that this will be a picture of a typical person's daily lifestyle at home. First, who are the people who live in that house? Ask for someone to volunteer a list of the members of his or her household. Typically, the list might include a spouse or partner, one or more children, and one or more friends or relatives in an extended family.

Things

Next, find out what things available in a household are valued by the hypothetical typical person. Ask the group to generate a sample list of things that might be reasonable and that sound like the kinds of things an adult might appreciate having at home. Do not record everything in a typical house on this list, just those things that are most valued by the individual who is the focus of this exercise. For example, the list might include the kinds of things that generally are available in most households, like a television, telephone, favorite chair or couch, stereo, the ingredients for a good meal or preferred snack, decorations that are highly valued, money, and various other items that a given individual might care most about (e.g., something that was received in childhood from a close friend or family member).

Activities

The last column to be filled is Activities. Again, have the group generate a list of the kinds of activities that are both enjoyable and expected to be available on a fairly typical day. It might be helpful to focus on a Saturday or Sunday—days that generally allow greater flexibility to do what is enjoyed at home. Encourage the group to be honest about the ac-

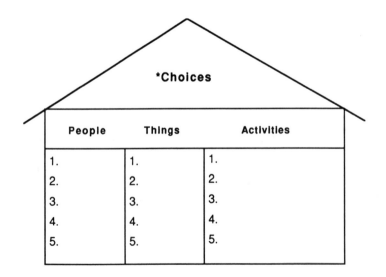

People	Things	Activities
1.	1.	1.
2.	2.	2.
3.	3.	3.
4.	4.	4.
5.	5.	5.

FIGURE 3.1. Lifestyle map.

tivities they list, rather than worrying about impressing others. For example, while any given weekend might include a special event like a party or an activity that might be regarded as constructive like exercise or mending clothes, if the group is candid and open, the list will be a bit more mundane. A typical weekend is most likely to include things like taking a nap, going for a walk, watching television, talking on the telephone with a friend, cooking and eating dinner, reading the Sunday paper with someone, talking with a child, working in the garden, and so forth. In fact, someone should mention sex as an activity! Encourage the participants to develop a realistic list that truly reflects the kinds of things people appreciate about being at home, the place where they are most likely to be able to do what they want.

Community Experiences

If it has not already been raised, now is the time to address the various community experiences of this typical person. Ask the group to suggest people, things, and activities that are available outside home, and write each of these down around the outside of the house in the figure. For each item, draw a line from the house to the item, and note how many times this outside experience is available in an aver-

age week. Thus, the group might list the following: 1) movies—1 time/week; 2) work—5 times/week; 3) grocery shopping—3 times/week; 4) eating at fast food restaurant—2 times/week; 5) church—1 time/week; 6) visiting relatives—variable, perhaps once every other week; 7) shopping for personal items—variable, perhaps once every other week; 8) going out to dinner—perhaps twice a month, and so forth.

Choices

Ask the group to return to the three lists of people, things, and activities and put a star by each item that the group members could expect to be able to choose for themselves. (Remember that the total list includes many items, most of which will reflect preferences of one sort or another, but that still might not have been chosen originally). Again, encourage the group to be open. When the activity has been done, at least one participant will provide some humor in discussing whether having his or her child was a conscious choice. Having some fun with the exercise will indicate that participants are interested and involved in thinking about the issues.

When the exercise is completed, the drawing should look something like Figure 3.2.

FIGURE 3.2.   Completed lifestyle map for typical person.

Discrepancies

Now compare this lifestyle map for the typical person with the actual lifestyle of a person who has a developmental disability and severe behavior problems. If the group is composed only of one team so that a particular client would be known to everyone, select the client regarded as the most difficult to manage and ask everyone to contribute as a second house for this real client is drawn and filled in. If the group is a larger one where not everyone will have personal knowledge of any one client, simply ask for a volunteer to fill in the lifestyle map for an individual who can be described very briefly for the group. When the second house has been filled in with people, things, and activities both at home and in the community, go back and put a star by those experiences that are known to be choices made by that client.

Summary

At this point, there should be little need for a great deal of discussion. If the exercise has been done thoroughly, the discrepancies in lifestyle will be obvious, indeed painful, for everyone to see. Encourage the group to name some glaring deficiencies in the disabled person's lifestyle that would seem most important to address first, and tell the group that they should return to these ideas whenever there is a need to design an intervention plan for an individual. Ask the group whether or not it seems reasonable to propose that persons with disabilities should be able to have experiences and exercise choices in a manner similar to those taken for granted by the hypothetical typical person.

At the completion of this activity, each participant should be aware of the kinds of daily and weekly opportunities available to most individuals in society to enjoy people, things, and activities they consider meaningful. If, however, a typical person became aware that his or her personal lifestyle was not, in fact, enjoyable, what would happen? For example, how much satisfaction does the average person feel when having to share living quarters with someone he or she does not like? How important are the things and activities available at home and in the community? Would he or she be happy without enjoying these dimensions of daily life? The authors believe that a starting point for addressing the needs of persons with developmental disabilities and problem behaviors is to ask these same questions about their lives. If there are significant discrepancies between the opportunities available to these individuals and opportunities other people appreciate and even take for granted, then addressing those discrepancies will be critical to the success of any effort to remediate problem behavior.

SOCIAL ROLES

Chapter 2 emphasizes that social attitudes toward persons with disabilities greatly influence what happens to those individuals. In a very interesting study subtitled, "What They See Is What We Get," Bates and his colleagues showed slides of a young woman with Down syndrome to teacher trainees, after which they were asked to report their attitudes toward and expectations for her (Bates, Morrow, Pancsofar, & Sedlak, 1984). The two groups of trainees saw the very same woman in the slides, but one group saw slides in which she was engaged in functional, integrated, and age-appropriate activities, while the slides that the other group saw showed her doing nonfunctional, segregated, and age-inappropriate activities. Although both groups held similar attitudes toward persons with disabilities in general and were equally knowledgeable about persons with mental retardation, the group who viewed the young woman engaged in the more normalized activities was more optimistic in evaluation of her competence and expectations for her future. This group reported, for example, that they felt she was capable of earning a higher wage in comparison to the level of employment that the group who saw the less positive situations believed possible.

The groups also differed in their predictions of where she eventually would be able to live, with the positive group seeing her in a more normalized, family-scale group home, while the negative group anticipated her living in a larger facility with up to 20 residents. What people saw about the very same person affected their judgments about what she could do and be!

Many persons who have disabilities such as severe mental retardation and autism are expected to live in institutions, attend segregated, disabled-only schools, and, as adults, attend day treatment programs or work in sheltered workshops. The reader most likely has experience in such a setting so assuming a layperson's perspective might be difficult, but what would be the impression of someone the reader knows who is not a professional and who saw a person with disabilities for the first time in, for example, a large institution? Would the image typically presented by such a facility make the average person feel comfortable about the potential for persons who have mental retardation to live in a home in a typical neighborhood? In fact, would even several visits to a large state institution—particularly to a unit for persons with behavior problems—make this typical person more or less accepting if a group home for persons with behavior problems were to open its doors on his or her street?

Now imagine an alternative picture. A child with Down syndrome attends a community recreation program with her older sister in the reader's own neighborhood center. She participates fully in the various activities that are enjoyed by the other children in the recreation program. In fact, she generally plays with two other children who are about her age but are not disabled. They know her well because she also attends school with them. They ride the same bus and eat lunch together every day. One of these other children is the reader's own daughter, and she says that she likes to play with Amy, the child with Down syndrome.

Coincidentally, the employer of the reader's spouse (who works in a chain grocery store as an assistant manager) suddenly announces that a young man with Down syndrome will begin training to bag groceries. The reader and spouse think of Amy and what she will be like as an adult: As a result of personal knowledge of Amy, would the reader feel supportive or hesitant about working together with this new employee?

Continue to take a layperson's perspective and now imagine seeing a television news broadcast about a special program for young adults with problem behaviors. The individuals in the program have various labels: autistic, deaf-blind, and mentally retarded. The news program shows brief glimpses of two young men and a young woman who engage in self-injurious behavior. A professional is then interviewed by the television reporter and explains that an electric shock device is being used to stop these young people from hitting themselves. Then there is a short segment on one of the young men wearing the shock device. He hits himself, and receives a shock. Later, he is seen working at a bench by himself putting blocks into a bucket, and the newsperson tells the audience that when Mr. Smith is not hitting himself he can participate in this prevocational program learning to sort objects. What would be the reader's impression of Mr. Smith? Suppose he were going to be trained to bag groceries at the local store? Based on the news program, would the reader be supportive or cynical about Mr. Smith's abilities and behavior?

Either positive or negative attitudes toward and perceptions of the capabilities of persons with disabilities can be promoted. Seeing a person with disabilities in a negative situation affects the way other people view that individual. Thus, demeaning living conditions, meaningless activities, and materials that are not appropriate to someone's age are not only unacceptable circumstances for the individual, they contribute to the maintenance of such unacceptable circumstances because of the image conveyed about the individuals in those situations. Simply because persons with mental retardation do not live in a certain community, the lay public comes to believe, after a time, that these persons *cannot* live there. Parents and teachers have lowered expectations for children and youth with autism when, in their region, such young people have no opportunities available to them that these adults would value for children who are not disabled.

Finally, persons with disabilities who are forced to live in congregate care facilities, work on repetitive and often meaningless jobs, and are not even provided with fashionable clothing and encouraged to look stylish and feel attractive clearly are not in the best position to view themselves in a positive manner. The authors believe that most persons with disabilities are well aware when their circumstances are demeaning. Even an individual who is diagnosed as severely retarded can quickly conclude that sorting popsicle sticks or buttons into bins that are then emptied in his or her presence by staff is not real work. Not only are such tasks likely to be as boring to a person with developmental disabilities as they are to other people, they sometimes can be the precipitating circumstances behind problem behaviors.

Table 3.1 lists some typical questions that can be asked about the opportunities available to persons with disabilities in each of the environmental domains. Check over this list, and evaluate the examples listed. Which are positive and which are negative, from the reader's perspective?

PATTERNS AND PERSPECTIVES ON THE ENVIRONMENT AND BEHAVIOR

As discussed in Chapter 2, the presence of behavior problems can actually represent skill deficits. Because an individual has not learned how to use a more adaptive or appropriate behavior for a particular situation, a behavior problem might be that person's strategy for communicating needs and preferences to others. Along these lines, recently there has been a great deal of interest in teaching alternative communication skills to replace excess behaviors that seem to have communicative intent. Such strategies are important and represent some of the more significant developments in establishing a proactive, positive approach to behavior problems. However, like other good ideas, this approach must make sense for the individual situation and should be incorporated into the context of general social, emotional, and motivational patterns for each person. The previous section discussed how some broad and general issues and opportunities can have a profound impact on one's lifestyle. This section discusses some more specific contextual patterns and suggests how the design of meaningful intervention programs must take these patterns into consideration.

Control

The first contextual pattern considered is *control*. It is very likely that extremely negative behaviors such as self-injury and aggression serve a general controlling function for the individual. In other words, though the specific function of an aggressive behavior could be narrowed down and identified as being used by the individual to escape or avoid people, places, or situations, it can be even more helpful to realize that the more general purpose of the behavior is to exercise control over what happens to oneself. The aggressive or self-injurious behavior is being used by the person to manipulate his or her environment.

Is it reasonable to allow the individual to exercise control over his or her environment? The average person would say that it

Table 3.1. Evaluating opportunities in the environmental domains

Domain	Questions	Example
Home	Would I want to live here?	Institution Group home for 15 persons Family-scale community residence
	Does my home include things I like to have and do?	Bedroom with twin beds Plain white sheets on my bed Plastic couch in the living room
	Did I choose and do I like the people I live with?	12 other persons with autism A friend A partner
Work	If I didn't do this job, would some-one else do it?	Sorting beads into separate containers Cleaning sugar water from the vocational area floor Washing cars at the police station
	Am I paid a reasonable wage for my work?	One token for every 5 minutes on task 50 cents for a 6-hour work day Minimum wage
	Would I be proud to tell my family and friends what I do?	Work at the grill at a fast food restaurant Clean up refuse at the city park Clean headphones for a national airline
Recreation	Is my leisure time activity something I personally want to do and enjoy?	Group trips to the bowling alley in the van Summer handicapped-only camping Playing videogames
	Do my leisure time activities give me things to do with my friends and family?	Playing videogames in a shopping mall arcade Going shopping Taking photographs
	Do my leisure time activities keep me occupied and happy during different kinds of free time across the life span?	Listening to a portable tape deck Leafing through magazines Special Olympics
General community	Are there things I can do outside my home?	Banking at the branch in the institution Making a meal from items purchased by staff Riding the public bus system

is, of course; some decisions are so important that it would be unacceptable to have others make them without one's consent or even involvement. Table 3.2 lists basic choices that most persons should have the opportunity to make. Most of these are day-to-day decisions like what clothes to wear or when to get up in the morning on a day off from work. Three of the decisions on the list, however, reflect major issues of control: Would not the average person resent having no say about whom to live with throughout life or what job to hold year after year? Similarly, sexual lifestyle is generally regarded as an issue of personal choice. The average person does not have total control over any of these choices, of course, but within certain budgetary guidelines, once someone is an adult, he or she generally does decide issues such as how to dress. And while the choice of a spouse obviously is dependent on whether the potential spouse also chooses the other person, few people would disagree that happi-

Table 3.2.   Questions that reflect daily and lifestyle choices

1. Can I decide what to eat for a meal or a snack, or must I eat what someone else decides I should have?
2. Can I decide what to wear, or are my clothes picked out for me each day as I dress and even purchased for me without my involvement?
3. If I have a day off (like a Saturday or Sunday) or have free time after dinner during the evening, can I decide for myself or with my friends/family what to do? Or is there a schedule I must follow on a regular basis?
4. Can I choose what television show to watch at least several times a week, so that I can usually watch all my favorite shows?
5. Can I decide on my own how to spend any of my money that is not committed for things like food and rent? Is this amount of money meaningful (i.e., more than a few dollars a week)?
6. Is it my decision whether I want to participate in a group activity?
7. Can I make a phone call to a family member or friend when I want to?
8. Can I decide for myself whether to stay up later or go to bed earlier than usual, or must I adhere to bedtimes decided by others?
9. Have I made a voluntary decision about whom I live with, and am I happy living with that person/those individuals?
10. Have I been able to select the job I want to have based on my interests and preferences in addition to my abilities and the availability of that job for me?
11. Can I decide whether to entertain others at home or visit family and friends at their homes?
12. Does my sexual lifestyle reflect my choices?
13. Is it my decision whether I drink, smoke, and/or engage in other "bad habits"?

Adapted with permission from a measure reported in Meyer, St. Peter, and Park-Lee (1986).

ness is greatly affected by the extent to which people *want* to live with those they do live with.

How much control over these decisions does a typical client have? A client who has spent a long time in institutions probably has had few opportunities to have an influence on his or her environment. The routines are rigid and almost never individualized. In addition, the assumption is generally made that the more severely disabled a person is, the less able the person is to make choices. Consequently, control is by definition not considered to be relevant for persons with severe disabilities. Perhaps the person has few skills that are really effective in manipulating the environment. For this person, staff might consider choice and control to be beyond the individual's capability. But is it?

Ironically, even community living may close off most opportunities to exercise reasonable control over one's environment. Persons with disabilities are seldom asked with whom they want to live. Instead, they are placed into group homes in the commu-

nity based on openings, shared places of employment and transportation patterns, and so forth. In the authors' experience, it is rare for persons with severe intellectual disabilities to even be involved in making such important decisions as where to live, with whom to live, or even which furniture to buy or which bedroom he or she prefers. Can persons who have severe intellectual impairments make such decisions? The authors think they can. There are curriculum strategies available to teach people with even the most severe disabilities to make choices, and some examples will be provided in Chapter 7.

Clearly, many of the most serious behavior problems in persons with disabilities can be attributed to issues of control. A person who is living in a restricted setting such as an institution or a group home may have few skills available to him or her. There are a few behaviors that work for the person who wants to exercise control because the person does or does not like what is happening to him or her. In situations like this, a behavior problem can be the most powerful tool available. Some excess behaviors, particularly the ones that have been described, are dramatic in their ability to effect change. A moment's reflection will support this, as one recalls how many times aggressive or self-injurious behavior has produced a major reaction from the person's social environment.

If this general point has merit, it is interesting to think of some of the logical implications. Consider, for example, the attempts that some researchers have made to regulate inappropriate behavior through a generalized compliance training procedure (with labels such as compliance training or pretask rehearsal). At first impression, training a person to be more compliant or cheerful about having to do things would seem to make sense, particularly if professionals are convinced that what the person is being expected to do is perfectly reasonable and even good for the person. If someone's difficult behavior can be interpreted as refusing to obey commands, follow directions, or complete work, then an effort to establish a strong class of responses in which the individual becomes more willing to comply sounds like a possible strategy to deal with the problem. However, from the viewpoint of the control issues just discussed, compliance training would be an even further reduction of the person's opportunities to exert control. Indeed, compliance training would be the exact opposite. The individual would be expected to become totally unable to exert control over others and his or her environment. Ultimately, if the authors' control interpretation makes sense, compliance training should backfire even if it seems to work initially. Someone might be forced at first to obey, or work, or follow, but when the conditions change, the authors would expect that the person would again use whatever behaviors the person has command of to stop doing things he or she basically dislikes or to demand to do things that he or she wants to do but is prevented from doing.

What might be an alternative that recognizes the importance of having reasonable control over one's environment? First, persons with disabilities can be provided with the training needed to be able to make the kind of choices listed in Table 3.2. In Chapter 7 of this manual, there is a sample program for teaching choices such as these (pages 113–115). But on a broader perspective, the authors also recommend generalized *influence-your-own-environment* training. This would be a relatively simply contingency to arrange. It would involve setting up a series of opportunities for the client to exercise some control and thus learn the general rule that one does have some power over the environment by using behaviors other than aggression, self-injury, and other extreme and inappropriate behaviors. These opportunities for control could take a number of different forms. At the most basic level, they would be situations in which the social environment was extremely responsive and sensitive to the person's needs.

For example, if the client is looking at something as if interested in it, rather than moving it out of reach, pick it up and bring it over for the client to touch, handle, eat— whatever is appropriate depending on the circumstances. This is very different from simply being positive to the client. The client must be able to exercise some degree of control, so it is necessary that he or she initiate some kind of attempt. Also, before saying "no" to a client, see whether it really matters that much if he or she does or does not do some proposed activity. After all, a self-injurious person might be taught to communicate and use the sign for "Leave me alone," but unless people actually leave the person alone when he or she uses the sign, what value will this skill have? Ultimately, creating such responsive environments will require some formal structures and serious changes in the ways that services and programs are conducted. But right now every environment, situation, and staff person can go a long way toward removing the artificial boundaries that restrict clients from exercising even simple preferences for objects, activities, and people.

A similar argument can be made about the physical environment. It too must be responsive to efforts made by the individual to have some influence over what is happening to and around him or her. For persons with very severe disabilities, special efforts would have to be made to ensure that voluntary control could be exercised, such as by using switches and other electronic or computer technology resulting in environmental responses such as playing music, making coffee, calling a friend, going to another part of the house, and so forth. It has been suggested by many psychologists working with nondisabled adults who are diagnosed as depressed that an important initial therapeutic strategy is to ensure that the client's environment is responsive. If it is not, the person might gradually strengthen the belief that nothing he or she can do will change events —an attitude that is called an *externally oriented locus of control.*

These same ideas can be extended to persons with severe disabilities. Thus, another level of intervention is to teach the client some simple assertiveness skills, such as being able to get caregivers and others to listen to requests or to agree to suggestions or to respect preferences (regardless of whether the caregiver thinks something is good for the client). Most other people are able to say, "Oh, let's not go shopping today; I don't really feel like it," and have others around them consider their feelings and acquiesce to their wishes, at least some of the time. In fact, the average person would be unhappy if forced to participate in multiple activities that others in the family wanted to do but the person hated doing and that were not balanced in some way by participation in activities that the person enjoyed. Effective assertive behavior not only allows people to control their environment some of the time but at other times provides another equally important function. It allows people to express anger or other strong emotions (pleasure, displeasure, etc.) in a socially appropriate manner. Again, if it is reasonable to suppose that much aggression and self-injurious behavior is motivated by anger or other strong feelings, then learning to be assertive and thereby either getting what one wants appropriately or at least expressing in an appropriate manner one's displeasure with what is taking place is a particularly useful alternative general skill.

The self-advocacy movement represents an even more sophisticated version of being able to exercise some control over one's destiny. Self-advocacy really is a more advanced form of assertive behavior. The goal is not only to be able to stand up for one's rights but also to advocate for oneself and change social expectations. Although there are not yet any empirical demonstrations of self-advocacy being conceptualized systematically as the alternative to excess behavior, the logic is compelling. Clearly, if one is to be an effective self-advocate and be capable of eliciting better treatment from others, then using socially undesirable power tactics like physical aggression is not likely to be very effective.

Again, it is imperative that the social environment actually respond to these new forms of behavior. If appropriate assertiveness and self-advocacy are to replace inappropriate excess behavior that in the past has been at least somewhat effective for the individual, the client must really be empowered. An analogy to young children can be used (not because persons with disabilities are like young children regardless of age—they are not—but because parents have experiences with their children that make sense to them and that will help them understand the point). Effective parenting involves providing increasing opportunities for children to regulate their own environment responsibly. Thus, children are given lunch money and a small allowance at first and later are trusted to make larger purchases and manage larger amounts of money. So-called overprotective parents who do things *for* the child all the time actually reduce the child's learning experiences and opportunities to recognize that it is one's own behavior that is responsible for the achievement of a given outcome.

Settings and programs that provide services for persons with disabilities often resemble the kind of caregiving environment that very young children experience. There are no opportunities for democratic decision-making, and all major activities and functions are performed by professionals, the adults in charge. Perhaps people underestimate the extent to which children are taught systematically to make increasingly responsible choices and given increasingly more complex opportunities to exercise appropriate control. As any parent of a teenager knows, failing to recognize increasing needs for choice and control will generate friction, while allowing for more democratic interrelationships between one adult (the parent) and the other, newer adult (the child) makes for a more harmonious household.

As persons with developmental disabilities also grow older and become adults, they must experience and practice positive strategies for similar control patterns in their lives. Being severely retarded does not mean that one cannot exercise control and choice. It is simply a matter of how constructively control and choice will be exercised. Other people must share the responsibility if serious behavior problems are maintained as the individual's major or sole strategy to influence his or her environment. To change the situation and replace serious behavior problems with new, positive skills and prosocial behavior will require that legitimate rights and needs to exercise control and choice be recognized.

Social Relationships

Another broad contextual pattern, that of social relationships, also requires consideration of specific social skills, which are most important. However, the context in which they are meaningful is one that incorporates one or more relationships. In many large institutional settings it is not uncommon for a staff member to take a special interest in a particular resident, and many close bonds develop as a result. However, staff turnover is typically high; staff are assigned to other programs, and so forth. One of the most striking characteristics of adult services, for clients whose families may be very isolated, elderly, or deceased, is that the adult clients often do not have stable or meaningful social relationships with a range of other people. So while discrete social skills are significant, it is also true that efforts must be made to ensure the emergence of friendships and more stable personal relationships across time.

Obviously this is easier said than done. Professional service staff are by definition paid for their role. Despite their personal feelings and best efforts, they often are not the ideal source of more normalized social relationships. The development of a variety of relationship possibilities, with peers and with appropriate others must be encouraged. Friendships, as previously discussed, are very important, but other types of relationships also can be fostered. The average person has ongoing relationships with people at work, neighbors, relatives, and so forth. These individuals have roles more extensive than simple friendships provide. For example, an older relative might be someone on whom one can rely for advice or help in a crisis or difficult time. Adults with severe developmental disabilities similarly need a range of relationships. In other social service areas this might be called one's *social support network.*

Most of the work on social development has been done with school-age children, and thus there is a great deal of interesting research on peer relationships and friendships. Children's support by adults tends to come from teachers (who may work with a student for a number of years) and the family, especially parents and siblings. But in the adult community the situation changes. An advocate, a job coach, a group home staff member, a member of the clergy, a volunteer, a buddy, might all provide social support. While the relationships with these persons might not always be in the form of traditional friendships that imply a more reciprocal social relationship, they do involve another caring person who is interested in the client's welfare, success, or happiness, and who is available to the client to fulfill a variety of social needs. Edgerton referred to some of these individuals as "benefactors" and found that such persons played a significant role in supporting persons who had been deinstitutionalized (Edgerton, Bollinger, & Herr, 1984). These benefactors made it more likely that persons with mild retardation could blend naturally into their neighborhoods and community, rather than remaining dependent on professionals to meet all their needs. Before initiating any kind of formal intervention program focusing on social skills, staff should examine the client's social ecology to see whether opportunities to form such relationships are in place. Adding this requirement to the principles of exercising control requires ensuring the availability of a range of social contacts and opportunities from which the client can select those interactions that he or she would enjoy.

Some years ago Landesman (Landesman-Dwyer & Berkson, 1984) did a series of studies of the opportunities for peer social interaction in different types and sizes of group homes and Intermediate Care Facilities (ICFs). Using direct observation methodology, she and her associates recorded the number and types of social interactions that took place in such facilities. They concluded that small facilities were not necessarily better, since the opportunity for social interaction often was greater in larger facilities, where there might either be more individuals that a given resident likes or wants to be friends with or simply more people likely to initiate and reciprocate social approaches. In trying to apply these interesting findings to the design of positive and habilitative services, it is important to apply the principles, not the superficial conclusion. A superficial conclusion would be that there should be more group homes that are larger in size, since one apparently is more likely to find a soul mate in a larger random group rather than a small one. This is, of course, not the logical implication. The proper conclusion to draw is that people with severe disabilities need opportunities to choose their social relationships, particularly the person(s) with whom they live. Residents must take an active role in selecting housemates to share very small group homes or apartments. Then, in addition, the smaller facilities need the kinds of contacts with the outside community that will provide alternative sources of social interaction.

Affection and Approval

By now the reader will have an idea of what is meant by contextual patterns. They refer to important characteristics of the environments within which clients with severe behavior problems are expected to function. Another such pattern can be described as something like the density of positive reinforcement available in the environment. The authors have been struck by this consideration for a number of years, ever since, in fact, they conducted detailed studies of the interactions between young severely disabled children with behavior disorders and their teachers. One of the categories coded was positive teacher affect, that is, touching the child in a supportive way, smiling, verbal praise and encouragement, and so forth. It was surprising that, although the teachers were all very well trained in principles of behavior modification and had their master's degrees in special education, the percentage of intervals in which positive affect was coded generally was very small. In many settings it is not uncommon to find that most of the comments and remarks of the teachers, caregivers, therapy aides, and so forth, are negative or the activities selected are not those preferred by the students or clients. This general contextual pattern could be thought of as being similar to what is known as classroom climate in regular schools or atmosphere variables in mental health facilities.

The pattern of affection and approval may also be defined as the density of unconditional positive opportunities. In other words, these are not reinforcers in the conventional sense of something that must be earned; instead, they serve as noncontingent positive opportunities. Associated with this is the absence of noncontingent negatives—hostile or critical remarks that are not related to particular behaviors exhibited by the client. In the research on the successful adjustment of deinstitutionalized psychiatric patients, who are often people returning to their own families, there is growing interest in the concept of expressed emotion (Leff & Vaughn, 1976). Roughly speaking, this refers to the degree to which the family members talk about the former patient in critical, rejecting, or hostile terms. In families that have high levels of expressed negative emotion, the patients do not make a good community adjustment.

There might appear to be some discrepancy between the concept of unconditional positive regard and principles of behavior modification that emphasize the importance of contingent reinforcement. Thus, it is worth explaining that these atmosphere variables are extensions of behavior theory, not in opposition to it. First of all, it is obvious that the positive affect and fun activities and other pleasing experiences should definitely not be contingent on undesirable behavior. In that sense these events would not occur at random. Thus the contingency is certainly one of exclusion—a bit like a very long-term Differential Reinforcement of Other Behaviors (DRO) contingency in which there continue to be high levels of reinforcement as long as negative behaviors do not occur.

It is critical to recognize also the eliciting function of atmosphere variables. In addition to being consequences, reinforcers can also be eliciting stimuli for positive emotional responses (cf. Staats, 1975). Positive events elicit such responses as feelings of pride and self-worth, positive affective responses such as happiness, and feelings of acceptance and comfort. It is obvious that when adult clients exhibit severe behavior problems, the surrounding atmosphere tends to be quite negative. Staff expectations are those of fear and suspicion. Even the frequent and regular prior planning meetings that might be required on behalf of a client with excess behavior can strengthen the notion that the client is difficult or dangerous. Eventually, it becomes almost impossible to create an atmosphere of acceptance and constructive opportunity. When such clients first come into a setting everything is centered around the negative: What will be done if there is an outburst; who will be responsible for handling the client; is the physician standing by with medication? Try thinking about what it was like coming home after a long trip or one's first semester away at college. Were there favorite foods or flowers from the family or a greeting at the bus stop? These are the types of experiences that are denied to persons moving into a new group home setting when staff expectations are of difficulty and problems. While the authors know of many settings that do create the kind of accepting atmosphere that makes a resident feel welcomed and wanted, it is interesting that there are no studies documenting the effect of atmosphere variables on severe behavior problems.

CONCLUSION

This section has discussed lifestyle perspectives that seem to be critical to one's quality-of-life: Is the environment responsive, socially enriched, and positive in atmosphere? These aspects have been referred to as contextual patterns because they are the contexts within which some of the more interesting positive treatment strategies must be embedded. The authors would not claim that these factors alone can remediate severe behavior problems, but they are necessary background conditions. More important, perhaps, these principles help to validate that a particular intervention strategy is being implemented appropriately and sensibly. Many specific behavioral intervention tactics are well-

intentioned but implemented in an illogical way. For example, a client's behavior reveals that he or she is angry, bored, or upset, and so staff attempt to regulate it by the use of aversive or punitive events. Or clients' behavior problems indicate that they have little control over their lives, and so a positive contingency is introduced that serves to control them more. By thinking of these contextual variables the professional is really asked to use criteria from the natural environment in the design of programs. What are circumstances like for nondisabled people? Can these general conditions be used as guidelines for planning interventions? In this sense, a social validation of intervention plans is being constructed, not by taking artificial plans and asking judges to rate their acceptability, but in the more fundamental sense of realizing what life would be like for anyone if they lived under adverse conditions. How can the environments of adults with severe behavior disorders be normalized? A family style group home may be a start, but this is normalized only in the physical sense. It is what happens in that home—socially, in terms of rules, and in terms of positive atmosphere—that defines a setting as habilitative, personally meaningful, and socially valid.

chapter

4

Assessing Priority
Target Behaviors

OVERVIEW

Chapter 4 begins with a process that caregivers and professional staff can use in order to identify which problem behaviors are priority targets for behavior change based on decision criteria regarding the nature and seriousness of behavior and its effects.

The second half of the chapter focuses on assessment strategies to guide intervention planning to address priorities for change. Data collection procedures are included that help to identify the conditions and circumstances in which the behavior is least and most likely to occur. This information is summarized to develop hypotheses about the function of a behavior for the individual, with each function suggesting a different intervention need.

TRAINEE OBJECTIVES

At the completion of this unit, participant trainees will be able to:

1. List several reasons that have been offered to support decisions to change behavior.
2. Identify three levels of seriousness of behavior problems, and recognize the decision criteria that apply to each level.
3. Given examples of behavior problems, decide which level of seriousness is involved, and describe the appropriate planning process that should follow.
4. Describe how a cost-benefit analysis might be used to supplement decision-making for Level II behaviors.
5. Describe how a cost-benefit analysis might be used to supplement decision-making for Level III behaviors and how it would differ from that used for Level II behaviors.
6. Identify data collection strategies that can be readily used in typical community and residential settings to assess behavior.
7. Summarize information on the occur-

rence of behaviors to identify when they are most/least likely to be a problem.

8. Identify three possible social communicative functions of behavior, and give examples of each.

9. Identify possible self-regulatory and self-entertainment functions of behavior, and give examples of each.

10. Given an hypothesis regarding the function of a behavior, describe a general process for how that information would be used to design an intervention.

INTRODUCTION

Persons with severe developmental disabilities who also have behavior problems are a challenge to services, settings, their families, and professional staff. In addition to the complexities of the learning and behavioral needs these individuals have, they also are least likely to enjoy daily participation in the kinds of meaningful experiences available to other people in society. They may live at home with their families, but these individuals are also those most likely to be placed outside the home into environments that are not at all home-like. And persons with complex disabilities typically have few meaningful personal relationships. Parents may continue to maintain contact with their child, and persons with disabilities may form friendships with one another, but it is far more likely that, over time, these individuals will have contact primarily with paid staff and professionals. This is, of course, very different from the kinds of personal relationships and social interaction experiences that other people enjoy and even take for granted.

This means that not only does a person with multiple disabilities have many programming needs because of his or her disabilities, he or she is also least likely to enjoy a full and rich daily life and

participation in meaningful experiences throughout the life span. Chapter 3 described a map of the average person's home life for comparison of the experiences of such a person with those available to a client who exhibits excess behaviors. It is important always to use any discrepancies between the two when making decisions about what will happen to someone with developmental disabilities that can reduce or eliminate those discrepancies. Sometimes the changes that need to be made involve changing the environment as well as changing that person's behavior.

SELECTING PRIORITIES

Subsequent chapters of this manual will describe the kinds of changes in social relationships, environments, tasks and activities, and behavioral programs that might be used to address behavior problems. But some decisions must also be made regarding which particular needs are of highest priority for the individual at present and in the future.

Some excess behaviors are so serious that there is no question that an effort must be made to decrease and eliminate them as soon as possible. Such behaviors might also be so serious that they should be included in a child's Individualized Education Program (IEP) as deceleration goals along with the various skill-building goals designed for instruction. Other behaviors are only slightly less serious, so that there is agreement that something should be done, but it may be possible to modify those behaviors primarily through skill development goals on the IEP. Similarly, for an adult, it might be possible to address certain behavior problems by selecting and teaching alternative skills to replace them over time. Finally, as mentioned earlier in this manual, there are many other behavior problems or excess behaviors that, for various reasons, may not be targeted for intervention at any given time.

Table 4.1. Summary of ratings of importance of criteria for selecting target behaviors

Decision criteria item	Teachers' mean rating ($N = 36$)	Teachers' rank order ($N = 36$)	Educational assistants' rank order ($N = 101$)	Psychologists' rank order ($N = 21$)
14. Dangerous to child	19.86	1	5	1
12. Dangerous to others	19.42	2	3	2
6. Interferes with learning	18.50	3	2	7
8. Replaces negative behaviors	17.97	4	7	4
9. Increases independence	17.92	5	4	9
1. Immediately functional	17.58	6	9	8
17. Prerequisite to other behaviors	17.42	7	8	5
11. Increases acceptance	17.31	8	1	6
15. Multiple effects	16.50	9	10	3
5. Parent concern	16.19	10	6	10
7. Enjoyable activity	15.81	11	12	14
10. Adequate resources	14.53	12	11	12
2. Damages materials	14.36	13	13	13
13. Age-appropriate	12.81	14	15	17
3. Weakness compared to other behaviors	12.60	15	17	16
16. Developmentally appropriate	12.56	16	14	15
4. Easy to modify	11.06	17	16	11

From Evans & Meyer (1985), p. 52. Copyright © 1985 by Paul H. Brookes Publishing Co.; reprinted by permission.

Logistically, however, even if there seemed to be a need to attempt to change every behavior problem that a person has, this simply would not be possible! Some individuals have many behavioral needs, and not all of them could possibly be addressed at one time. In other cases, attempting to address all behavioral problems would mean valuable time away from learning new skills. Because persons with severe developmental disabilities have so little habilitative and program time in proportion to their learning needs, because they have so few positive skills, and because most behavior problems actually will be decreased most effectively by the teaching of new skills rather than direct intervention with the behavior, deceleration goals should be considered a priority *only when unavoidable*.

Evans and Meyer (1985) identified 17 reasons that typically are offered as a rationale for identifying priority goals that might be included in a habilitative program for an adult or child. The authors asked various professionals (teachers and psy-

chologists) and paraprofessionals to identify those reasons they found most *compelling* for including a particular goal in someone's program. Table 4.1 lists these reasons from the highest rated to the lowest rated according to the teachers' ratings and the ratings of educational assistants and psychologists. Note, for example, that "dangerous to child" was most important, with "dangerous to others" close behind. In contrast, "weakness compared to other behaviors," "developmentally appropriate," or "easy to modify" were not regarded as very important reasons to change behavior. Based on this and other research on decision-making in programs for persons with disabilities, the authors have proposed three levels of seriousness of behavior that can be used to select priority target behaviors whenever a learner has multiple needs.

Determine which Behaviors Are a Priority

Any behavior can be categorized into one of three levels of seriousness that have implications for whether or not an intervention will be planned and what the intervention will be like. Step 1 of behavior assessment involves applying these categories:

Level I: Urgent Behaviors Requiring Immediate Attention
Level II: Serious Behaviors Requiring Formal Consideration
Level III: Excess Behavior Reflecting Normal Deviance

Level I: Urgent Behaviors Requiring Immediate Attention   Urgent behaviors that demand immediate efforts to intervene are those that are health or life-threatening. These behaviors might be described as self-injurious or self-abusive and include such things as head banging; slapping or hitting oneself; biting one's hands, fingers, and other body parts; rumination and vomiting; picking at skin so that tissue damage results; placing sharp objects into one's shoes; and many other behaviors. These behaviors can cause tissue damage, infection, malnutrition, and chemical imbalance in the body. They can lead to, for example, blindness (eye poking and head banging), hearing impairments (putting objects into one's ears), and even death (serious head banging and vomiting). There is also no ambiguity regarding these behaviors. Almost everyone would agree that they are of serious consequence for the individual person and that it would be in the person's best interest to eliminate these behaviors.

Thus, there are clear intervention implications for Level I behaviors. First, the behavior is serious enough that it should be dealt with in the individual's program plan through the inclusion of a deceleration goal. There should also be one or more alternative skill acquisition goals designed to teach the individual alternative positive behaviors to replace the self-injurious behavior over time. In summary, intervention is always needed and the self-injurious behavior should be monitored formally.

Level II: Serious Behaviors Requiring Formal Consideration   Serious behaviors that require formal consideration are those that represent one of four risk characteristics: 1) the behavior interferes with learning, 2) the behavior is likely to become serious in the near future if not modified, 3) the behavior is dangerous to others, and 4) the behavior is of great concern to caregivers.

Any behavior (such as screaming and crying, which interfere with activities and tasks) that is truly serious enough that it interferes with learning obviously could jeopardize an individual's program in all areas. Sometimes learners engage in behavior that is not actually self-injurious but that *looks* a great deal like self-injurious behavior. Examples might be self-biting, which does not result in any tissue damage, light face slapping, and pushing fingers against the eyes. These behaviors look like low intensity self-injurious behavior, and many clinicians and researchers believe that self-injury probably starts out looking like these examples. If so, it is crucial to intervene with the behavior before it becomes a strong habit that is prominent in the person's repertoire and more difficult to change *and* before injury does occur.

Obviously, behavior that is dangerous to others, such as hitting peers and staff, presents many problems for the individual and the program. It is perhaps only slightly less alarming than self-injurious behavior only because behavior that is dangerous to others can be controlled depending on what others do. It is also possible that behavior such as hitting or biting others can be so severe and difficult to control that it will be judged a Level I (not Level II) behavior requiring urgent attention.

Finally, some behaviors are priorities for the person's family and caregivers, in that what they care most about is a particular behavior. It is possible that the professional staff might not even agree with the family that the behavior is important, but the issue is that the behavior is indeed important to the family. For example, the parents might say that they are most concerned by their child being noncompliant and tantruming in public places. This has become such a problem for them that they feel they no longer can take the child out in public; this in turn means that the family cannot go out together and must always have a sitter in order to do anything without the difficult child. The stress of such a situation might well lead to a decision to place the child outside the home. Ironically, then, the child might learn many new skills in a school program and still become institutionalized because this concern of the parents was the "straw that broke the camel's back." Thus, if professionals cannot persuade the parents that a behavior is not really serious (which, of course, it might be even though the professionals may not often witness the behavior), it is crucial that they commit to helping modify such a behavior to support the integrity of the family and the child's security at home.

In each of these cases, the behavior is serious enough to be reflected indirectly on the Individualized Program Plan through the identification of alternative skill acquisition goals. It may also be necessary to add separate behavior deceleration goals, though these should be in addition to a comprehensive skill acquisition program plan. Professionals should never substitute deceleration goals for skill building goals. In addition, at this level a cost-benefit analysis should be done, which is described briefly at the end of this section. Therefore, the general rule is that intervention most typically is warranted with Level II seriousness behaviors, and the behaviors should be monitored formally along with any potentially equally or more serious behaviors that might be related to the target behaviors. (See the cost-benefit section.)

Level III: Excess Behavior Reflecting Normal Deviance There are several other reasons that might be offered to justify intervention with a behavior problem that falls into the category of normal deviance and that might not be serious enough to be reflected in the individual's program. These include the following characteristics: 1) the behavior is not improving or getting worse (e.g., screaming and crying during noninstructional times), 2) the behavior has been a problem for some time (e.g., thumb sucking), 3) the behavior damages materials (e.g., throwing items on the floor), 4) the behavior interferes with community acceptance (e.g., echolalia in public places), and 5) an improvement in the behavior would generate another behavioral improvement (e.g., a reduction in teasing peers might lead to positive interaction with peers).

While each of the behaviors in these categories might be important enough to justify a priority target for change, they are less compelling than Level I and Level II behaviors. Some analogies to behaviors displayed by nondisabled individuals might help to illustrate. Someone might be slightly overweight and continue to eat too much (the behavior is not improving or getting worse or the behavior has been a problem for some time). This individual might decide to start dieting, but then decide not to do so because of the costs involved. The person might have other responsibilities and things to worry about and not care particularly about being slightly overweight. He or she may also be unwilling to give up eating snacks in front of the television during the evening, gourmet meals at home, and eating out in restaurants with friends on a regular basis. Similarly, another individual might damage materials, for example, by chewing on pencils when working so that the pencils definitely are ruined. Again, however, there could be reasons why the person elects not to worry about changing the pencil-chewing behavior. The authors have listed "interferes with community acceptance" at Level III for a slightly different reason. It seems that the community actually is quite accepting of minor discrepancies in behavior and even some rather major differences among people. Sometimes it is far easier and perhaps even more correct to expect the community to become more tolerant of a behavior such as echolalia than to require the person to refrain from it. And, finally, it might be that an improvement in one behavior would lead to other beneficial changes, but it might be far more appropriate simply to identify skill acquisition goals that more directly lead to those improvements.

For Level III behaviors, the behavior is not serious enough to occupy valuable programming time on an IEP or IPP. If consistent with skill acquisition goals already reflected on the program plan, staff might identify alternative skill acquisition goals. Whether or not a deceleration goal would also be included would depend on a cost-benefit analysis similar to the Level II cost-benefit analyses, but also including costs to staff time and program resources. (See the section following on this concept.)

The general rule is that intervention most typically is warranted only if all other needs are being met (which is not very likely). It might be important to monitor some of these behaviors informally even if there is no intervention, and if an intervention is planned, there should, of course, be some monitoring of the target behavior.

The Cost-Benefit Analysis

Although behavior modification has not traditionally recognized the existence of the phenomenon of symptom substitution, the field has come to realize that excess behaviors and skill behaviors are related to one another in sometimes complex ways within the individual. For example, a staff person might notice that whenever someone is required to spend long periods of time at a seat-work task, the person becomes increasingly agitated and finally erupts into a self-injurious episode. Another individual almost always follows

shouting with a direct physical attack on someone else. In other cases, when restrained from engaging in a behavior such as body rocking, the person might instead engage in face slapping or some other equally serious behavior. At Level II, it is particularly important to think about possible interrelationships between such behaviors and be watchful that a successful deceleration program with one behavior does not actually result in a serious escalation in a more serious behavior. In such a case, the costs of intervening may outweigh the benefits. At Level II, the cost-benefit analysis should be restricted to forming hypotheses regarding consequences for the learner's repertoire; these behaviors are serious enough that it would be inappropriate not to intervene simply because it would cost the program or staff too much in terms of staff time and program resources.

On the other hand, Level III behaviors simply are not as serious for the individual, and the cost-benefit analysis here can reflect program resources. The first costs considered should, of course, be possible detrimental changes in the individual's behavior. But, in addition, it would be appropriate to decide not to intervene with a Level III behavior based on a lack of staff time or resources to effectively implement a responsible intervention. This is true only for Level III behaviors. Level II and Level I behaviors are so serious, based on objective criteria, that resources must be provided and staff time must be arranged. Otherwise, the consequences potentially would be so greatly damaging to the individual (and the program) that the ultimate costs incurred would be overwhelming.

ACTIVITY

Break into small groups of six–eight staff people. In each group, have someone identify a person with developmental disabilities who also displays many behavior problems. Describe the individual briefly and list the person's behavior problems. Have the group then classify the problem behaviors as Level I, II, or III behaviors.

For any Level II and III behaviors, have the group specify whether or not they would recommend intervention even though the behavior is not as serious as Level I.

Do a cost-benefit analysis for at least one behavior at Level II and another at Level III.

Have two groups report back to the larger group. Discuss the cost-benefit analyses in particular, and be sure that the examples clearly differentiate the procedures chosen for Level II and III.

ASSESSING BEHAVIOR

Careful Description

As discussed in Chapter 2, behavior problems can be described in various ways. For example, it is fairly common to classify excess behaviors into broad categories using labels such as disruptive, self-injurious, and stereotypic. Other behaviors might be referred to as uncontrolled, including various socially undesirable behaviors that seem to represent delays or a failure to develop typical regulatory skills; bed wetting and drooling might fall into this group. But for Step 2 of behavior assessment, behaviors should be described in objective and measurable terms. Usually this is a topographical description, but care should be exercised when giving only the form of a behavior. Consider the following descriptions of forms of behavior. (These examples are taken from Evans and Meyer, 1985, p. 25.)

1. Raising his right arm, the child repeatedly extends and retracts his fingers toward his palm in a gripping/releasing type of motion.
2. An adult male repeatedly pushes his hand hard against his eye, making a fist and rubbing his eye rapidly with his knuckles.
3. In the middle of an activity, the individual suddenly begins shouting, jumps

up, and runs crying to a corner of the room.

How would these behaviors be labelled? Actually, only one of them represents something that might be regarded as a behavior problem. Which one? The first is a nondisabled toddler waving goodbye; the second is an adult with a severe allergy problem that causes his eyes to itch and water; and the third is a girl with autism, whose extreme sensitivity to high pitched noises caused a reaction to the sound of a lawn mower outside; she ran to escape the noise. These behaviors might be labelled with terms such as stereotypic (the first example), self-injurious (the second example), and disruptive (the third example). And it is certainly possible that the behaviors fit these categories in principle. But in the first case, the ritual actually represents something that is socially acceptable, desirable, in fact. And in the second and third examples, knowing more about the circumstances changes the observer's perception of the behaviors themselves. In general, knowing the forms of a behavior does not give enough information to make intervention decisions. It is necessary to find out what the function of that behavior is as well.

Motivational Analysis of Behavior: Identifying Likes and Dislikes

This section addresses Step 3 of behavior assessment, the analysis of information needed about a behavior problem that has been identified as a priority for change. Traditional behavioral assessment strategies emphasize the importance of doing a *functional analysis of behavior*, sometimes described as an A-B-C analysis:

A. What are the *antecedents* that reliably predict when the behavior problem will occur?
B. What is the *behavior* itself?
C. What are the *consequences* that typically follow the behavior?

Systematic use of A-B-C procedures requires knowing as much as possible about antecedent and consequent events surrounding instances of the behavior. It is equally important to identify antecedents that reliably predict that the behavior will *not* occur.

In the past, much emphasis has been placed on using an A-B-C analysis of problem behavior in order to identify consequences that are either reinforcing or punishing to the individual. A consequence is considered to be reinforcing if a behavior increases in rate or intensity following instances where the behavior leads to that consequence. A consequence is considered to be punishing if, following instances where the behavior leads to such consequences, the behavior decreases in rate or intensity. Thus, typical interventions to decrease the occurrence of a negative behavior would be to remove reinforcing consequences and/or to introduce punishing consequences, which would always be specified for an individual. Knowing something about which consequences motivate an individual in what ways may even be used as the primary basis of an intervention plan directed to modifying a behavior problem.

At the very least, general ideas about the individual's likes and dislikes are necessary before the design of any intervention plan. Go back to Figure 3.1, the Lifestyle Map. What people does the individual care most about? What are the things and activities that the individual presently likes and dislikes? How could more of the people, things, and activities that the person prefers be introduced into his or her daily lifestyle if this were important to an intervention plan? The average person is sufficiently motivated at home, for example, to do the dishes and change the bed sheets because of appreciation for eating a good meal on clean dishes and the feeling of clean sheets. And the average person may be likely to reward himself or herself with a preferred activity or new outfit after successfully dealing with a particularly challenging week when many important and stressful things had to be done. It is also true that when the negative aspects outweigh the positive aspects of some domain of our life—job, marriage, house—people may either seek some major changes or become increasingly dissatisfied or even depressed. Knowing the likes and dislikes of an adult with developmental disabilities in relationship to the lifestyle currently available to that person might provide information critical to improving problem behavior.

It is possible to be somewhat successful in producing behavior change using a strategy of manipulating contingencies without actually addressing the function of a behavior. For example, suppose certain valued privileges are taken from the person with autism (who could not tolerate high pitched noises) whenever she displays the behavior in the earlier example. One could probably control her behavior so that she would learn not to jump up and yell whenever she is in the room with anyone who typically delivers such consequences. But if the function of her behavior is incorporated into the intervention design, there might be more success in producing a lasting change in her behavior that would be generalized to situations where the trainer is nowhere in sight. Knowing that she engages in the behavior because she cannot tolerate the noise, perhaps a long-term intervention strategy would be to teach her to self-regulate in various ways. First she might be taught to anticipate antecedents associated with her problem so she could prepare herself. She could be taught to cover her ears, perhaps even to use a portable cassette player for her favorite music not solely as a leisure time activity but also as a reasonably socially acceptable strategy to block out stimuli (the loud lawnmower noises) that are a problem for her. In fact, this may be a strategy that other people sometimes use to deal with environmental events that are difficult to tolerate.

Thus, while a traditional A-B-C analysis can reveal important information for the design of interventions, more information regarding motivation is even better. First the A-B-C analysis should be done not only for occurrences of the behavior (B), but also for times when the behavior typically does not occur. In addition, however, it is crucial to develop a hypothesis about the possible function of the behavior for the individual.

Identifying the Function of a Problem Behavior

Step 4 of behavior assessment is to develop some hypotheses about the function a particular behavior problem has for the learner. As discussed earlier, in almost all cases, the behavior problem is used by the individual to accomplish something to meet certain needs or desires. It might not be a very appropriate behavior, so it is regarded as negative by others. Yet, the individual engages in the behavior at a high rate, suggesting that no matter what others think about the behavior, it is a reasonably successful strategy for the learner, at least some of the time.

Evans and Meyer (1985) summarized several functions that behaviors might have:

1. *Social-Communicative:* These behaviors clearly are related to social interactions. The behavior seems to be a method of nonverbal communication, and might involve the following different types of messages in different individuals or at different times: 1) "Leave me alone," or "I don't want to do this" (maybe the task is too difficult, the person is tired, does not like the other person); 2) "Pay attention to me!" (the staff person might be spending time with someone else); and 3) "I want that [object/activity]" (maybe someone just asked the person to stop an enjoyable activity, or the person wants someone else's sandwich).

2. *Self-Regulatory:* Behavior serving this function varies with environmental circumstances and perhaps how the person feels physically (e.g., tired, overstimulated, sexually aroused). The behavior seems to be a strategy to adjust arousal level, pay attention to something that is very interesting (when there are distractions) or very boring (when the person is tired).

3. *Self-Entertainment or Play:* This behavior may be related to social situations (i.e., it looks like an attempt to play with others) or occur only when the person is alone. It might be, for example, a way for the person to entertain himself or herself when left alone or waiting for something. Or, perhaps it is a strategy for playing with others, even when the behavior is actually regarded as negative by them. This can explain the otherwise confusing situation when a learner seems to prefer to tease or even hit a peer whom he or she is known to like.

ACTIVITY

As a large group, give examples of behavior problems that seem to fit one of these functions. Be sure to include examples in which the very same behavioral form seems to have different functions—perhaps even for the same individual at different times.

The discussion might reveal that it is not always easy to figure out what the function of a behavior might be. Ask the group to think about what further information might be of assistance in these cases. How can additional ideas about possible functions of behavior be generated? (See next section.)

GENERATING HYPOTHESES ABOUT THE FUNCTIONS OF BEHAVIOR

Table 4.2 is adapted from Meyer and Evans (1986) and provides some examples of a process that might be used to generate hypotheses about functions of behavior and then test them by determining what really happens under different circumstances. The table suggests more than one possible explanation for the same behavior. When planning programs to remediate these particular behavioral difficulties, staff and others who know the individual well should be encouraged to do this kind of brainstorming in order to consider adequately all the reasonable explanations. Then certain questions should be asked in order to test them. It might be possible to complete this process based on informal and day-to-day knowledge of the individual, but it would be helpful also to collect some data to assist decision-making. This might include keeping daily logs; objectively measuring certain specific behaviors at different times (particularly using a scatterplot technique developed by Touchette, MacDonald, and Langer, 1985), using a checklist like the Motivation Assessment Scale, developed by Durand (1988), and even using required Incident Records as a source of information.

In keeping with the approach of this manual to encourage local decision-making by all those concerned with remedying excess behavior, it is always helpful to encourage everyone who knows the client well to make suggestions about the possible functions of behavior. Posing the question, "Why do you think this behavior is occurring?", can produce quite a variety of answers. Not everyone thinks about the world in behavioral terms and principles! In general, it is worth encouraging more rigorous thinking about behavior by trying to use sound behavioral and psychological principles. However, this may discourage people from speculating about causes of behavior that may be very insightful, and based on their ordinary knowledge of everyday behavior. A somewhat similar argument has been made by Wahler (1980), who claimed that mothers' reports of their children's behavior disorders gave important clues as to the possible maintaining variables. A comment such as, "He just does it to annoy us," from a staff member, may say quite a lot about maintaining factors (negative attention), lack of alternative entertainment (the client is bored), and the attributions of the staff regarding the client's behavior. If malicious intent is attributed to the behavior by the care provider, the intervention design clearly will have to focus on much more than teaching positive alternatives, since such a plan probably will not be carried out by staff.

Parents, staff, and others who interact with an individual on a frequent basis will have a reasonable intuitive understanding of excess behavior, so it is necessary to listen with a trained ear to descriptions of the behavior. Behavior described as "totally unpredictable—it just seems to come from nowhere," may need to be explored more carefully to determine direct organic causation. Trait labels, such as, "She's so stubborn," often indicate a general noncompliance or inflexibility that might have to be targeted for intervention or might reveal some serious problems in the client's lifestyle such that there simply is no incentive to be compliant. Explanations that do not seem very sophisticated, such as, "Well, I think he does it because he is severely retarded," or, "because he doesn't know any better," at least indicate that the observer recognizes the relationship between excess behavior and the failure to acquire certain social rules, conventions, or skills.

Listening carefully to laypeople's notions about behavior may yield some strange ideas, but often these are more valuable than baseline data recording carried out by individuals who are not dedicated

Table 4.2. Generating alternative explanations to identify the function of excess behavior at home, at work and in the community

Description of excess behavior	Alternative explanations	Corresponding function test—Will excess decrease if:
After approximately 15 minutes of work (sorting items into small plastic bags for a contract), Mr. James begins yelling and throwing the materials on the floor; he then runs away from the work bench toward the coffee area.	1. He dislikes the supervised situation, a particular trainer, or the task itself.	1.1. Demands to work are alternated with low-demand interactions? 1.2. Trainer or task is changed?
	2. He tires quickly, and loses control after a short period of working or being on task.	2.1. Work sessions are shortened, then increased gradually to longer periods? 2.2. Work sessions are alternated with easy and enjoyable activities?
	3. Task is too difficult, and he is unable to cope with stress, errors, and so forth.	3.1. Task is broken down into smaller steps? 3.2. Errorless learning strategies are used? 3.3. Another equally important task is substituted that is less difficult?
When walking in the room (or indoor environment), Ms. Teall makes the rounds, pushing objects off tables and shelves onto the floor.	1. She enjoys (is reinforced by) attention from peers and/or direct care staff that results from excess behavior.	1.1. Staff ignore behavior? 1.2. Staff say "No"? 1.3. Peers are not present in the room?
	2. She enjoys watching and hearing objects fall onto the floor (and may be otherwise bored).	2.1. Floor is carpeted or objects themselves are soft? 2.2. She is busy with a novel or preferred activity?
	3. She needs more physical activity and exercise.	3.1. Walking across room occurs after a more active versus a sedentary activity? 3.2. She is tired?
After approximately 10–20 minutes in a community training experience such as a trip to the grocery store, teenager hits a peer and/or begins to shout at others.	1. Teenager cannot tolerate relatively unstructured settings (with multiple stimuli, etc.) for more than a short time.	1.1. Community experience is initially shortened to 10–15 minutes? 1.2. Supervision and structure is increased?
	2. A specific peer is making him or her angry.	2.1. Peer is absent, or another peer is closer, interacting more, etc.? 2.2. Any aversive behavior by specific peer is interrupted in some way?
	3. When peer or another person does not respond as she or he wishes, teenager is attempting to "get his/her way."	3.1. Peer is taught to respond positively when possible and: 3.2. Peer taught to move away when she or he cannot respond?
	4. Teenager is attempting to communicate with others, but is not understood or is ignored unless she or he tantrums.	4.1. Attention is provided on a consistent schedule? 4.2. Any request or initiative is responded to versus ignored?

Reprinted with permission, with some revisions, from Evans and Meyer (1985).

behavioral observers. (These individuals may even resist this kind of recording. Perhaps the assumption that direct service staff can be trained to perform another version of what a specially trained psychologist does is not only unrealistic but may fail to take advantage of the very real strengths that these staff persons do have in other important areas.) In order to go beyond the naiveté that may sometimes emerge when speculation is encouraged, it is possible to follow up with questions that shape thinking in constructive ways. For instance, if the observer/informant uses a great deal of trait descriptors, then systematically asking questions such as, "Can you give me an example of him being stubborn?" helps focus attention on specific behaviors. Questions regarding the client's affect ("Does he usually laugh or smile when he is engaging in the stereotypic behavior?") point to sources of information that can help in the analysis of behavior. (Smiling or laughing indicates the possibly self-reinforcing nature of the behavior.) Most important, however, one can establish the concept that explanations are always hypotheses that need to be tested, by carefully asking, "If your explanation is correct, what predictions can we now make about how the client will behave in such-and-such a situation?"

EXAMPLE

David is 25 years old, lives in a large institution, and is enrolled in a job training program in a community college. David's residential program is therefore very restrictive, while his work training program is much less so. Because the work program is community based, David spends a great deal of his day program time learning not only vocational skills but also participating in community recreation activities, and learning general community skills, such as how to shop in a grocery store. David is diagnosed as severely mentally retarded; he walks with an awkward gait and has engaged in serious head banging for many years. This behavior was at its worst sev-

eral years ago when David was living at the institution but his educational program was highly structured and included response-cost and seclusion time-out for negative behaviors. The structured program was associated with an escalation of the behaviors and was discontinued the following school year. Subsequently, David's day program activities changed rather dramatically and now emphasize the acquisition of new skills in the context of a variety of functional and typical activities in various environments. This program might be characterized as a *distributed trial instructional format*, rather than the *operant conditioning format* of the earlier program that included repetitive practice of isolated skills and immediate, consistent consequences. Although his negative behavior now occurs far less frequently than it did, David still engages in head banging. Sometimes he does this several times a week (in a short episode of two or three impacts), and sometimes the behavior occurs at a high rate for days at a time.

Generating some explanations for David's head banging behavior in order to guide the intervention plan for David would require a great deal more information than what was just provided. More explicit information on the nature of David's head banging and its exact rate could be added but even this might not be helpful in terms of identifying possible functions of this behavior. Therefore, following is an example of a Daily Log (Figure 4.1) (completed three times weekly, always on Monday, Wednesday, and Friday regardless of events or behavior) and an Incident Record (Figure 4.2) that staff keep for David. These data collection strategies were specifically designed to be relatively easy to use, meet state reporting requirements (i.e., the Incident Record), and at the same time provide a rich resource of information that might be used to identify the function of a behavior. At the very least, this information should give staff and caregivers some ideas regarding what might be motivating David's head banging, which could then be tested by systematic observation of his behavior in different circumstances and under different conditions.

Based on the information provided in the log and in this single Incident Record, what

Daily Log (Form 1)

Client name: _David_   Date of week/date: _Monday, April 12_

Log entry by: _Dan_   Community experience: _Shopping trip to the grocery store_

Comment briefly on the day's events and the student's behavior. Note any incidents that occurred that seem important to you. Give your impressions regarding what the client enjoyed/did not enjoy and tasks on which he worked well.

David did fairly well on his typical Monday schedule but had a serious problem in the early morning just before we started work. He was sitting at a coffee table and listening to a tape, and Tony came up to him, stared at him, and tried to take the recorder away. David got very upset and started yelling. Tony continued to bother him and David began to hit his head on the coffee table. I was able to get his attention and he calmed down when we went for a walk.

He especially enjoyed the grocery store in the afternoon and was okay after that.

1. Overall, what kind of day did the client have? (Circle one number only.)

1	②	3	4	5
Very bad day	Not okay	Not sure	Okay	Very good day

2. How well did he do on tasks while at work today? (Circle one number only.)

1	2	3	④	5
Very poor	Not okay	Not sure	Okay	Very good

3. How well did he do on community activities today? (Circle one number only.)

1	2	3	④	5
Very poor	Not okay	Not sure	Okay	Very good

Comment on any behavior that occurred that was positive or negative.

_____

FIGURE 4.1.   Daily log kept for client three times weekly, always on Mondays, Wednesdays, and Fridays (Form 1.).

Incident Record (Form 2)

Briefly describe what was happening just before the behavior occurred:

It was a "free time" period in the room.

What was the client doing:

Listening to a cassette tape recorder by himself.

Was anything being said to him, was he being prompted, or? (describe what):

No, he was pretty much alone until Tony interrupted him.

Describe in detail what the client did and what happened through the incident:

Tony came up to David and started bothering him—he came really close, stared at David, and then tried to take the tape recorder away. David got upset and looked angry at Tony— he wouldn't give up the tape recorder. He yelled a couple of times and then got really agitated and immediately started to bang his head on the coffee table. I had gotten close to him by now and told him to stop. He banged a couple more times and started to cry. I told him to use his handkerchief to wipe his nose. He did and stopped banging but seemed like he was still really upset.

Briefly describe what happened to the client immediately after the incident (Include any "consequences."):

I asked him to come with me to take something to Donna's room. He cried most of the way down the hall, but he didn't bang anymore.

FIGURE 4.2. Incident record kept for client (Form 2.).

Figure 4.2. *(continued)*

SUMMARY DATA

Activity:

Free time

Location: **Date/Day of week:**   **Time:**

Job site   Monday, 4/12/86   9:15 a.m.

Staff present when incident occurred:

Me, Kevin, Mary — also, the delivery clerk was there talking to Kevin.

Nonstaff present when incident occurred:

12 other clients were in the room.

Why do you think the person behaved as he or she did and the incident occurred? (What do you think set him off?) This hypothesis should be written by the staff person who was most directly involved in the incident:

I think he was kind of agitated when he got here — he seemed to be in a bad mood when he got off the van. Also, he doesn't really like Tony, and today it was just too much for him when Tony bothered him.

How do you think the behavior should have been prevented or handled, and how might it be prevented or handled next time? (Again, the person most directly involved in the incident should fill this out.):

Maybe there was too much going on in the room at the time? It was very noisy; maybe I should have taken David for a walk as soon as I noticed how upset he was in the morning.

Additional space for comments or anything left over from previous questions:

Who completed this record (name): Don Smith (direct service worker) could be suggested as a possible explanation for David's head banging behavior? That is, what function might this behavior have for David? Suggest some other situations that might be examined for the purpose of testing this hypothesis.

Why Assessment to Determine Function Is Important

Obviously, the reason to attempt to determine what the function of a behavior problem is for the learner is that this insight will be crucial to the design of the intervention. Most typically, an excess behavior being used to solicit attention, as a play strategy, to communicate fatigue or difficulty with a task, and so forth is used because the individual simply does not have the appropriate alternative skill to accomplish that same purpose. This means that the presence of an excess behavior is a certain clue regarding a primary skill deficit need in many instances. The individual needs to learn a new skill and needs to learn that the new skill will be *more* powerful in satisfying his or her needs and wants. If this happens, there will no longer be a reason for the behavior problem to continue. Again,

the most meaningful and lasting approach to remediating behavior problems, in the majority of cases, is to identify the purpose they serve and teach the missing skills that will allow the learner to accomplish those purposes in a more socially acceptable manner.

These issues will be addressed in more detail in Chapter 7. However, one point can be made now and kept in mind for future reference. The caregiver may know the purpose of the problem behavior in the person with disabilities but not agree that the person should be able to exercise the option to fulfill that purpose. This is an important issue. In fact, it is possible that at least some behavior problems arise simply because persons with disabilities have so little personal choice or options in their daily lives. Staff often deem it inappropriate to give in to the individual even though everyone is aware of the person's purpose for the behavior and agrees that the *purpose* is legitimate. It is important, nevertheless, to convince staff that the critical first step is to teach a new, appropriate skill to fulfill the purpose and also that learning when and how to use that skill is a process that takes some time.

chapter

5

Design of Intervention Plans

OVERVIEW

This chapter provides a framework for the process and content of intervention plans. First, four intervention components are described that must all be considered in a comprehensive treatment plan. Such a plan includes procedures for: 1) short-term prevention, 2) immediate consequences (including crisis management), 3) establishing adaptive alternatives, and 4) long-term prevention.

Next, four criteria are described for judging the usefulness and potential effectiveness of an intervention plan; these include the grandmother test, the Cheshire cat test, the test-drive test, and the wimpy-hefty test. Finally, a team decision-making process and intervention plan format are described and applied to a specific example.

TRAINEE OBJECTIVES

At the completion of this unit, participant trainees will be able to:

1. Describe the four intervention components for a specific individual given information regarding excess behavior

and its function from the assessment process.
2. Recognize the difference between an intervention and a crisis management plan.
3. Apply the four criteria for judging an intervention plan to a specific case involving a familiar client's program.
4. List the specific steps involved in the development of an intervention plan.
5. Participate in a team meeting to identify the critical components necessary in the design of an individual client's intervention plan.
6. Identify an intervention plan form that includes all relevant information on the specific and general procedures to be followed for an individual client.

THE FOUR INTERVENTION COMPONENTS

The authors think that it is unrealistic to expect that successful remediation of a long-standing excess behavior will be achieved by implementing only a one-shot effort to manipulate that behavior. This can be illustrated at a more personal level by means of a common, everyday example.

Suppose a person has been overweight by about 20 pounds since childhood. The person often has made efforts to lose the weight, sometimes giving up after a few weeks, so that before anyone really noticed, it was all regained. Once or twice the person made a dramatic effort, maintained a weight loss diet for many weeks, and managed to keep the weight off for a few months. But for some reason, by the end of the year, the weight was steadily being regained.

If genuinely serious about losing weight and keeping it off, how should the person go about doing so? Some possibilities are exercising vigorously for a short time while drastically cutting back on eating; a special regimen of eating special foods on a special schedule; following the plans in weight loss books or an aerobics tape; going to a health spa; using a rowing machine; or following other suggestions from friends. But interestingly enough, the pattern of the message about how to lose weight effectively has become fairly consistent. The way to lose weight and keep it off is to *change one's lifestyle*. The person's weight problem is not an isolated event in the person's life. It is the logical product of how much and what the person eats, habits of liking to eat during particular activities, and the absence of a physical fitness program. The person may even have encouraged or camouflaged the weight problem with a style of dress that is comfortable and creates a thinner look, never trying on certain styles of clothes and resisting even the temptation to be interested in looking thinner.

The person needs to do far more than following one diet or even a diet plus an exercise regimen for a few weeks. Eating less and exercising more for a period of time may be necessary, but, in addition, serious changes in the person's activities and daily habits are required. The person would need to break some strong habits that have resulted in feeling the need to eat snacks during certain activities and overeat with friends and colleagues. Finally, various contingencies should be arranged so that the person is continuously reinforced for efforts. Perhaps admitting the interest in being able to wear a certain style of dress after all would be an excellent motivator.

For a person with developmental disabilities who has a particular problem behavior, these same kinds of issues are relevant. A behavior that has existed for many months or even years might be controlled overnight, but not truly changed until many things happen. The environment and activities must be such that positive alternatives are supported and the negative behavior is not. The individual must be motivated to change his or her own behavior, so that when the trainer is not around or something happens that really provokes the behavior (e.g., the availability of the box of favorite cookies for the person trying to lose weight), he or she can resist the temptation to fall back into old habits. And, perhaps most important of all, unless the person has learned new habits, he or she will have nothing to do instead and the old ones will return as soon as the special intervention program is over. Finally—and this is something similar to relapse prevention training in alcohol abuse programs—if an incident does occur, everyone has to know how to deal with it and avoid becoming discouraged and abandoning a program that actually is doing rather well.

Thus, fairly generic principles that apply to effective behavior change for anyone can be applied to addressing problem behavior exhibited by persons with mental retardation and other developmental disabilities. Four levels of intervention that seem essential to any effort to change behavior can be identified.

1. Short-Term Prevention

It takes time for anyone to master new skills. Thus, as noted earlier, a person with disabilities who needs to learn replacement skills as alternatives to problem behavior will continue to be at risk for using negative behavior to solve problems in the early stages of an educative program. While these adaptive alternatives are being learned, some efforts will have to be made to reduce the frequency of occurrence of the negative behaviors. Most short-term prevention strategies are ecological. Environmental conditions are arranged or reorganized to reduce the number of situations likely to trigger the excess behavior. For example, a young child might be very disruptive on a long car journey. Since a lengthy journey is likely to be a situation involving high risk of discomfort for anyone, particularly a child, generally parents try to prevent difficulties by taking along a few special activities or toys so the child will have something to do that is enjoyable.

Prevention can be achieved by total avoidance of the situation. Families may resort to this tactic in community situations. If the individual is likely to have a tantrum at a nice restaurant, the parents stop going out to such places with the child. This is, of course, unfortunate for all concerned, even if it is understandable. After a history of such experiences, often it takes some persuasion to get parents to try outings with the child again. Measures less drastic than not going at all would include selecting a quieter restaurant (if noisy restaurants are the stimulus for the outburst) or to a noisier restaurant where it is acceptable to eat with one's fingers (if difficulties with manners are the problem). Thus, selecting a pizza parlor rather than a more formal establishment might be an ecological strategy to prevent problems.

Short-term prevention also can mean very close supervision in situations that are associated with problems. Such supervision would later have to be faded. An example of this involves a client who shoplifted when making other purchases in department stores. Until more positive behaviors were mastered, it was necessary

for the instructor to shadow the individual closely, gradually allowing more and more independence around a given store. The issue of fading such control is especially important when dealing with restraints, a quite common form of short-term prevention. Any form of physical restraint is very hard to remove once it is applied, so it is crucial to plan for the eventual removal of any artificial restrictions from the very beginning of an intervention plan.

In some cases, it may not matter whether an ecological intervention becomes more or less permanent. If a client rips only certain types of clothes, it might be a good idea to take away such clothes permanently. This response would be most appropriate if the results of the functional analysis indicate that a certain material is irritating to the individual's skin or the person intensely dislikes clothing that has a particular fit. In these cases, allowing the client choice and simply removing the troublesome items seems a reasonable move. Similarly, if a client's behavior is particularly troublesome at the beach, at baseball games, at church, and so forth, it may simply be that he or she dislikes the activity. If the client is an adult, it would seem fair to recognize his or her right not to attend such functions. Not all situations can be gradually faded back into the individual's life and schedule of activities. Each person should have some say in choosing to participate in certain environments and activities.

It is worth remembering that behaviors themselves can serve a short-term preventive role. For example, the client may be less likely to become disruptive when relaxed or physically tired. Perhaps a normal period of physical activity, such as taking a walk, physical education class, jogging, aerobics, and so forth, can be arranged to precede essential activities during which excess behavior is most likely to occur. This is not the same as a contingent exercise program in which the individual is forced to engage in an activity as punishment for disruption. Instead, natural movement variations are arranged throughout the day as a change of pace according to patterns typical for a person's age range.

Finally, it might be possible to predict fairly reliably when problem behavior is *about* to occur. In fact, direct service workers who know the client very well often are able to tell when something is about to happen even before the client realizes it. Anticipating problem behavior in time to interrupt or distract the individual in some way can be a highly effective short-term prevention strategy if the staff member's actions are timely and sufficiently motivating to capture the person's attention.

2. Immediate Consequences

But when the excess behavior *does* occur, it is necessary to respond to it, even if the situation is not serious enough to call for some type of emergency crisis management procedure (which will be discussed later). When the client is asked to board the public bus and refuses, when the client throws something across the room, when the client grabs a peer's food in the dining room of the group home, or when the individual will not remain seated at the fast food restaurant and the rest of the group is not yet finished, then something must be done.

In the behavioral literature, there has been considerable emphasis on ignoring such behavior. This is a good principle if: 1) the function of the behavior is attention seeking, so that ignoring it should decrease the effectiveness of the negative behavior; 2) the client has a more appropriate way to gain positive attention, and will move on to using that behavior if there is no response to the less appropriate strategy; and/or 3) the behavior can indeed be ignored, because it is not disruptive, harmful, intrusive, and so forth. Since these conditions are rarely all true, a more active conse-

quence when the behavior actually takes place is needed. These specific consequences might include quite normalized strategies such as a verbal reprimand (e.g., "No, don't leave yet."), simple restitution (e.g., requiring the individual to return food to its owner or pick up the materials that were thrown), or a brief response interruption (e.g., moving to position yourself so that the individual cannot continue to grab objects or throw materials). With each of these procedures, the general rule is to ensure that the excess behavior will not work for the client. That is, when the individual tries to accomplish something using problem behavior, he or she is not successful. This lack of success should then enhance the probability that more adaptive behaviors will begin to be used in such situations.

Many of the more active consequence procedures are also difficult to use. For example, restitutional overcorrection assumes somehow that a client, who a moment ago angrily threw a chair across the room, will cheerfully retrieve the chair when told to do so by a direct service worker and return the situation to its original state. Of course, things are not that simple. Usually, what ensues is a power struggle between the staff person and the client, and sometimes this rapidly becomes a physical power struggle once the staff member is committed to getting the client to comply. To avoid such situations, it is crucial to have a good sense either that the individual is likely to comply or can easily be convinced to do so without a physical struggle. This is particularly important in community situations when insisting that the person do something (e.g., having the client thank a cashier) may be more trouble than it is worth unless it clearly involves something that should be enforced (e.g., having a client return an item in a doctor's office before leaving).

Mark Durand has suggested that, if it can be carried out, the ideal strategy is to ensure that there are no consequences from the client's perspective that reliably follow the behavior. The idea is that problem behavior must cease to be functional for the person, such that when the person exhibits that behavior, there is simply no change whatsoever in the events taking place. The activity continues, the conversation continues, the task requirements continue, and so forth. This is quite different from ignoring the excess behavior. Instead, the trainer acts as if it has not happened. In extreme cases, this would mean doing nothing different even if the individual is engaging in serious behaviors such as throwing objects or hitting the trainer. Such an approach would only be recommended in conjunction with teaching replacement skills (which will be discussed next). The plan would be that while the tantrum produces no response from the environment, if the individual suddenly utilizes the new skill that he or she is learning, the environment will respond immediately. Durand's approach is intriguing, and theoretically should be quite effective if staff can remain neutral while the negative behavior is taking place.

Finally, there will be occasions when a very serious behavior occurs that requires the use of *crisis management* procedures to prevent harm to the individual and/or others.

It is important to make a distinction between intervention directed to producing behavior change and crisis management procedures used to deal with immediate, emergency situations. Perhaps every effort is being made to prevent a very serious behavior from occurring in the early stages of an intervention, while the individual is acquiring some new skills that eventually will take the place of the excess behavior. For example, an individual might engage in severe head banging, and, should an incident occur, a strategy is needed to prevent injury. In such cases, it is necessary for staff to design and monitor certain crisis

management procedures very carefully. In many cases, the very last resort is to physically prevent the head banging by holding the person. This is usually referred to as personal restraint, and might be the only way to prevent injury until the individual has calmed. But this technique involving physical contact might actually contribute to the episode. The authors know of several instances, for example, where the individuals become even more agitated and upset when anyone physically interrupts or grabs them in any way, so that an episode lasts even longer and becomes more serious than ever. Thus, personal restraint is a last resort; it should be used only if other procedures fail to prevent or interrupt the episode.

Using a procedure such as restraint in order to stop a serious behavioral incident is not, however, an intervention. It is something that might have to be done, but only as part of an overall plan to intervene with the behavior through other, more active intervention plans and goals. If these intervention plans—including positive programs to teach the person new coping skills—are working, there should be a decrease in the behavior and a decline in the number of times crisis management procedures are necessary. The crisis management procedure might be needed until the intervention has succeeded in reducing a serious problem to near zero levels. Furthermore, the number of times that crisis management procedures are needed provides an indication, over time, of how successful the intervention efforts really are. But the crisis management procedure is not a substitute for an intervention plan.

3. Adaptive Alternatives

In terms of short-term versus long-term effects, adaptive alternatives are at the intermediate level of intervention. It often takes time to teach adaptive behaviors that are the precise alternative to the excess behavior. For example, if it is felt that the excess behavior has a communicative function, then teaching a specific appropriate alternative, such as asking for help, may take a little time, particularly if the verbal or signing skills themselves have to be taught. However, in many cases the instruction in the adaptive alternative takes place not only in the formal teaching situation (as exemplified so ideally by the curricular approach), but also at the time the excess behavior has occurred (or is about to occur). An individual who is being aggressive, for instance, might be taught more socially desirable assertive or self-advocacy skills in the context of a social skills training group after work at the training site. However, if the client does physically attack a co-worker, the trainer might be able to intervene rapidly with the more appropriate assertive skill and rehearse it with the client in that given situation. Much of this manual's discussion of curricular strategies involves instruction in more adaptive alternative behaviors, so no more will be said about this intermediate intervention level here. However, there is one aspect of adaptive alternative instruction that really involves a different level of intervention: long-term prevention strategies.

4.   Long-Term Prevention

Think once again about the example of the young adult who is aggressive in the work place. Such behavior suggests deficits in social skills—in being able to obtain what is desired from other workers and in coping with their teasing or other habits that the client finds annoying. If, for instance, physical aggression is triggered by criticism from other workers, the adaptive alternative might be an assertive social skill such as being able to ask the co-worker not to say such things because they are offensive. But the behavior also reveals more fundamental problems that, in this case, can be thought of as having a number of dimensions: 1) poor impulse control (not being able to ignore or shrug off remarks);

2) lack of empathy for others (not realizing the consequences for others when pain or harm is inflicted); and 3) poor judgment regarding the significance of joking remarks, well-intentioned corrections, and so forth. Knowledge of the individual's total pattern of behavior problems would help one decide which of these more basic skill deficits are most in need of remediation. Thus, if the individual shows poor self-control abilities in other areas (e.g., being very impulsive while working or not being able to control eating behavior) then a more general training in self-control in different situations is needed.

Such a training program would also, of course, be curricular in focus but would be directed to the more general difficulties and deficiencies revealed by the excess behavior. Teaching these very basic aspects of socialization seems nonspecific to the given behavior problem. Learning how to form and keep relationships, concern for others, self-control behavior in different situations, and having a general understanding of what is right and what is wrong in different circumstances take considerable time. That is why this is considered a fourth level of intervention. Yet, these skills are necessary to achieve permanent, long-term benefits and reductions in excess behavior. Researchers have sometimes approached the issue of adaptive alternatives to excess behavior as if therapy or rehabilitation involves some sort of one-for-one replacement of negative behaviors with positive alternative substitutes. The authors believe that this approach is far too narrow. It ignores the complexity of behavioral response relationships and the different interactions within each person's repertoire. The authors have summarized the evidence of these interrelationships in the intervention literature addressing behavior problems in learners with disabilities (Evans, Meyer, Kurkjian, & Kishi, 1988) and believe that ultimate success in addressing such problems is dependent on understanding and appreciating these complex behavioral interrelationships, even in individuals with the most severe disabilities and cognitive deficits.

A comprehensive intervention plan, then, must contain a strategy for each of the four intervention components delineated above. The following brief overview of a typical plan for two different behaviors illustrates how this can be accomplished.

AN EXAMPLE

Problem 1: Throwing Objects

Whenever he is reprimanded or thwarted in some way by his parents or teacher, a young child grabs the nearest object and throws it across the room. The *short-term prevention* procedure involves a number of elements such as teachers trying to reduce frustrating situations by being more careful about the difficulty level of tasks presented to him, and having his parents learn to anticipate times when he is apt to throw something so they can physically interfere with his grabbing of objects simply by blocking his movements or quietly removing objects from his reach. The *immediate consequence* designed involves making him retrieve the object after receiving a sharp verbal rebuke and a statement of the rule that throwing indoors is not allowed. Any time he seems frustrated but does not throw something, he is praised and specific mention is made of something that he did, instead of throwing, that was positive. (Please, never say, "That was good not throwing objects indoors"!) The *adaptive alternative* is to teach him a better way to express anger (e.g. verbally communicating that a task is difficult). The *long-term prevention* involves building up his frustration tolerance by playing games that he cannot always win, encouraging his parents to tease him more and joke with him, and so forth, so that not getting exactly his own way will become something he can handle.

ANOTHER EXAMPLE

Problem 2: Stealing Food

A group home resident steals food from the kitchen. As incidents are not generally discovered until much later, the consequence is not entirely immediate but is the eventual consequence of the behavior that had been in place already. This consisted of a rather tedious verbal lecture from a senior staff member (alone in a remote part of the house) as well as a loss of telephone privileges for the day. The original short-term prevention plan of locking the refrigerator door was dropped because it was so disruptive for other residents. Furthermore, this last component seems particularly unnatural given that most adults take for granted the right of access to food at any time. Thus, the person's access to food remains unaltered, but more control over the amount (size of helpings), variety, and availability of snacks between meals, has been imposed; as long as he does not steal food, he is allowed to eat what he wants. The adaptive alternative is his learning how to request food, having control over funds to buy his own snacks, learning where to keep them at home, and becoming involved in more food preparation for everyone in the group home so that he learns to save certain food items when they are needed for a planned meal. The long-term prevention involves greater emphasis on teaching property distinctions: which items belong to him and which belong to others.

CRITERIA FOR JUDGING AN INTERVENTION PLAN

Obviously, the major measure or acid test of an intervention plan is whether it effectively reduces the excess behavior and produces other collateral positive changes, including permanent benefits in the adaptive skills programmed as part of the curricular component. However, in keeping with the original statement that an educative approach is sensitive to values beyond simply technical efficacy, there are other criteria to be applied to judge an intervention plan, before and during its implementation.

Is the Plan Socially Acceptable?— The Grandmother Test

In the 1980s, rather extensive literature appeared on the social acceptability of different methods of behavioral intervention

(Witt & Elliott, 1985). However, the authors think that social acceptability goes beyond what parties with vested interests consider acceptable. Parents, teachers, service providers, and even ethics boards might be overly influenced to judge procedures to be acceptable because of their own involvement in a particular situation. Acceptability should be more widely defined in terms of standards that are common for nondisabled persons and in terms of the degree to which the intervention plan is normalized. In other words, if the major aspects of the plan were described to a grandmother, would she consider it sensible, humane, and credible? This test assumes that the grandmother is kindly, so it is not foolproof.

Can the Plan Be Faded or Blended into the Overall Habilitative Effort?— The Cheshire Cat Test

After a while it is not possible to tell whether a good plan is in effect or not; it will have blended into the general efforts to assist the client in achieving his or her maximum potential. This is quite different from traditional behavioral interventions that were required to be removable, clearly occurring or not occurring. Educative approaches, in contrast, can pass the Cheshire cat test. Do they, indeed, gradually disappear, leaving only the smile?

Is the Plan Likely to Work?— The Test-Drive Test

Obviously effort would not be put into a plan that did not seem likely to work, so the test-drive test comes very early on, when the plan is first put into effect. Generally speaking, the plan has to work well the first time. When trying out a new car, the test-drive cannot really indicate that the car is going to run for the next 50,000 miles without problems, but it is a better measure than kicking the tires or admiring the digital displays on the dashboard. The car

should, for instance, start the first time and be able to make it back to the salesroom without any problem. Similarly, the first attempts at using the intervention plan should not make excess behavior worse, cause five staff members to resign, and so forth. Educative behavioral strategies do take time, but some positive benefits should be evident immediately.

Is the Plan Potent Enough to Tackle the Problem?— The Wimpy/Hefty Test

Chronic and long-standing behavior problems, particularly those defined as Level I, are serious. As explained at the beginning of this manual, they often are behaviors that cause enormous administrative difficulties and utilize vast professional and technical resources. Such substantial behavior problems should not be tackled by weak strategies, anymore than a lot of heavy wet garbage can be put into a wimpy trash bag. One television advertisement says that a garbage bag should be "hefty, hefty, hefty." There is no point in starting with a minimal effort and constantly having to intensify it. That results in staff becoming disillusioned and increases the demand for supposedly more effective and immediate strategies, such as restraint, medication, or aversive contingency procedures.

DESIGNING THE INTERVENTION

Chapter 3 described a general process for evaluating a client's lifestyle and deciding whether his or her experiences and opportunities seem to be normalized and sufficiently enriching to motivate individual participation and interest. Before proceeding to assessment and intervention planning for an individual client, it will be helpful for the team to have participated in at least one training session dealing with these general lifestyle issues. This could be done by only the team members to be involved in planning for a particular client, or the team could be part of a larger group of staff attending the series of training sessions up to this point.

Similarly, Chapter 4 presented assessment strategies for use in identifying and describing problem behaviors, involving the planning team's participation in a training session dealing with these assessment strategies as part of a larger staff grouping. In addition, however, it is important for each planning team to apply these assessment principles and practices to the very real needs of the individual client who is the focus of the intervention plan. Mastery of the assessment strategies presented in Chapter 4 should mean that key staff have collected sufficient information to identify priority behaviors, describe them objectively so that changes in these behaviors can be monitored over time, describe the conditions and circumstances that reliably predict when the problem behavior is most likely to occur and not to occur, and develop specific hypotheses about the possible functions of those behaviors for the individual. The final section of this chapter describes a team planning process and the steps involved in developing a behavioral intervention plan to address serious excess behavior. (See Table 5.1 for a summary of these steps.)

The Team Planning Meeting

Gathering and summarizing the assessment information (see Chapter 4) traditionally has been considered to be sufficient for the design of a specific intervention for an individual client who exhibits problem behavior. Generally, a staff member with programmatic authority and perhaps some prerequisite level of expertise would be responsible for organizing this information and proceeding through the necessary steps to design an intervention plan. A chief psychologist in an institution or a staff psychologist or psychiatric social worker, for example, might assume this responsibility on behalf of many, perhaps dozens, of clients.

The authors have found it extremely useful to diverge somewhat from this model for two reasons. First, it is not realistic for one professional, no matter how expert, to have sufficient personal knowledge of each client and day-to-day contact with those clients to design and monitor interventions that are likely to be effective for large numbers of individual clients. Second, even the most perfect intervention will fail if those expected to carry it out do not understand the procedures, do not agree with the plan, follow the plan inconsistently, and so forth. These are all issues of procedural re-

Table 5.1. Steps in planning an intervention for problem behavior

Order of steps	Step	Procedures described
1.	Identify priority excess behaviors for intervention	Chapter 4
2.	Describe target behavior(s) objectively and in measurable terms	Chapter 4
3.	Identify the conditions and circumstances that predict when the behavior will/will not occur	Chapter 4
4.	Generate hypotheses regarding possible functions of target behavior(s)	Chapter 4
5.	Conduct team planning meeting to evaluate client's overall program and identify: 1) the Wish List and 2) the Now List	Chapter 5
6.	Design individual client's behavioral intervention plan[a]	Chapter 5
7.	Identify procedures to evaluate intervention outcomes	Chapter 9

[a]Chapter 5 outlines the Behavioral Intervention Plan format, while the various intervention strategies that will be part of this plan are described in Chapters 6, 7, and 8.

liability or treatment integrity (Voeltz & Evans, 1983), and they require that the direct service staff have both the ability and motivation to follow recommendations made by someone else who is simply not present the majority of the time.

To some extent, issues of treatment integrity have been addressed by having staff trained in specific strategies for individual clients and by having various data collection procedures set up that involve some objective record of both what the client does and how the intervention is implemented. However, neither extensive training nor periodic monitoring of the implementation of an intervention is a guarantee that the agreed-upon procedures will be followed (Berkman & Meyer, 1988; Janney & Meyer, 1988). What is needed to ensure treatment integrity is for all staff who will be involved with the client to be invested in the treatment plan. For this to occur, those staff who have close contact with the client must be part of the intervention planning team. This recommendation is not being made, however, solely as a strategy to entice staff into believing that everyone involved in services has played an important role in deciding what to do. In the authors' opinion, input from the various individuals who have day-to-day contact with the client is indispensable to the design of a valid intervention plan. These staff members are, simply stated, the only individuals in a position to know what is happening for the client, and failure to involve these key individuals in the design of intervention plans will make it difficult, if not impossible, to achieve a successful outcome.

Thus, the next step in the design of an effective Behavioral Intervention Plan is to convene the Team Planning Meeting. This meeting will provide the forum for developing a Wish List and a Now List on behalf of the client. These two lists represent the immediate and longer term (if necessary) changes in lifestyle and represent the individualized program design that will be the context of the specific intervention to address serious challenging behaviors. Following the Team Planning Meeting and the development of these two lists, the designated case manager, working in collaboration with the relevant supervisory and consultation professionals, will draft the Behavioral Intervention Plan. (See Figure 5.1.)

What Should Be Done Prior to the Team Planning Meeting As briefly discussed previously, all staff who might be involved in a specific Team Planning Meeting should have received some general training covering the material in Chapter 1 (overview of an educative approach), Chapter 3 (lifestyle planning), and Chapter 4 (assessment). In addition, a professional staff member with overall programmatic responsibilities for the client in question should have organized readily available and additional information to identify the priority target behaviors (Step 1), described those behaviors in objective and measurable terms (Step 2), identified the conditions and circumstances that predict when the behavior does/does not occur (Step 3), and generated hypotheses regarding possible functions of the target behavior (Step 4). Each of these steps involves communication with direct service workers, review of written records and past interventions, and some direct observation of the client.

As this information is gathered and organized, someone to fill the case manager role should be identified and involved in these preliminary steps. The authors suggest that each professional staff person who is available on a full-time basis in any given setting be designated to fill this case manager role for a limited and realistic number of clients. If all professional staff are involved in this way (vocational trainers, educational staff, occupational and physical therapists, psychologists, social workers, rehabilitation specialists, recreation therapists, speech pathologists, etc.), it should be possible to reduce the

Behavioral Intervention Plan (Form 3)

Name: *Sara Mason*

Home address: *Northern Training Center*

Residence phone: *999-999-9999*

School/work program: *Day treatment program*

Address: *Town Road Everyplace, N.Y.*

Transportation (describe): *Van to and from day program*

Client diagnosis/level: *Severe mental retardation*

Any medication (type/dosage): *Haldol (-) Tegretol (-)*

Any restraint used (describe): *For severe incidents of head banging a basket hold is used.*

Date of birth: *3/21/1959*

Sex: Male (Female)

Own guardian: Yes (No)

If no, name/relationship of guardian: *father: Sam Mason*

Client role: *Trainee in vocational program*

Supervisor: *Donald Heath*

Phone: *999-949-9999*

PART A: Referral Priorities

1. List problem behaviors, definition, summary of baseline frequency/duration in order of priority, from highest to lowest priority for change:

BEHAVIOR	DEFINITION[a]	BASELINE DATA[b]	PREVIOUS TREATMENTS
1. Head banging	Hits head against wall or floor	3-4 incidents daily with 2-3 hits each	DRO, Restraint, overcorrection
2. Head hitting	Hits head with fist	5-6 incidents daily, with 6-8 hits each	As above
3. Aggression	Hits others with hand or fist	1 incident every 1-2 days	Time-out; restraint
4. Non-Compliance	Refuses to do work, move with group	5-6 times daily	Verbal reprimand, overcorrection

[a]This definition must be objective and measurable.

[b]This should include information on frequency and duration.

2. Identify intervention target(s) from above list (top priority):

   Head banging & head hitting : aggression

3. Rationale for priority decision:

   These behaviors injure Sara and can be dangerous to others.

FIGURE 5.1. Behavioral Intervention Plan (Form 3.).

(continued)

PART A (continued)

4. Persons to be involved in the Team Planning Meeting (NOTE: At least one direct service worker who knows the client well and is liked by the client must be present):

WHO	ROLE	RELATIONSHIP TO CLIENT[c]
1. *L·V·H·*	Case Manager	Staff psychologist (daily contact)
2. *W·J·M·*	Chief Psychologist	Supervises psychological personnel (weekly contact)
3. *S·D·*	Program Coordinator	Ward supervisor (daily contact)
4. *A·S·H·*	Direct Service Worker	Day shift worker (daily contact)
5. *S·M·T·*	Direct Service worker	Evening shift worker (daily contact)
6. *G·K·V·*	Speech, OT, PT, etc.	Language consultant (biweekly contact)
	Job Coach/Supervisor	Day program coordinator

[c]Why it is important for this person to participate in the meeting.

PART B: Intervention Design

1.0.   *Short-Term Prevention*

    1.1.   Environment/schedule/activity changes:

> All changes in the <u>Now List</u> to be implemented.

    1.2.   Individualized prevention strategies:

> Redirect & distract Sara when she becomes agitated.

    1.3.   Specific distraction and interruption strategies:

> Ask her to help with something; change activity; initiate a conversation about something that interests her.

2.0.   *Immediate Consequences*

    2.1.   Redirect instructions (behavior about to occur):

> Say "Sara, look at this," or ask her to help with something. Ask her if she would like a break.

(continued)

PART B (*continued*)

2.2. Consequences (behavior has occurred):

Tell Sara to stop. If she does not stop after 2 hits, use personal restraint until calm.

2.3. Crisis management needed: (YES) NO

If YES, attach detailed description of procedures to be followed.

3.0. *Adaptive Alternatives*

3.1. Initial target replacement skill goal (instructional level and cue(s) corrections apply):

- *When asked "would you like a break" Sara will request "Can I take a break?"*
- *When presented with different options, Sara will make a choice.*

3.2. Long-term outcome replacement skill goal (rate/duration are normalized and natural cues/corrections apply):

- *Sara will take a break on her own initiative for every ½ hour of work (approximately).*
- *Sara will indicate preference in different situations.*

4.0. *Long-Term Prevention*

4.1. Self-regulation goals:

- *Use a schedule for daily activities & initiate reasonable changes in activity.*
- *Select appropriate solitary activities at home when she wants to be alone.*
- *Take a break from required tasks on a reasonable schedule.*

4.2. Community integration goals:

- *Actively participate in community activities & environments (e.g., shopping fast food restaurants, going to bank).*
- *Increase peer interactions, including social dating.*

4.3. Residential goals:

- *Live in a supported apartment with two preferred roommates.*

(*continued*)

PART B (*continued*)

    4.4. Employment goals: *Supported employment in an integrated work situation.*

PART C: Informed Consent and Professional Review

1. Level of review required: *Crisis management procedure requires Human Rights Review*

2. Consent required/obtained: *Yes*

WHO?	NEEDED?		HOW OBTAINED?
(Parent)/Guardian	(YES)	NO	*Signed informed consent form*
(Self)	(YES)	NO	*Verbal explanation of procedure and, if possible, signature mark*

(Note: Sara can be taught to make a signature)

PART D: Staff Training Needs

WHO	WHAT		BY WHEN
Direct service workers	INTERVENTION *Chapters 6-8 of manual*	EVALUATION *Active participation in activities. Listing of choices Sara can make daily. Existence of adapted schedule system for Sara.*	*December 10*

PART E: List of Attachments

Always Required:
1. Instructional program to teach replacement skills
2. General guidelines for prevention
3. Data collection forms/procedures

May be Required:
4. Crisis management procedures (requires 5–8 also)
5. Incident record form
6. Signed informed consent form
7. Summary of professional review
8. Previous Treatments Summary (must be attached for any behavior that is regarded as Level I or Level II behavior).

case load of any one case manager to no more than a few clients with serious behavior problems. This is important to ensure that the case manager is able to maintain close contact with the individual clients and staff working with those clients. Thus, consultation staff (e.g., part-time psychological or psychiatric personnel) or professionals who are basically supervisory and do not have daily, direct service responsibility for the client (e.g., a chief psychologist), should not serve as case managers, even though these individuals should continue their broader review, supervisory, and consultation roles over all such behavioral intervention plans within ioral intervention plans within the agency.

In selecting the professional who will serve as case manager for the individual client, some of the factors to be considered include the following:

1. The amount of contact he or she has with the client during a typical day makes a difference (the more the better).
2. The extent to which a particular discipline is likely to be primary to the intervention plan is important. For example, a speech therapist might be ideal for a client who requires systematic communication training as part of the intervention plan, while the recreation therapist might be the best choice for someone whose excess behavior suggests the need to learn appropriate leisure time skills.
3. The motivation or interest of the potential case manager in the individual client is significant. One professional may have a particular interest in the client. Alternatively, when a professional has had extensive contact with a client over a long period of time, it might be important to switch responsibility to someone new. This can be a strategy to provide a fresh perspective on long-standing difficulties as well as

to give the staff member at risk for burn-out a break from a demanding situation.

Who Should Be Involved in the Team Planning Meeting Part A of the Behavioral Intervention Plan (see Figure 5.1) provides a potential listing of the individuals who should be involved in the planning meeting. First, the designated case manager should be present, as should anyone who has overall programmatic and supervisory responsibility for the clients' behavioral programs (e.g., the chief psychologist and the program coordinator). At least two direct service workers should be identified who have a great deal of contact with the client and can provide input crucial to the intervention plan design. One or both of these staff members should be someone who is known to like and/or be liked by the client. Generally, it is possible to identify one staff member who has taken a special interest in even a very difficult client and/or who is clearly liked by the client. No Team Planning Meeting should proceed without these key individuals.

Additional professional personnel who are involved in the client's program should also participate. For school-age children and youth, both the teacher from school and a key caregiver from home should attend. If the child is receiving related services such as occupational therapy or speech therapy, professionals from those fields must also be involved in this important, initial planning meeting. For adults, a job coach or work supervisor needs to be present along with someone from the client's living environment. These individuals might overlap with someone identified in the role of case manager or with the direct service workers described above. If this is the case, at least one additional staff member from the client's day and residential environments should be included. Finally, the client's guardian should be present, as should his or her advocate if there is someone in this role.

Conducting the Team Planning Meeting Schedule approximately one hour for the Team Planning Meeting, ideally in a comfortable room (e.g., a seminar room) arranged so that all team members can see one another and with a chalk board or large flip chart for recording information. Someone from the administration (perhaps a program coordinator or the chief psychologist) should act as facilitator for this meeting, and should be prepared to direct the group through the meeting process, keep the meeting on schedule, and record the information on the chalkboard. Generally, the case manager should not perform this role, as this individual is a major source of information about the client and should be free to contribute to the discussion. The facilitator, however, should strive to remain neutral throughout the planning process and resist the temptation to talk at the group and/or make decisions for the group. It is important that the facilitator elicit group input on each step and remind the group of the goals involved at each step.

At this meeting, the group begins with a very brief presentation of the client's difficulties and current program. Following this presentation, the facilitator states, briefly, that the purpose of the meeting is to start by looking at the client's present lifestyle and then to describe major, future goals for him or her. (Remember that the staff should have already participated in Chapter 3 activities.) Finally, the group is asked to generate two lists.

1. The Wish List Based on what they agree are the ideal program options and life experiences for this client, the team members make up a Wish List. This is a Wish List in the sense that the needed resources or opportunities may not currently be available to implement the changes involved. Remember, the items included in this list should not be limited by lack of opportunity, lack of resources, lack of staff, or even concern that the client does not have the ability to do something. For exam-

ple, it is sometimes said that choices are not relevant to persons with profound retardation. Yet, there are curricular components designed to teach persons with the most severe disabilities how to make choices (cf. Wuerch & Voeltz, 1982), and, in the authors' experience, these individuals do have preferences and can be taught to reliably indicate their choices to others. Similarly, in any particular geographic region, there may be limited opportunities for persons with severe mental retardation to live in family-scale homes in the community or participate in supported work. However, there is evidence that in other areas such options are available and these individuals are doing well under these circumstances, so they should not be excluded from the list of possibilities simply because they do not now exist everywhere. A Wish List should reflect realistic goals for the future for the individual, not the limitations of the present.

At the same time, the intention is not to imply that this Wish List be unrealistic in the sense that it involves expectations that are unreasonable. In constructing this first list of goals, it is helpful to continuously remind the group that the list is similar to what would be reasonable goals for any person the same age as the client. Thus, even though a nondisabled adult might not now live in a particular environment, the person might have a personal career goal and plans about the kind of house where he or she hopes to live in the near future. This would be part of a Wish List. It should include goals that the person could reasonably achieve, but almost always would also involve the best of what the person could achieve. In this context, then, what would be reasonable goals and opportunities for the client if the various supports and services needed to achieve them could be arranged?

The purpose of the Wish List is to show what an ideal program will look like for this client and what kind of lifestyle it will reflect if it can be put together. Although there may currently be significant obstacles to accomplishing the kind of program and daily lifestyle the Wish List entails, team members should agree that its content represents the true needs of the client and, therefore, will work toward implementation as opportunities present themselves.

2. *The Now List* The agreed-upon directions for the client's program now should be reflected in the Now List. It is most likely to reflect many existing circumstances, activities, and environments but should also include any and all of the goals stated in the Wish List that can in fact be implemented immediately, using existing resources and expanding available opportunities. Thus, the Now List will somewhat resemble the client's existing program and situation but will also include some important goals for changes that should improve the daily lifestyle and quality-of-life for the client. Making this list is the final activity to be accomplished at the Team Planning Meeting, and the group should leave the room with a clear understanding about the kinds of changes that will be made immediately.

It may be, for example, that the client could immediately be included in an activity that is already occurring for other clients, though he or she had not been considered for participation previously, for whatever reason. Or perhaps a positive program component that requires more intensive staffing could be implemented even one half hour a day, which would be less than the level stated on the Wish List, but a good beginning nevertheless. The point about the Now List is that the planning team members must have a commitment at the planning meeting to implement the goals and opportunities included on this list without delay. Thus, it is crucial that this list be realistic. If a suggestion generates disagreement about whether it can be accomplished, the group should avoid argument and move on to another suggestion.

The facilitator may at this point prompt the group with suggestions about each of the items on the Wish List.

The purpose of the Now List is to ensure that the limitations of current circumstances are not allowed to interfere with accomplishing at least some aspects of the improvements in lifestyle and program opportunities that are essential to long-term behavior change. At the very least, a change in program and the introduction of some degree of novelty in the daily lives of persons with developmental disabilities allows everyone a new start, both client and staff. Because this list is to reflect changes that definitely are going to happen and a commitment is being made to administratively support those changes that are indeed possible, staff should leave the meeting with a sense of optimism about both the agency and the client. (Remember, it is important that someone in authority to make the necessary administrative decisions be at this Team Planning Meeting.) At the same time, there should also be a clear sense that the Wish List is indeed the real goal, and that the current inability to achieve everything on that list does not justify a failure to work toward such goals for the future.

The main point is that what now exists for the client may be so far from ideal and from meeting his or her needs, that it cannot be known which of the client's behavior problems are in fact the result of being required to live a lifestyle and participate in activities that would cause anyone to protest. If, on the other hand, staff work toward the kinds of changes that would provide the client with a reasonable lifestyle, they are then in a better position to identify those behaviors that truly stem from the client.

Following is a brief outline of the steps involved in the Team Planning Meeting process and a script from a case history of an intervention plan that actually evolved for a client as a result of such a meeting.

A TEAM PLANNING MEETING FOR SARA MASON[1]

Step 1: Brief History

The case manager, who is the supervisor on the institutional ward where Sara lives with 24 other clients, briefly presents Sara's case history.

"Sara Mason is 30 years old, and she is diagnosed as being severely mentally retarded of unknown causes. She weighs 128 pounds, and is currently on daily dosages of Haldol and Tegritol, prescribed due to her behavior problems. She has been blind for 5 years as a result of her self-injurious head hitting. She both hits her head with her fist and bangs her head against the tile walls and floor of the institution and in her day treatment program. She does walk fairly independently, she knows her environment rather well and uses the walls to guide herself. Also, she is extremely noncompliant and often refuses to participate in the activities scheduled in her day treatment program. Finally, she occasionally is aggressive toward others, which usually takes the form of hitting someone and often occurs when she is being difficult or noncompliant."

"A major concern is her head hitting, which has not improved as a result of the medication or previous behavior programs. Also, she has shown a 35% decrease in self-help skills over the past year. A protective helmet is planned to prevent further injury if the next program is unsuccessful in reducing her head hitting and banging. On the positive side, she has gained some skills in taking care of her personal things in her room area. She has very little contact with her parents, who see her perhaps once a year."

Step 2: Brief Summary of Agenda

The facilitator gives a brief summary of the Team Planning Meeting agenda.

"We're having this Team Planning Meeting to review Sara Mason's program and try to identify some goals for her that would both reflect improvements in her behavior and allow her to have the kind of lifestyle she could enjoy."

"Rather than starting by looking at her behavior problems—we'll do that later—first we want to look at her lifestyle. What are the kinds of things that she does every day? Does she like those things? How many times each day or week can she do or have the kinds of things she likes? Are her activities functional? Do they have meaning? In other words, do her daily schedule and lifestyle seem to be motivating for her? Particularly since her self-injurious and aggressive behaviors seem to occur when she is noncompliant, it's going to be particularly important to see what kinds of choices and options Sara has on any typical day."

"Next, we want to list our major goals for Sara Mason. What are the kinds of things she could do and participate in by the end of the year? What kind of future could we see for her?"

Step 3: Develop a List of What Sara Mason Likes

The facilitator asks the group to call out things that Sara likes and writes the list up on a board. This list includes the following:

	Sara's likes	How often does she do this now?
a.	Being left alone when she wants to be	?
b.	Taking a nap	Maybe twice weekly
c.	Wearing pretty clothes and being told by someone else (staff or anyone else) that she looks pretty	Varies
d.	Music: radios, popular music, the disco	Once to the disco
e.	Social attention from staff or anyone else	Varies
f.	Going dancing in the gym (there are dances at the institution held twice a month for residents)	1–2 times monthly
g.	Trips to the community (e.g., fast food restaurant)	1–2 times monthly
h.	Visits with her family	Once a year

[1] The client's real name has not been used.

Step 4: Mark the List of Sara's Likes with How Often She Can Do These Things

Look again at the above list. The number of times Sara gets to do things she likes has already been filled in, based on group input. Notice that the number of times filled in accurately reflects what really happens at the present time for Sara Mason, not what might happen if everything were ideal.

Step 5: Mark the List of Sara's Likes with How Often She Could Do Those Things

Now go back to the list and add a column to the left of the list of Sara's likes. Write down how often she *could* do those same things. Remind the group that this new list should reflect what would be reasonable for a typical person of Sara's age; they should not limit their estimate because Sara has a disability. And the *could* estimate should not be restricted by lack of resources, existing schedules, the institutional procedures, and so forth. For example, how often would a typical 30-year-old woman be able to take a nap? The group said "daily," and agreed that if a typical adult desired it, a brief nap at the end of the work day could be an option. Listed below are a few other samples of what the group decided could be opportunities for Sara Mason:

Wear pretty clothes and be complimented by others

This provoked a great deal of discussion. Everyone agreed that Sara liked dresses, yet she seldom got to wear them. In fact, Sara did not seem to like any of her clothes, and spent much time pulling at her blouse and shorts (her typical attire) as if she were uncomfortable or hot. The group thought that it would be reasonable to wear dresses nearly every day if one wants to and talked about things like a real hairstyle for Sara (she currently has an unflatteringly short, plain cut) and learning to use makeup, perfume, and body powder (which could also make her clothes more comfortable on a hot day).

Trips to the community

The team felt that a typical adult would go to a fast food restaurant twice weekly, on the average. In addition, more attention to her wardrobe and her grooming would also involve trips to stores for shopping and to the hairdresser for cuts and styling.

Social attention

This item prompted some discussion about whether Sara had friends other than staff and, in particular, a boyfriend. It was agreed that there were almost no opportunities for clients to see one another or date. Apparently, Sara did seem to like a man about her age who lived in another building, and he seemed to enjoy her company. The group felt that this friendship would be beneficial for Sara and her potential friend and discussed ways to allow a more normalized social dating pattern to occur for them. Particularly because Sara seemed to be so responsive to being told that she looked nice, positive social opportunities and her own interest in looking nice were viewed as potentially affecting her self-injurious behavior. (It has been the authors' experience that, logically enough, clients can become invested in their own appearance just as other people are, and that this can affect not only grooming habits but even serious behaviors such as self-injury.)

Remember, it will probably be necessary for the facilitator to remind the group that their estimate of how often she could do things should not be limited by how often things are possible now. Instead, it should be based on what would be reasonable for a typical, nondisabled individual of the same age.

Step 6: Identifying Sara Mason's Present Daily Activities

For this step, organize the contributions of the group into four major categories of activities —work, leisure/recreation, home, and community. Under each category, ask the team members to list what Sara now does on a typical weekday.

What real work does she do? This should include both the actual job task she might perform as well as work habits (e.g., taking a break, going to and from work). For Sara, it was clear that she had no real job. Her day program did not involve anything that could be considered meaningful work by anyone. Someone volunteered that she could imagine Sara learning to work on a job at the shopping mall within walking distance of the institution if there were a supported work program available to assist her. In the area of work habits, the group agreed that there were few opportunities to even develop these in her day program. Breaks were scheduled and directed by staff, so she had no opportunity to learn how to initiate breaks on a reasonable schedule; in fact, she was described as being noncompliant and aggressive when it seemed that her intention was to stop working, suggesting that learning to take a break might be an ideal constructive alternative. She was able to go to her work area independently on site, but transportation to and from the work area was provided and directed by others and she also needed to be prompted to work once she was in the work area.

Her *leisure/recreation* list was equally short. Sara seemed to have few options available to her to occupy her leisure time. The things that she liked such as music were totally controlled by others; she did not have her own radio or stereo. Social events were organized by staff and occurred infrequently (perhaps once or twice a month). Occasionally, the entire group walked to a nearby park, but, again, this activity was totally dependent on staffing and scheduling at the institution.

In the *home* domain, personal grooming and management, household chores, and even eating and going to the bathroom were restricted by institutional routines and physical arrangements. She could eat independently but almost never ate family-style as meals were delivered on special carts and served cafeteria-style on individual trays. Grooming was basic only, with little time or attention given to style and fashion. She did keep her own personal cabinet and chest of drawers neat and enjoyed helping direct service staff place residents' blankets neatly at the foot of the beds and on the shelves when they were stored; interestingly enough, this was not really a job but was something discovered by a direct service worker who had taken an interest in Sara.

Finally, in the *community* domain, Sara's opportunities were even more restricted. She seldom went anywhere outside the institution and, when she did, she went as part of a relatively large group of clients with transportation provided both ways.

Step 7: Develop the Wish List for Sara Mason

The team felt that Sara's actual needs were not being met in any of the domains, nor was she able to do most of the things she enjoyed doing. They decided that her ideal habilitation plan should look something like the following:

Home

More focus could be put on appearance, including stylish grooming and dress. Sara could have a housekeeping job that was her responsibility (along the lines of the blanket task that had already been identified).

Personal management for Sara would include learning more self-control and how to make personal choices, for example, learning a schedule, choosing when to take a nap, picking out clothes at the store, and so forth.

Eating could be done family-style. Sara could learn how to pass serving bowls and take reasonable portions for herself. She could also learn how to make a snack for herself (a sandwich, or even popcorn in the microwave with an adapted keyboard).

Work

Sara could learn to do a real job in the community, with the assistance of a supported work program and a job coach. Sara could learn work habits, such as how to travel to and from her job site using public transportation, when and how to take a break at work, socializing with co-workers, calling in sick, and so forth.

Leisure/Recreation

Sara could become involved in dating and social events with peers. Contact with the family could be increased. (The group decided that it would be reasonable to talk to family members on the phone once every one–two weeks and visit perhaps once or twice a month. A plan might be developed to reinforce Sara's family for more contact to make it more likely that they would be willing to interact with her more often.) Solitary leisure activities could be encouraged for Sara. She could have a portable cassette deck and radio for her personal use. Sara could become more involved in peer interaction activities. She could learn to shop with a friend and a staff member. She does engage in brief verbal interchanges, and the group felt that she could learn to have a social conversation, whereby someone would deliberately engage her in a verbal interchange that involved back and forth discussion about an event, for example. This also would enable her to talk on the telephone, a skill she could use to communicate with her family.

Community

Sara could learn to shop at the neighborhood shopping mall. Eating at a fast food restaurant could be encouraged. Sara could learn to ride the public bus.

Step 8: Develop the Now List for Sara Mason

At this point, the group should be ready to realistically identify those things that can and should be done to change the client's day and lifestyle. The facilitator should mention once again that the purpose of the Now List is to approximate the Wish List as much as possible, to try to bring as many different things as possible into Sara's life that she likes and that seem meaningful to her. Once this was done, then staff would be in a better position to deal with what was left over in terms of her behavior problems. If Sara is noncompliant in her present program—exhibiting refusals that often escalate into aggression or self-injury—staff does not know how much of this noncompliance is actually her strategy to try to avoid engaging in what clearly are not meaningful activities anyway. While noncompliance, self-injury, and aggression are not appropriate and constructive strategies to disengage from meaningless activities, perhaps they are Sara's only strategies. Sara might indeed need to learn better ways to communicate her needs and wants, but in the meantime, an improvement in her lifestyle could significantly reduce her present difficulties while she is learning new strategies.

For Sara, the team agreed that several things could be done immediately. First, Sara could be given more choices over what she wore, and be taken on some shopping trips almost immediately to purchase some new clothes. Her institutional haircut could be replaced by a more stylish cut (her hair would look better longer), and she could learn to use perfume, powder, and even nail polish. Staff agreed to identify another housekeeping job for Sara that she would enjoy. This would be something that Sara could use if she were to move to an apartment in the community. Finally, she would be offered the choice of taking a nap or being alone at a designated time each day after her day program ended.

Staff also agreed that Sara could spend more time with the one individual she seemed to like and that staff would attempt to engage her in social conversations (in which comments would be given back and forth so that an exchange takes place) several times daily. She could be assisted in calling her family on the telephone once every 2 weeks to start, and staff could structure this carefully to ensure that the experience was positive for the family. Once each week, a favorite staff member would be given an opportunity to walk individually with Sara to the neighborhood fast food restaurant for a supper offgrounds. And while this might not materialize for some time, Sara's name would be submitted for consideration by the state agency for supported employment training. In the meantime, the staff at her day program could attempt to identify types of jobs that might be similar to real jobs and try out her participation in each of these; she could also be taught to ask for a break from her existing tasks.

At the end of the Team Planning Meeting, the facilitator should have a Now List of the things to be done immediately to change Sara's program and lifestyle. A written summary of the Wish List and Now List should be prepared after the meeting and circulated to everyone who attended with a request for additional ideas.

Developing the
Behavioral Intervention Plan

Once the changes suggested at the Team Planning Meeting are in place, the case manager should be ready to do a first draft of a Behavioral Intervention Plan. This plan will incorporate the various opportunities and experiences available to the client but will specify the precise intervention procedures to deal with the priority target behaviors that were identified for the client. Figure 5.1 shows a format for a Behavioral Intervention Plan that incorporates the various required information and reviews along with a comprehensive treatment design.

This form for Sara has been filled in. (A blank form is included in the appendix.) Note that the plan for Sara includes attention to all four components of the interven-

tion: 1) short-term prevention, 2) immediate consequences, 3) adaptive alternatives, and 4) long-term prevention. Chapters 6–8 describe various strategies and how to determine which of them are appropriate for a particular client based on the assessment data. The authors recommend that the case manager complete a first draft of suggestions for each of these components, and talk over these suggestions with each key staff member individually to solicit input for the revised draft. After these individual consultations, a second team meeting should be held to review and discuss the revised draft, and final changes should be made at that meeting. If the team has participated fully in the process to this point, this stage will proceed smoothly and there will be many ideas for this plan that are consistent with the direction taken at the initial Team Planning Meeting.

chapter

6

Ecological and Consequence Procedures

OVERVIEW

This chapter addresses the various environmental modifications of antecedents and consequences that may be needed as part of an intervention plan along with the more direct and long-term efforts to replace problem behavior with new skills that are described in Chapters 7 and 8.

These short-term prevention (ecological) and immediate consequence procedures are designed to limit the occurrence of problem behavior while new, adaptive behaviors are being learned to take their place.

This chapter also discusses the distinction between intervention and crisis management, and makes recommendations regarding the use and re-evaluation of crisis management techniques whenever they are used to deal with very serious behavior problems that might otherwise result in harm to the individual and/or to others.

TRAINEE OBJECTIVES

At the completion of this unit, participant trainees will be able to:

1. Recognize examples of environmental conditions that might need to be changed as part of an intervention plan for problem behavior.
2. Differentiate those environmental changes that might be needed temporarily (only until the individual's behavior has improved) from environmental circumstances that require permanent changes in program, staff, and activities.
3. List examples of antecedent and response prevention strategies that can be used to limit the occurrence of problem behavior.
4. List examples of nonaversive consequence-based procedures that might be used in conjunction with environmental modifications and/or skill instruction, and identify those that are potentially appropriate based on individualized assessment information.
5. Recognize examples of techniques or practices that are not acceptable for use in habilitative and educative programs and services for persons with disabilities.

6. Explain the difference between intervention and crisis management and describe how information on the use of crisis management procedures should be incorporated into the evaluation of the effectiveness of the intervention.

7. Identify cases in which a crisis management procedure may be needed as part of a treatment plan based on evidence of potential harm to the individual and to others.

8. Identify area resources for information on the design and use of safe crisis management procedures.

9. Suggest examples of possible short-term prevention and immediate consequence procedures that might be appropriate for a Behavioral Intervention Plan based on individual assessment information.

INTRODUCTION

This manual emphasizes throughout that most behavior problems exist to serve a purpose for the individual. Even though these behaviors are not socially appropriate or desirable, and may even be dangerous to the individual and to others, they are functional in that, at least some of the time, they accomplish something that is needed or wanted. Of course, it is possible that some behaviors are not purposeful but are instead the result of a physiological or biological condition, and some examples of such behaviors were given in Chapter 2. Yet, even in those cases where a behavior clearly is part of a syndrome and is largely involuntary (e.g., hand wringing in Rett's syndrome or self-biting in Lesch-Nyhan syndrome), there are examples in the literature of successful efforts to reduce such behaviors by teaching the person to do something else instead, and thus exert some control over the behavior by replacing it (Anderson, Dancis, & Alpert, 1978; Duker, 1975; Evans & Voeltz, 1982). And, in the majority of cases, excess behavior does

have a function for the individual, so that it is logical to suppose that if the person had a more efficient and effective means (an alternative, positive behavior) to achieve that function, the excess behavior would no longer be needed. That is, it would become less functional than the new, replacement behavior and, therefore, cease to be used.

This means that a true intervention almost always has to involve teaching replacement behaviors and the use of those replacement behaviors until they are fluent, that is, at least as efficient and effective as the problem behaviors they are meant to replace. But learning and mastering new behaviors and skills takes time. What can caregivers and staff do about problem behavior while everyone is waiting for new skills to become fluent? In fact, how can staff even teach someone those new, replacement behaviors if he or she is continuously or almost continuously displaying disruptive, aggressive, self-injurious, dangerous, and/or self-stimulatory behaviors that seem to make instruction, or even learning, almost impossible?

The antecedent and consequence manipulations that are described in this chapter are important components of an intervention plan. However, they have not typically resulted in lasting and meaningful behavioral improvements when used alone. The Behavioral Intervention Plan format introduced in Chapter 5 requires all four of the following:

1. Short-term prevention (discussed in this chapter)

2. Immediate consequences (discussed in this chapter)

3. Adaptive alternatives (discussed in Chapter 7)

4. Long-term prevention (discussed in Chapters 5, 7, and 8)

The environmental, antecedent, and consequence strategies described in the following sections are not, therefore, designed to be used in place of or even prior to the more direct and long-term instructional and behavior change strategies covered in Chapters 7 and 8. They are meant to be: 1) *preventive* in that they reduce the antecedent stimuli that have provoked the problem behavior in the past (and thus, it is hoped, would prevent the behavior from ever taking place), or they *interrupt* the behavior early on before it escalates and becomes serious; 2)*immediately useful* in that they enable caregivers and staff to react appropriately and safely when behaviors do take place; and 3) *temporary* because the simple manipulation of only those antecedents and consequences in the environment that control behavior cannot really lead to changes in behavior unless the learner has mastered other, more positive behavioral responses to use. In fact, true mastery has to mean that even if the old antecedents returned and only normalized, natural consequences were in place, the behavior problem still would not recur.

ECOLOGICAL
CHANGES AND PREVENTION

The assessment should provide information on the kinds of circumstances that predict whether or not the problem behavior will occur. Based upon this information, staff should be able to identify the environmental antecedents that seem most likely to provoke the problem behavior. There may also be other behaviors that the client does, that are themselves not terribly serious or difficult but also seem to be antecedents to problem behavior. For example, it might be noticed that head banging almost always follows certain kinds of vocalizations that are somewhat different from other vocal behaviors. Identifying such antecedents, whether they are part of the environment or even another behavior in the client's repertoire, can be helpful in two ways. First, it might be possible to pre-

vent certain antecedents from occurring and, consequently, prevent the problem behavior from occurring as well. If, for example, proximity to a particular co-worker is almost always followed by aggression, keeping the client away from that co-worker might temporarily eliminate the aggression (temporarily because the problem is not really solved until the client can handle such situations without being aggressive with others.) Similarly, staff could perhaps control self-injury by interrupting or distracting the individual the minute they notice that his/or her vocalizations have started to sound like those that seem to precede head banging. (This is control because, presumably, if staff were not there to interrupt the vocalizations, the behavior would once again escalate into head banging.)

Second, knowing the antecedents that predict a serious problem behavior can help staff and caregivers prepare for such an incident in those instances when it cannot be prevented. If, for example, the client cannot be distracted from engaging in the vocalizations that seem to lead to head banging, staff can perhaps at least make certain that he or she moves some distance from any hard or dangerous breakable surfaces (e.g., a metal stall door in a restroom, a plate glass window) that could result in serious injury.

If the assessment has been comprehensive enough, it should also identify the situations in which the problem behavior is least likely to occur. The authors have found the Daily Log procedure to be extremely helpful in providing this kind of information (see Chapter 4). Staff might notice after a period of time that the client almost never is aggressive with a particular staff member, when eating out in a fast food restaurant in the community, sitting quietly listening to music in a certain location, and so forth. Knowing when the behavior is least likely to occur can be helpful in understanding the behavior. Comparing these situations with the kinds of situations in which the problem is more likely to occur should give more information to develop some hypotheses about the purpose of the behavior. For example, if the client often is aggressive during the morning at work when sorting materials at a workbench, but almost never is aggressive on those mornings instead spent sweeping up, what might be the cause for the aggression? Clearly, it is not just dislike of the setting. It could be dislike of table-top activities, finding the sorting task too difficult or boring, or dislike of a particular co-worker who is seated close by at a work station. Certainly, there are several variables involved that make the sorting task different from the sweeping task, and it could be any one or some combination of these variables that is causing the problem. But having some information about variations in the behavior under different circumstances will at least narrow down the possibilities.

For example, for a client who will be discussed in more detail in Chapter 7, Mr. Jordan, self-injurious behavior was high in the institutional setting. It seldom occurred while he was on a walk outside the institution or in a community environment such as a fast food restaurant. Clearly, the pattern seemed to involve institution versus community, but these two types of general situations varied on other dimensions as well. The institutional situations were highly routine, and there was little tolerance for noncompliance to the routines, while the community experiences generally were undertaken in the company of his advocate, who treated him as a friend and allowed Mr. Jordan to do what *he* wanted to do. Thus, by careful analysis of the problem behavior in relationship to these differences in the environment and social contexts, it was decided that the adaptive alternative skills Mr. Jordan needed to learn involved decision-making, communication,

and self-regulation. Obviously, it should be easier to learn such skills in community environments and more normalized social interactions than those that exist in an institution. But it seemed important to identify the more precise features that needed to be reflected in the planned changes. Simply to have emphasized community living as the goal, based on an initial look at the patterns in his behavior, might have missed the point. To have forced community living on Mr. Jordan that was almost as highly routine as institutional living would not have worked. Instead, the emphasis was on self-determination in the community— quite a different focus.

Mr. Jordan's situation also provides an illustration of a case where modifying the environment permanently is the appropriate strategy to follow. If someone is being expected to perform meaningless, boring tasks, or tasks that are far too difficult for him or her, then clearly it is important to recognize this and identify a new job that is appropriate for the client's needs and interests. If an individual typically hits other residents in the group home, for example, only when they attempt to take away items that belong to him, it would seem reasonable to suggest that not only does the individual's behavior need to change, but the behavior of the other residents needs to change as well. If a self-injurious behavior occurs only when an individual is neglected for long periods of time, then surely the environment should be changed as soon as possible to ensure that he or she both receives the needed social attention from other people and is busy doing important and preferred activities. In cases such as these, ecological changes may be long overdue and all that are needed to prevent future occurrences of the problem behavior.

Yet, even when the environment is clearly inappropriate and making unreasonable demands on someone, the existence of a problem behavior may support the need for additional interventions along with making the necessary environmental modifications. It may be understandable that someone engages in behaviors such as self-injury, aggression, or disruptiveness when provoked or bored or frustrated, but it would be preferable for everyone involved if that person could master adaptive alternatives to deal with the problem situations. Even when environmental changes clearly are needed, problem behavior may still indicate that critical new skills and behaviors are also needed.

Consider a different possibility. Suppose the assessment information identifies the antecedents associated with a problem behavior, but it seems that these conditions are not unreasonable for the individual? If this is the case, environmental changes still may be needed, at least temporarily. These temporary ecological alterations would be designed to eliminate powerful stimuli that would otherwise lead to the problematic behavior. As new replacement skills are learned, the kinds of antecedents that once predicted problem behavior could be gradually reintroduced using systematic fading procedures. This is, in fact, an important process to ensure that, as the individual is becoming more fluent in using the new adaptive alternatives, he or she is also learning how to use those skills in the kinds of situations that were a problem in the past.

Broad-Based Ecological Modifications

Various macroenvironmental or broad-based changes can be made in the environment that will cause improvements in problematic behavior even though the precise antecedent stimuli directly relevant to a particular individual's behavior remain a mystery. Lazar and Rucker (1984) discuss these issues in their report on the remediation of serious rumination behavior. They were able to show significant improvements in this behavior by changing a variety of circumstances simultaneously, including: 1) reducing the amount of liquid that the child was allowed to consume with food at mealtimes and for an hour afterwards (the quantity of liquid was carefully monitored to ensure that sufficient liquid was consumed each day overall); 2) introducing chopped food as a substitute for strained food; 3) changing the nature of the mealtime experience itself, so that it became more of a social event for the child; and 4) moving on to alternative positive activities, that required active involvement from the child, immediately after the meal, rather than allowing the child to sit with nothing to do for even a few moments after the meal was over. By the use of this combination of changed circumstances, the rumination was significantly reduced. While it might be more precise to know the exact causal antecedent for rumination for the child, it may not be essential to have all the answers in order to have an impact. Because the kinds of changes that Rucker and Lazar discuss were fairly appropriate and normalized, it was also easy for staff to make them, and, in fact, some of them were things that should be done anyway. Those changes that were more unusual, such as restriction of the amount of liquid consumed along with the food at the meal, were gradually altered back again after the rumination behavior had been reduced by substituting the alternative activities.

Chapter 3 discussed the kinds of lifestyle issues that should be considered in evaluating whether or not a client is actually being expected to comply with and tolerate unreasonable environmental circumstances. Sometimes all that is needed to reduce behavior problems dramatically is the provision of a long-overdue improvement in the individual's quality-of-life. More often, the solution is not quite that straightforward, and even after the environment has been significantly improved, excess behaviors may continue. But at

Table 6.1.   General guidelines for David's worksite[a]

A. General observations about David
1. David wants to be able to direct his interactions with people.
2. David wants to initiate talking and interacting with people, rather than being the recipient of the initiations of others.
3. David values his own space and reacts negatively when intruded upon.
4. David enjoys being talked to like an adult, and being given the opportunity to do things as independently as possible.

B. Rules for greetings and interactions with David
1. Keep greetings brief and matter-of-fact.
2. Greet at least one other person first.
3. Before extended interactions with David, wait for him to initiate. He might physically approach, begin vocalizing to someone, look intently, or stare.
4. If David vocalizes from a distance (does not seem to be talking to anyone) it is best to ignore.
5. David seems to become more upset when more than one activity, staff person, or task is involved. To prevent confused messages avoid interacting with David when he is involved with assigned staff.

C. Specific procedures
1. To make interactions with David more consistent, try to follow this staff order: Dan, Karen, Mary, Kevin. One person will deal with David. Do not intervene unless asked.
2. When David begins to get upset:
    a. Don't panic; remain as calm and matter-of-fact as possible.
    b. Try not to react with alarm or with comforting tone; it seems to make him more upset.
    c. Avoid touching him (either comforting or restraining), as this seems to make matters worse.
    d. Distract him with something different to do. For example, tell him to pick up his handkerchief, carry a laundry basket to Donna's room, go for a walk, and so forth. This works best when done early in the incident.

[a]We wish to thank Sara Jenkins who developed these guidelines for David. (See also Chapter 4, where examples of David's Daily Log and Incident Record data are included.)

least it is fair to assume that if the environment is first evaluated to ensure that the expectations for the client are reasonable, then the job of designing an individual Behavioral Intervention Plan does not become a bandage for what actually are signs of a much larger problem.

Finally, the authors have found it useful to look more closely at the general social climate of the environment and try to identify some broad-based changes that might be made in staff behavior overall. Somehow, it seems to be easier for staff to implement more broad-based changes in program design or practices than it is to be consistent about delivering particular consequences for an individual client. Table 6.1 provides a sample summary of general guidelines developed by staff for dealing with David, the young man whose Daily Log and Incident Record appeared in Chapter 4. How do these guidelines match the assessment of David's behavior in Chapter 4?

Individualized Ecological Modifications

In addition to the more general environmental and programmatic changes that might be made, often it is necessary to modify some very specific antecedents to problem behavior for the individual client. This section follows the model and categories for these modifications described in *An Educative Approach to Behavior Problems* (Evans & Meyer, 1985). Basically, such individualized modifications may fall into three categories: setting factors, activity-related task modifications, and response interruption.

Setting Factors Perhaps the assessment strongly points to particular places, persons, and/or activities that almost always seem to predict the behavior problem. In David's case, for example, it was discovered that being with Kevin (a staff member) was reliably associated with head banging, while being with Dan (another staff member) resulted in the fewest incidents. Thus, the general guidelines for the worksite included making it less likely that Kevin would be responsible for David. It may well be that David simply did not care for Kevin and thus used a head banging incident to end these interactions. It did seem to be the case that David's head banging occurred mostly when he wanted someone to leave him alone or there was more activity or involvement than he could handle. Staff felt, though, that actually Dan was more sensitive to David's difficulties with very intrusive social behavior. That is, Dan had some skills that were useful for interacting with David that could perhaps have been learned by others, including Kevin. But in the meantime there was the need to reduce the number of serious incidents as much as possible, so that the ecological strategy was to decrease contact with the staff person, Kevin, who seemed to represent some difficulty for David. As Kevin becomes more skillful at following the general guidelines for interacting with David, and while David himself is acquiring more constructive strategies to back away from people when he needs to, a short-term prevention strategy is to reduce the number of risky situations for David by limiting his contact with Kevin. Remember, though, that this is a temporary measure, as eventually David must learn better ways to cope with situations he dislikes. In fact, a good test of success in teaching him to do so will be how he handles an interaction with Kevin at a later stage.

Similarly, for Mr. Jordan (discussed earlier in this chapter), certain setting factors were predictive of self-injurious behavior. His behavior varied as a function of which staff member he was with, and he was far more likely to have a behavioral incident on the ward at the institution than when on a walk outside. Knowing these variations in behavior should lead to temporary (and sometimes permanent) changes in environment, schedule, and activities in order to avoid problem antecedents until Mr. Jordan has mastered more positive behaviors. If the setting factors associated with problem behavior are judged to be reasonable, the client should eventually learn how to deal with them as they are carefully and systematically reintroduced over time. But if the setting factors are actually unreasonable, they should be changed permanently. Why should David be expected to receive directions from any one of perhaps 30 different adults on any given day, or Mr. Jordan be expected to earn the right to take a 5-minute walk off the unit of an institution by spending 25 minutes putting pegs in a pegboard? These are unreasonable environmental circumstances, and the individualized modifications that are made immediately should also reflect more appropriate long-term environmental expectations.

Task-Related Factors Many problematic behaviors occur in task-related situations, so that one's first interpretation is that the individual is being noncompliant. An alternative explanation is that there is something about the task that troubles the person. Perhaps his or her communication skills are fairly limited, but the individual has learned over time and in many personally difficult situations that displaying problem behavior brings about a change in routine. For example, by tantruming or engaging in self-injurious behavior, the person is able to avoid being forced by others to do something and/or have others leave him or her alone.

Other tasks might be so easy or boring for the individual that problem behavior could be a strategy to have a good time when things are dull. Provoking a reaction from a supervisor, direct service worker, or other client can be an antidote to boredom and hour after hour of meaningless activity.

Whenever excess behavior seems to be clearly related to particular activities or tasks, it calls for a re-evaluation of the extent to which the individual's day and activities match his or her needs and interests, and are therefore likely to create motivatation for the person care about the task. The task might be too difficult for the individual. Perhaps the assessment has also documented clear signs of stress or emotional upset when a particular job starts. In a case like this, the task or job should be closely examined in relationship to what the individual is generally able to do. Could some changes be made to adjust the difficulty level, such as breaking the task down into smaller steps, giving the individual some extra assistance on certain steps that are more difficult, or providing some instruction using an errorless learning procedure (e.g., time delay, which is described in Chapter 7)? Whenever the task itself seems to be appropriate for the individual, these kinds of instructional modifications are required to provide some extra assistance until the person is better able to cope with the demands of the activity.

Sometimes a *change in position or posture* is needed. Persons with physical disabilities, for example, might be under a great deal of stress if they are expected to stand or even sit without extra support while doing their work. Ordinarily, standing or sitting without support might not be a problem for short periods of time, but once the person must both stand and use his or her arms and hands for a particular task, the motor coordination demands can be quite overwhelming. An analogy to driving a car is illustrative. Ordinarily, driving a car does not require full attention in the sense that a person can both drive and converse at the same time. Suppose, however,

that the traffic conditions change or it begins to rain or snow. Generally in heavy traffic or poor weather, complete concentration on driving is necessary, and a conversation probably will stop until conditions improve. Similarly, a person with a physical disability may need to devote full concentration to a task, so that also having to independently maintain a standing or sitting position simply is too difficult. Arranging for the person to do the very same task while sitting and with some additional supports could solve the problem.

A *change in scheduling* might be the issue for both individuals with physical disabilities and others who perhaps have difficulty doing one thing or staying in one position for long periods of time. For a person with physical disabilities, some kind of schedule adjustment might be needed indefinitely. For example, therapists recommend that at least three stationary postures be identified (in consultation with a therapist) for individuals who are nonambulatory, and body position should be changed every 20 minutes or so using these three postures. Furthermore, rest or break periods are needed more often, and it might be unreasonable to expect an individual to work long periods of time without a break, regardless of changes in body posture. Returning to the driving analogy again, driving in heavy traffic or poor weather can be difficult but becomes even more so during a drive under such conditions for extended time periods. Thus, the driver would stop for a short break when driving in a snow storm for more than an hour or two. Schedules might also need to be modified for those who have a short attention span or who have simply never before been expected to work on a task for any length of time. Initially, the work time periods might be kept quite short, interspersed with breaks and changes in location or position. The total length of the work day might also be shorter at first, with a goal to lengthen it gradually over time as the individual's physical stamina and tolerance are built up. For these cases, of course, it is important to gradually normalize the schedule so that eventually it reflects the kinds of expectations that are both necessary and reasonable for someone of the person's age range working on a given task or job.

A final individualized change that might work in cases where unsuccessful attempts have been made to identify the specific antecedents to problem behavior would be to *simply change everything*, or change as much as possible. It is often the case that a person with severe behavior problems has been removed from program after program, so that his or her typical day has become very restricted with little variety in schedule, activity, social opportunities, or even location. The person might be assigned to particular staff and spend his or her day in a behavior management unit, perhaps not even being considered for things like job training or community outings because of his behavior. A trial period involving drastic changes in these conditions can be very revealing. It should be possible to completely alter the individual's day for a 2-week period or to do so for several hours a day for a period of time. The person might be included in various community-based activities, for example, even though it was thought he or she was too disruptive for such experiences. This will usually require the assignment of one-to-one or even two-to-one staff initially. Though the staff might already have other assignments, they could perhaps be made available for a limited trial time period. It is possible that the individual's behavior will be completely different under the new circumstances, so that increased staff ratios could be systematically normalized fairly rapidly.

Why such overall changes in location, scheduling, activities, and so forth should result in improvements in behavior might remain a mystery. The problem antecedents might have been eliminated by such changes (see the principles for habit breaking discussed in Chapter 8), or perhaps instead the new stimuli are so distracting and interesting that the person is more motivated to be attentive and participate. In either case, an old and long-standing behavior pattern will be temporarily interrupted. If, during this interruption or honeymoon period, the individual can be engaged successfully in the new activities and work to establish alternative positive behaviors, the problem behavior might never again occur or might occur only very rarely in the new activities, environments, and situations.

Response Interruption   Response interruption procedures are exactly as one might expect. They involve preventing a problematic behavior from occurring or interrupting the behavior. This can be done by using some kind of prosthetic device, by manually blocking or restraining a movement, and/or through verbal cueing. *Prostheses* can be used at particular times—for example, using mittens to prevent hand-biting while riding the bus or van. Unfortunately, prostheses might be needed almost continuously, as with the use of padding, splints, arm restraints, or a helmet to prevent certain self-injurious movements like hand-to-head, or to reduce the likelihood of tissue damage from blows. (Noncontingent mechanical restraints such as four-point or five-point restraints technically might also be placed in the latter category, but as these procedures totally restrict all movement and are highly aversive, the authors do not consider them acceptable even for temporary use.) *Manual blocking* can consist of blocking someone's efforts to hit his or her head or actually holding the person's hands down momentarily when there are signs that the person is about to self-inflict a blow or hit someone else. A variation of this procedure is using body position to reduce the likelihood that a behavior will occur. For example, a client can be moved away from another client who seems a likely victim, or the staff member can move close to be positioned so that the client cannot hit someone else. Of course, the latter procedure should be used ideally when one is reasonably certain the client will not attack the staff person, but the procedure might also be necessary to prevent injury to another client even if the client might hit the staff person instead. *Verbal cueing* can also work quite well. Perhaps the person seems agitated, showing all the signs that typically predict problem behavior. Saying something like, "I'm waiting for you to be quiet," might be sufficient to interrupt a behavior chain that otherwise would have escalated into an incident.

These kinds of response interruption procedures might be used whenever it seems essential and it is possible to prevent attempts at problem behavior from taking place. For example, if the problem behavior will result in injury to the individual or to others, then staff should prevent it from occurring whenever they can. Following are discussions of three principles that must be incorporated, however, into the use of such procedures.

1. Response interruption procedures should never be used in such a way that they could act as contingent restraint or punishment for the behavior. This argument could be made on purely ethical grounds, in that response interruption procedures can otherwise easily become aversive in their use. On habilitative grounds the argument can be made because these procedures do restrict the person's movement in some way, so that using them deliberately as a consequence for behavior can and often does result in a steady and dramatic reduction of the person's participation in meaningful activities. But a very important clinical reason for never using restraints as punishment is that, when used this way, the procedures themselves, and even protective clothing such

as mittens, arm splints, and helmets, seem to become reinforcing for the person. When this happens, it later becomes almost impossible to remove them. (This is discussed in number 3.)

To reduce the likelihood that this will occur, any use of prostheses or other response interruption procedures should be done in a completely neutral manner whereby no attention is focused on the device or technique; the person using it should show no emotion, acting almost as if nothing is occurring. For example, a shadowing procedure can be extremely useful to deal temporarily with a very difficult and dangerous behavior such as aggression toward others. Use of this procedure requires temporary assignment of a one-to-one shadow to the individual. The shadow staff person *absolutely may not engage in any social interaction with the client.* Instead, this staff person behaves in an almost robot-like way, doing nothing but watching unobtrusively much of the time. However, the shadow person must move very quickly to interrupt the client's attempt or movement to be aggressive toward someone else or engage in self-injurious behavior by manually blocking the movement, grasping and holding the client's arms until he or she relaxes, or actually using a crisis management hold procedure if necessary. (See the section on crisis management later in this chapter.) Meanwhile, the activities and even social attention from other staff persons—such as the direct service worker who might be the staff member typically responsible for the person during a particular time period or activity—continues as if nothing is happening. The shadow is dealing with the problem behavior, but because the other persons in the environment can therefore virtually ignore the behavior, the message being communicated to the client is that problem behavior simply does not provoke any change in that environment. Theoretically, the authors think of this as true extinction because it reduces the effectiveness of problem behavior for the person, while practically, it significantly reduces the chances of injury or damage. While this procedure may appear at first glance to be expensive from a staffing point of view, it can be faded rapidly, so that within weeks it should be possible to stop using the shadow person. And the strategy is beneficial also in that it does not involve any interruption in activities and the individual's program.

2. *The response interruption procedure used should be as normalized as possible.* If, for example, protective clothing is used, it can be very bizarre in appearance or, with a bit more effort, it can be made attractive and age-appropriate. A teacher the authors knew who became responsible for a new student who engaged in severe hand biting carefully selected a fashionable jacket pattern to replace the arm splints that came with the student. Since the student would bite her hands almost continuously whenever the splints were removed, and it was not possible for the staff to interrupt this behavior all day, the teacher designed a new schedule whereby no prosthesis was used for brief time periods scattered throughout the day while staff engaged the girl in alternative activities with her hands. But to prevent injury during the wait times in between these structured situations, the jacket was constructed with extra long sleeves and velcro connectors on the sleeves and pockets of the jacket to prevent hand-to-mouth movements. The jacket was quite attractive and similar to other clothes that might be worn by a teenage girl, so that it was easily faded over time (as the student's hand biting was reduced).

An important method for normalizing brief interruption procedures is to make them part of the instructional procedures. Obviously one would typically be in the best position to use brief interruption when engaged in one-to-one instruction close to the client. (This is because if you are not near the person when the brief interruption should be applied, then coming over and using the method is almost certain to serve as attention reinforcement; this effect will be the opposite of the effect desired.) Thus brief interruption can be expressed as feedback about the way the task should be performed. For instance, in one of the authors' research studies, a young woman was being taught a sandwich making routine. She loved to pound objects on hard surfaces and she would grab the plastic container of sliced turkey and pound it on the table very hard. The instructor then placed her hand over the client's wrist and said, "No, Anne, the turkey container goes back in the fridge," and followed that by a full physical assistance prompt to place the container gently in the refrigerator. In this way the brief interruption is really no more than guidance as to the correct behavior needed to perform the task being taught.

By focusing in these ways on how to make the devices or procedures as normalizing as possible, two purposes can be fulfilled. First, as illustrated in the jacket example, to the extent that prostheses resemble typical materials and procedures, they can be more easily faded and replaced by those typical materials and procedures. Second, an emphasis on normalizing prostheses should help to ensure that they will not further stigmatize the person with disabilities and highlight his or her differences from others. The use of restraint devices such as a shock headpiece, for example, is not only objectionable on basic ethical and clinical grounds, but also further stigmatizes, and thus socially isolates the person who wears it, in the eyes of peers and others who do not have disabilities.

3. *Response interruption procedures should only be used as temporary measures—never permanent—and a plan to fade their use should be included.* It is critical that response interruption pro-

cedures be viewed as temporary measures. A genuinely effective and successful intervention should mean that the behavior is improved even after any and all such artificial procedures have been faded and eliminated. These procedures and prostheses should *never* become a permanent part of the individual's lifestyle.

Occasionally, an individual enters a program in full mechanical restraints. Perhaps an adult has worn a helmet and been fully restrained, with both arms and legs strapped to his or her wheelchair for many years. It may be that previous intervention efforts were abandoned and the restraints were used to prevent the client from serious injury, so that they now are removed only for toileting or bathing and are replaced by bed ties at night. After such restraint procedures have been used for such an extended period of time, it is highly likely that their removal would result in an extreme burst of self-injurious behavior, which, of course, would further discourage any efforts to removed them permanently.

Romanczyk (in press) has argued that restraint may serve to increase the motivation to engage in self-injurious behavior due to classical conditioning. The application of restraints is immediately followed by a stimulus complex made up of cessation of the self-induced pain, physical and social contact, and removal from all existing demands. Thus restraints themselves become positive and serve as a discriminative stimulus or cue for no demands, safety, and so forth. Given this argument, staff must recognize that removal from restraint actually becomes aversive, and special efforts can then be made to ensure that the initially brief time periods out of restraints are as positive as possible. It might be preferable to concentrate on highly intrinsically reinforcing leisure activities, rather than work-related activities, since it is easier to structure leisure events to be totally nondemanding.

In such cases, a systematic fading program must be designed. Like the one described earlier to use with protective clothing, the restraints would be removed for only a few minutes at first, several times a day, and the time periods without them would be gradually increased. Whenever they are removed, there must be an active program occurring in which the individual is encouraged and even physically prompted to engage in the alternative positive behaviors. Several such alternative routines that the individual seems to like or at least tolerate should be identified, such as washing one's face with a wash cloth and putting on after-shave lotion, playing video games, making and eating a sandwich, and so forth. These activities might have to be totally guided hand-over-hand at first, and for some individuals, even the long-term goal on some of the activities might be partial participation with some assistance continuing indefinitely.

Partial participation means that even though the person cannot do the entire task independently, he or she can partially participate (Baumgart et al., 1982). The idea is that partially participating in meaningful activities is preferable to independence on make-believe activities or no participation at all. One of the goals of partial participation is to identify patterns of assistance that are as normalized as possible. Perhaps another client could later become involved who could do the missing steps or give whatever other assistance was needed. Alternatively, someone who is not disabled but who is typically available in an environment might be asked to help. For example, suppose someone is learning to ride the bus between home and work, but cannot readily identify the places at which to get off. Rather than indefinitely continuing efforts to train the person to do this or abandoning the goal of riding the bus, the bus driver could be asked to help. The client could carry a card that is color-coded and learn to show the bus driver the green side one way (which asks the driver to tell him when they reach the bus stop closest to work) and the red side the opposite way (which asks for the stop closest to home). Chances are, the individual will learn the correct stops eventually, but in the meantime the bus driver could help.

Whether the client eventually learns complete independence on the various replacement activities or partially participates, any artificial prosthetic devices or procedures that were once used to prevent problem behavior should eventually be eliminated completely. It should be possible (as has been the author's experience), using systematic instructional and fading procedures of this kind, to have an individual restraint-free within a year. But this is possible only if there is a clear commitment to the effort involved in both teaching alternative behaviors (see Chapter 7) and fading any artificial response interruption procedures.

CONSEQUENCES: WHAT TO DO WHEN THE BEHAVIOR OCCURS

The ecological changes discussed in the previous section are almost always needed as a component of an intervention plan, and in combination with the kinds of curricular interventions described in Chapter 7. If the ecological modifications are done well, it is possible that the problem behavior will almost never occur while the individual is learning new, adaptive alternatives. In many cases, however, even with good efforts at prevention, there will still be times when the problematic behavior will occur early on in an intervention program. This section is intended to address the question of what to do when the problem behavior does occur.

In applied behavior analysis, much emphasis traditionally has been given to the importance of consequences for determining whether behavior will increase or decrease in the future. If a behavior is judged to be positive so that it should increase, it should be followed with a reinforcer, something that the individual perceives to be personally rewarding, which is evidenced by the fact that any behavior followed by that reinforcer occurs even more often. Alternatively, if a behavior is judged negative and should be eliminated it should be followed with a punishment, something that the individual dislikes, which is evidenced by the fact that any behavior followed by that punishment occurs less often in the future. In addition, a variation of reinforcement procedures might be used to decrease a negative behavior by giving the individual a reward for not doing that behavior. Thus, someone who wanted to stop smoking might reward himself or herself with a special trip after two months of successfully not smoking. Any of these consequence procedures conceivably could be part of an intervention plan, again used in combination, with the kinds of procedures described in Chapter 7. And the use of any such procedure would be based on the assessment information for an individual client.

Finally, this section discusses crisis management procedures. These procedures might be needed to stop very serious and potentially dangerous behavior that might otherwise result in harm to the individual and to others. However, the authors emphasize the distinction between a crisis management procedure and an intended consequence such as a reward or punishment, especially because the crisis management procedure obviously does follow the occurrence of the problem behavior and thus could be confused with these other, intervention procedures. *Crisis management procedures are not interventions, as there is no expectation that use of such a procedure will have an impact on the future occurrence of problem behavior.* Instead the sole purpose of a crisis management procedure is to stop a behavior that is dangerous in order to protect the individual and/or others from injury or harm.

(In fact, since crisis management procedures involve physical contact with the individual, they may actually have the opposite effect of increasing the future probability of such behavior if the individual likes such contact, as is often the case). While such a procedure may need to be used in a particular case, it is never a substitute for a systematic intervention plan that should include teaching alternative replacement skills or behaviors and may include ecological and consequence modifications as well.

Acceptable Consequence Procedures

Some general principles can be offered regarding those consequence procedures that are acceptable for use in any program or setting. First, any consequence procedure included in a program for a person with developmental disabilities should be the kind of procedure that would be allowed for use with nondisabled persons who have not committed any crime against society. Rewards and punishments that might be used should: 1) be acceptable for use with a nondisabled peer, 2) represent typical and natural consequences likely to occur in the natural environment, and 3) be likely to be continued in the natural environment. Second, consequence procedures should only be used in combination with an effort to teach the person more positive strategies (as described in Chapter 7). It makes little sense to punish negative behavior or even reward its absence without some reasonable assurances that the person has better, more positive behaviors to use instead. In fact, the more severe a person's disabilities and cognitive impairments, the less sense it makes to rely on rewards and punishments unless one is willing to argue that the individual clearly has mastered all the necessary prosocial replacement skills and behaviors.

Third, the use of consequence procedures in general assumes that the individual is motivated by his or her circumstances and perceives that what the environment has to offer is, in fact, worth working for. Surely, the person's lifestyle needs to be meaningful and purposeful. The activities and tasks in which the individual participates must be meaningful and purposeful. Those tasks and activities that somehow are essential regardless of preferences (such as doing the dishes) must somehow be balanced by activities that are highly preferred (such as eating a good meal). And people are far more likely to be motivated to be positive in interactions with others if they like those people. If everything that happens to a person with a disability is meaningless and even distasteful to that person, it is difficult to imagine how any artificial rewards or punishments could make up for the absence of an acceptable quality-of-life or lifestyle.

Fourth, any consequence procedure used must eventually be faded to the kinds of circumstances or conditions that are typically present in the natural environment. There should be clear goals stated at the outset of the intervention plan regarding what the long-term behavioral objectives are for the individual under what kinds of natural conditions. If it continues to be necessary to use instructional rewards and punishments for weeks or months (or sometimes years) after an intervention plan has been implemented, it is safe to say that the intervention plan is not working. A successful intervention not only results in significant behavior change, but fades into the natural environment so that it is no longer needed.

Unacceptable Consequence Procedures

Some techniques are never permissible because they infringe on the basic human and civil rights of the individual. These include the following (adapted with permission from a list included in Durand, Meyer, Janney, & Lanci, 1988).

1. Deprivation of sleep, adequate nutrition as part of three daily normal mealtimes, privacy consistent with age guidelines, and appropriate environmental conditions (e.g., temperature)
2. Denial of reasonable contact and communication with family and friends, including visits
3. Locked seclusion or isolation time-out, including any circumstances in which the person cannot be seen by staff and/or cannot see staff
4. Contingent mechanical or physical restraint, except where such a procedure is part of a crisis management plan or where the person has been in continuous restraint and an intervention program has been developed that involves removal of those restraints
5. Discipline by other clients
6. Verbal abuse or any other actions that demean the person
7. Any decelerative technique designed to decrease or eliminate behavior when that technique is not guided by a functional analysis of the behavior and accompanied by a parallel positive program to teach alternative behaviors and skills
8. Any other technique that would not be considered legally acceptable for use with any other persons who have not committed crimes against society
9. Any technique for which the parent, guardian, or client refuses permission

Reinforcement or Positive Consequences

Reinforcement generally is used in two ways as part of an effort to remediate excess behavior. Perhaps problematic behavior actually is being encouraged because whenever the client exhibits that behavior, he or she obtains a reinforcer, something he or she wants. The authors have emphasized repeatedly that problem behavior is almost always functional for the individual precisely because it is a fairly successful, if not appropriate, strategy for obtaining what the individual desires. If this is true, then the desired reinforcement should no longer follow the problem behavior. Instead, the client should be taught positive alternatives to use to obtain those reinforcers. This alternative represents the second way in which reinforcement principles might operate in an intervention program. Rather than receiving the reinforcement after displaying the problem behavior, the desired reinforcement would come only when the person does not do the behavior or does some other behavior.

Thus, Differential Reinforcement of Other Behavior (DRO) and Differential Reinforcement of Incompatible Behavior (DRI) procedures might be incorporated into an intervention plan. A DRO program to deal with hand biting might involve a pat on the shoulder, something the person likes, for every 2-minute period in which no biting occurred. If biting had occurred, the clock would be reset so that 2 continuous minutes would have to pass in which no biting occurred before the individual received another pat on the shoulder. In a DRO program, generally it makes no difference what else the person does; as long as the target behavior does not occur, he or she receives the reinforcement.

In a DRI program, however, only behavior that is directly incompatible with the targeted behavior problem would earn the reinforcer. This means that for any particular behavior problem there needs to be agreement about one or more alternative behaviors that the person should be encouraged to do that are of such a nature that it is not possible to do both the problem behavior and the incompatible behavior at the same time. Thus, for a child who hits his or her face or who engages in hand biting, toy play might be selected as an alternative incompatible behavior. The child would then be encouraged or even taught to play with toys that required use of his or her hands and would be reinforced for time periods in which he or she not only did not do the problem behavior but did play with the toys.

The DRI program should be based on the functional analysis of behavior (see Chapter 4) so that the alternative behaviors to receive reinforcement both are incompatible with the problem behavior and match the function or purpose of that behavior for the individual. Furthermore, it is usually true that the individual needs to learn, that is, be taught, the functional alternative (see Chapter 7.). Unfortunately, the published literature on the use of DRO and DRI with persons who have developmental disabilities all too often assumes that the person already has alternative behaviors in his or her repertoire to replace the problem behavior. In addition, the issue of whether the replacement behavior to be reinforced accomplishes the same function as the problem behavior is often ignored. Evans and Meyer (1985) therefore emphasized how important it is to identify what they called an *equal power alternative skill.* Such a skill is equally powerful because it accomplishes the desired function and is an alternative obviously because it is a replacement for the problem behavior. A DRO or DRI reinforcement program alone that is not accompanied by an educative program to teach and establish fluency in the relevant alternative behaviors is unlikely to have lasting effects. Indeed, Favell (1973) found, in her classic study of reinforcement of toy play as an alternative to self-stimulatory behavior, that this was indeed a problem. Learners who had few play skills did not maintain the initial improvements (reductions) in self-stimulatory behaviors once the structured DRI program ended.

Whenever a program using reinforcers is designed, it is critical to use rewards that not only are preferred by the person but that also are likely to be available on a continuing basis. Use of a very artificial and unnatural reward that is very unlike any-

thing likely to occur outside the treatment situation creates problems later on when the person expects to continue receiving that reward elsewhere. What happens then is that because the reward is not given elsewhere, the very new good behavior is being virtually ignored from the perspective of the person. Because the new behavior has therefore ceased to be rewarded for the individual, it is greatly at risk for quickly deteriorating, with the client returning to use of the older, well-established problem behavior. However, in a very real sense, this issue of natural reinforcers is going to be addressed quite automatically if the behavior being reinforced is truly a replacement behavior because it accomplishes a particular function for someone. Presumably, that function is the reward for him or her. So if the new alternative is selected precisely because it is a replacement behavior that does accomplish what the person wants, the issue of reinforcement is resolved as long as the new behavior continues to be supported by resulting in the desired consequences for the individual.

General Guidelines in the Use of Punishment

By definition, a punishing event is something the individual does not like and would, if given the choice, seek to avoid. The use of punishment to remediate excess behavior is based on the theoretical principal that if something the person dislikes consistently follows the problem behavior, he or she will stop doing that behavior in the future in order to avoid the aversive consequences.

Theoretically, the principle of punishment as a motivator of behavior makes a certain degree of sense. However, some of the problems involved in the planned use of punishment with persons who have developmental disabilities include the following:

1. The person who is punished for a certain behavior is expected to do something

else instead. There will be a problem if the person has no other functional behavior.

2. Punishment typically is administered by someone else and may even be initially used in only one particular treatment environment. The person being punished will learn that punishment does not occur in other places and with other people.

3. Punishment that is very distressing to the person and/or even painful—such as isolation or slapping or shocking the person—may produce other emotional responses like anxiety, stress, crying, attempts to escape or strike back, and so forth. A person who is in pain or feeling a great deal of anxiety may not be able to pay attention to the message of punishment, and punishment sometimes creates side effects that might be even more serious than the original target behavior.

4. Punishment principles require that all direct service workers who are responsible for the client learn to use the punishment procedure. There are potentially very negative effects on staff who are taught and expected to do things like slap or shock persons with developmental disabilities as treatment.

Not all punishment procedures are extremely aversive, of course. Some of the kinds of punishments used with persons with developmental disabilities and behavior problems range from relatively normalized punishers (e.g., withdrawal of positive social attention, verbal reprimand, and deprivation of preferred activities), to more aversive procedures such as forced participation in nonpreferred activities, the contingent presentation of noxious stimuli (e.g., distasteful substances), electric shock, and corporal punishments (e.g., slaps). The authors believe that the reason punishment works has more to do with the information it provides than how aversive

it is. Punishment is *corrective feedback*, giving the person a clear message that the behavior just displayed was an error or somehow unacceptable to others. If the individual is reasonably motivated to perform correctly—to please others in the environment who are important to him or her—any corrective feedback that successfully communicates that something was an error should work. In the authors' experience, punishments more aversive than things like withdrawal of positive attention, verbal reprimand, and restricted access to preferred activities and materials simply are not necessary. Furthermore, neither these nor highly aversive punishments will work if the person is not motivated to do well and please others, does not enjoy his or her environment, does not have alternative behaviors and skills to use in place of the punished behaviors, and/or is so stressed, aroused, resentful, upset, and so forth that he or she simply cannot even pay attention to what is happening anyway.

The various side effects that may occur with the use of a punishment procedure include effects on other behaviors in the person's repertoire as well as the effects on staff who are required to carry out such a procedure. Suppose that a punishment leads to even more negative behavior, as the individual becomes extremely agitated or angry and begins to escalate negative behaviors as a reaction to, or in order to escape the punishment. While it might be possible to win the battle by increasing the strength of the punishment and making it clear who is in charge, such a process is likely to be very costly for everyone. Persons who are forced into compliance are not likely to appreciate their circumstances, and individuals (who may have nothing better to do, especially in a really poor program, than think of new ways to fight back) can be quite resourceful in developing yet another problem behavior for which another behavior management plan would then need to be developed. Equally serious is the effect on staff. Service workers are being asked to do things that make the person upset, angry, and so forth, so that the situation invariably escalates into a real struggle at least some of the time. The older and bigger the individual is, the more likely it is that an injury can occur; even very young, small children can become quite difficult and strong when they are very upset or angry. The situation represents a terrible potential for loss of control, injury, and even intentional abuse. From a safety perspective alone, it is always preferable to use an available alternative strategy that does not require physical contact between staff and client when both parties are likely to be emotionally upset.

Specific Techniques and Their Use

Several procedures are reviewed here that should be sufficient to both provide the person with corrective feedback and give staff and others reasonable strategies to use that are safe as well as acceptable for use in typical programs and community environments.

Time-out Particularly for highly disruptive or aggressive behavior that is motivated by social attention, a within-room and within-view time-out procedure might be developed. Guidelines for use of such a procedure include the following:

1. Ideally, a shadow staff member should be responsible for taking the person to the time-out area. This staff member should not be a source of any positive or negative social attention, but should be totally neutral while using time-out. If the negative behavior is motivated by social attention, the individual might be more rewarded than punished whenever the assigned direct service worker carries out the procedure. If possible, this staff person should remain uninvolved in the time-out situation.

2. If there is no shadow available, there should be a clear agreement on a day-by-day basis as to who is responsible for carrying out the time-out procedure each day. This person should, as described earlier, behave in as robot-like a fashion as possible, and all other staff should remain uninvolved in the procedure.

3. The time-out area should be within the room and within view, meaning both that staff can see the person at all times and he or she can see at least one staff person at all times. The authors believe that isolation can be frightening to a person who may not understand that he or she is not truly alone when unable to see anyone else. Isolation time-out can lead to extreme emotional reactions as well as an escalation of other serious behaviors, while a within-view procedure should not be alarming.

4. The ultimate goal of a time-out program should, in most cases, be directed toward teaching the individual to use a self time-out procedure whenever he or she feels a need to leave a situation that might otherwise erupt into a serious episode. (See Chapter 8.) Thus, the time-out area need not be incredibly comfortable and desirable, but also should not be extremely unpleasant. A chair that is a few feet away (more than an arm's reach) from objects that could be reinforcing, even tossed or broken, should serve this need fairly well. The staff person in charge of the time-out for that day should also stand more than an arm's reach away, but close enough to react quickly if the person tries to leave before the time is up or engages in some other behavior that must be interrupted. (But the staff person must remember to remain neutral and appear not to be looking at the person.)

5. The time period in time-out should be very brief, perhaps 3–5 minutes. A

timer could be set, and when the timer goes off, the staff person should move closer to eye level, and ask the person, "Are you ready to _____"? Some indication of an affirmative answer or a neutral response should result in a return to the group or situation, while a very negative reaction might require resetting the timer for another 3–5 minutes.

6. Time-out should work within a few days. If, after a few days there is no appreciable change in the behavior or if the time-out situation itself is as difficult as the target problem behavior that led to it, the program should be reevaluated.

Verbal Reprimand   Particularly when the person has a positive social relationship with the other people in his or her environment and is therefore motivated to please those significant others, a firm verbal reprimand may be all that is needed to stop even very serious behavior. A calm "No, stop hitting" can be quite effective if this verbal reprimand is used at the very start of an incident before the person has become extremely agitated. Incidentally, nondisabled peers, such as employers or coworkers or companions, should use the same kind of verbal reprimand they might use with someone else who is not disabled. Sometimes nondisabled people are hesitant to be frank with someone with disabilities, but such frankness can be highly effective and should be encouraged.

Brief Contingent Restraint   Response interruption procedures, which were described earlier in this chapter, are different from brief contingent restraint on two dimensions: 1) intent: brief contingent restraint is intended to be a mild punishment, while response interruption should be done in such a way that it will not be interpreted as a punishment; 2) timing: brief contingent restraint should immediately follow the problem behavior and continue for a predetermined period of time, while response interruption occurs before the behavior actually happens, as often as needed to prevent the behavior from occurring, but does not involve restraining the person for a period of time. Rather, the behavior is momentarily interrupted and then the person is released.

A very brief, contingent personal restraint can be used effectively as a mild punishment for various behaviors such as stereotypic hand mannerisms, hitting one's head with one's fist, and hitting others. To do the procedure, the staff member holds the person's hands down, perhaps on his or her lap or on a table, for a very brief period such as 20 seconds. After the 20 seconds has passed, the person's hands are released and an opportunity to do an alternative positive behavior (e.g., manipulating a preferred toy, using a wash cloth to wash one's face) is presented. This procedure does not work if the restraint procedure provokes a vigorous struggle or if staff cannot do it without becoming visibly upset. It must also be done with *neutral affect*—no emotion—so that the focus of attention remains on the activity at all times, never the restraint procedure. Finally, there is absolutely no advantage to the procedure to restrain for longer than about 20 seconds. If it works at all, it should work using this very brief time period.

Crisis Management

Occasionally, an incident may occur so that staff must do something to stop behavior that is dangerous to the person and/or those around him or her. When this happens, a crisis management procedure must be used. This procedure generally involves personal physical restraint—grabbing and holding the person until he or she is calm. There are various procedures that have been designed to make personal restraint as safe as possible. The state agency can identify published and other written training materials for using these procedures.

Remember that whenever an incident is serious enough to warrant use of a crisis management procedure, an incident record must be completed. The form and example provided in Chapter 4 (and the Appendix) is especially designed to provide useful information to attempt to determine what went wrong and how things can be handled better in the future. States and agencies require that an incident record of some sort be kept whenever crisis management procedures are used, but this compliance procedure can be very useful programmatically.

As emphasized earlier in this chapter, everyone must be clearly in agreement that a crisis management procedure is not an intervention program. It is something that might be necessary when the intervention plan is in place but the problem behavior still occurs. If the intervention plan is effective, there will be a pattern of significant or at least steady decline in the number of incidents over time and in different circumstances. But when the crisis management procedure steadily continues to be needed, this is the clearest evidence that the intervention plan is not working and needs to be revised.

chapter

7

Teaching Adaptive Alternatives for Home and Community

OVERVIEW

This chapter provides an overview of the critical components of an educative approach to behavior problems. This approach involves the teaching of positive alternative skills for use in the home and community. The adaptive alternatives must be identified based on the function of excess behavior for the client, who learns that the new prosocial skills are equally or more powerful than problematic behavior as a strategy to meet his or her needs.

Furthermore, the replacement of behavior problems by new skills must take place in the context of positive goals for the client that emphasize integrated and normalized home, work, leisure/recreation, and community environments. If such goals are not immediately attainable, they should still form the basis of long-term planning and should not be limited due to past perceptions of the client's abilities and behavior.

TRAINEE OBJECTIVES

At the completion of this unit, participant trainees will be able to:

1. List three major categories of alternative skills that might need to be acquired by the client as positive substitutes for problem behavior.
2. Give an example of assessment information that supports the need to teach a client each of the following: 1) social and self-regulatory skills, 2) communication skills, and 3) leisure or play activity skills.
3. State why it is critical to allow the client to use a new skill to accomplish a particular function as often as he or she wishes during the early phases of an educative approach.
4. Give an example of how use of a new skill to accomplish a particular function would be gradually normalized in rate or intensity to reflect typical en-

vironmental circumstances.

5. Recognize an example of positive long-term goals in the domains of home, work, leisure/recreation, and community on behalf of a client with severe mental retardation and serious behavior problems.

INTRODUCTION

Chapter 6 discussed in detail the various short-term prevention and immediate consequence procedures that may be needed as part of a comprehensive intervention plan to remediate problem behaviors. Many of these procedures reflect the best thinking from several disciplines and theoretical perspectives, and represent in particular the major contributions from applied behavior analysis as an emphasis within the theoretical framework of behavioral psychology. In fact, since the early 1960s, systematic intervention research has witnessed the validation of the many antecedent and consequence manipulations described in Chapter 6. Behavior therapists have sensitized the professional community to the strength that certain antecedent stimuli have in eliciting behavior, both positive and negative. And applied behavior analysis has amply demonstrated the importance of ensuring that the natural consequences of behavior support positive behaviors and discourage negative ones. Finally, Powers (1988) and Meyer and Janney (in press), among others, have emphasized that the exclusive focus on the immediately observable chain of events in isolated behavioral interactions involving one or two people must be expanded to include systems and complex social environments if applying these theoretical principles is to achieve meaningful treatment outcomes.

Similarly, practices that have evolved from disciplines such as vocational rehabilitation, therapeutic recreation, the communication sciences, and special education have articulated the kinds of alternative work, social, and academic skills that must be mastered by an individual who is expected to make a positive social adjustment to his or her society and culture. People learn many complex positive and prosocial skills to communicate, solve problems, socially interact with others, entertain themselves during free time, and deal with stress and symptoms of illness, for example. If an individual does not acquire these skills, does it follow that he or she will not have similar needs? On the contrary, it seems far more reasonable to suppose that no matter how serious his or her disabilities, every individual must deal with such situations using whatever personal strategies he or she has. Operating on this assumption, Public Law 94-142, the Education for All Handicapped Children Act, 1975, has mandated that students with even the most severe cognitive impairments have a right to receive an individually appropriate education and related services to assist them in acquiring the skills needed to achieve their maximum potential. Society has accepted the responsibility to not only create positive environments and appropriate educational programs for persons with disabilities, but also to provide whatever instruction is necessary to support their full participation in society. Unfortunately, these developments have come about only recently, even in comparison to the contributions of applied behavior analysis. As mandatory public education has been in effect only since the mid-1970s at the earliest, there has been little time to validate effective instructional and educational environments for persons with disabilities. Perhaps even more serious, many, if not most of the adults now receiving services throughout the United States did not have access to any kind of meaningful instruction and may not have experienced any educational program whatsoever. These adults have never had opportunities to "be the best that they can be," as Lou Brown has often put it. They have reached their adulthood status without systematic assistance to learn how to adapt to community environments. Even more tragic, large numbers of these adults have never even had the opportunity to adapt to community environments, but instead have spent their lives in substandard environments such as institutions and day programs that once were the subject of exposés such as *Christmas in Purgatory* (Blatt & Kaplan, 1966). Is it reasonable to assume that these individuals have, by and large, reached adulthood without developing some kinds of strategies to cope with their environment and, in many cases, even focused their efforts on trying to resist such environments in whatever way they can?

The fact that a person has never been taught a formal communication system (e.g., language) does not mean that he or she will not attempt to communicate. Think of a very familiar client who does not talk or have any formal communication system. Does he or she communicate nevertheless? How do people know when he or she wants something or does not want or like something? The person's system might involve moving closer, smiling, and pointing at the things desired. These would all be regarded as positive efforts to communicate, even though they are rudimentary and might be referred to as nonverbal. Or, the person's system might involve crying or yelling when desiring to be left alone, throwing materials on a job he or she dislikes, grabbing desired food, or falling limp to the ground to avoid boarding the van with everyone else in the morning. These too are rudimentary efforts to communicate, though these particular behaviors are referred to with terms such as noncompliance, aggression, and disruption-behavior problems. Knowing that these behaviors are actually efforts to communicate is important, not only because this information shows that these efforts must be replaced with alternative communication skills but also because the information identifies a

situation in which the client is highly motivated to communicate. Thus, presumably, he or she will be highly motivated to use the new skill taught, if that skill clearly is as effective for the person as the previous problem behavior was. For this effect, input from someone with expertise in communication sciences is needed to help design an individually appropriate communication system for this individual.

Similarly, think of an adult with moderate to severe retardation who is ambulatory and fairly active motorically. The person is assumed to be unemployable and never entitled to the services of the state's office of vocational rehabilitation services. Therefore he or she is assigned to a prevocational training program in a day treatment center. In that center, he or she is expected to sort objects, some of them functional (e.g., spoons, forks, knives) and others nonfunctional (e.g., popsicle sticks, blocks). But each time the person completes a sorting task, a staff member comes around and dumps the items into one pile and instructs him or her to begin sorting again. Even persons with very severe retardation can see after weeks and even years of this procedure that finishing a task does not mean that it is over, does not result in any kind of reinforcement, and does not seem to lead to any next step. (For an analogy, think of how difficult it is for people to force themselves to vacuum the rugs, knowing that it will need to be done again only a few days later.) Unless there is some clear purpose to the sorting task, unless it is preferred by some highly preferred reinforcer, and/or the individual enjoys sorting for its own sake (some individuals do seem to enjoy such activities), it is perhaps predictable that such an individual might learn that throwing the objects, falling limp to the floor, or even hitting oneself or the trainer will lead reliably to a change in activity. A vocational rehabilitation specialist can contribute invaluable information to identify something new and meaningful—real work—for the individual that might significantly decrease the causes of what might be reasonable task avoidance behaviors.

This chapter describes how various adaptive alternatives might be identified and taught to the individual to replace problem behavior that the individual is using because he or she has no other strategy to fulfill his or her purpose. Even though developments such as supported living, supported work, leisure education, and community integration for persons with the most severe disabilities are very recent, there have been many impressive demonstrations that challenge past beliefs that these individuals could not learn and participate. Not all of them can be covered here, but this chapter attempts at least to provide a summary of developments in three curricular areas: 1) social skills and self-regulation, 2) communication training, and 3) leisure education. Finally, this chapter provides example of an Individualized Program Plan (IPP) for an adult client that integrates these components as part of a plan to remediate severe self-injury using available resources.

SOCIAL SKILLS AND SELF-REGULATION

Although there are materials available that describe efforts to teach persons with developmental disabilities social skills, most of these deal with fairly discrete behaviors such as eye contact, compliance to commands, greeting others, and so forth. Teaching more sophisticated social skills such as taking turns, for example, is more rare in the literature on persons with severe disabilities. It is clear that, whatever social competence is, as a construct it involves some very important behaviors and integration patterns that are critical to doing well at school, work, home, and in the community. In fact, there is considerable evidence that persons with developmental disabilities are more likely to lose their jobs because of deficits in social skills than because of actual performance on particular job components (Greenspan & Shoultz, 1981; Wehman & Hill, 1985). Yet, what these social skills really entail and which ones are critical have not yet been identified.

Meyer, Cole, McQuarter, and Reichle (1988) have described the validation of a measure of social competence that addresses the range of social skills reported to have an impact on outcomes for persons with disabilities (Meyer, Reichle et al., 1985). Table 7.1 provides a listing of the 11 *social competence functions* delineated on their measure—the Assessment of Social Competence (ASC)—along with the definition for each function, definitions of two sample levels for each of the functions, and sample items. The ASC is hierarchically ordered, so that the higher levels represent more sophisticated and socially acceptable strategies to accomplish any particular function. However, within each function, behavior at any level may be effective from the individual's perspective in the sense that the purpose is fulfilled.

Thus, a client with few strategies to cope with negatives may throw objects or strike out at a trainer when told to continue working on a task he or she dislikes intensely. While throwing objects or hitting others are not desirable or appropriate, they may be the only strategies the individual has to escape work, and, in fact, they could be quite effective at least some of the time. Similarly, an adult who is never allowed to make reasonable choices about everyday issues such as what to wear, what to do during free time, whom to sit with, what time to go to bed at night, and so forth, may well protest in inappropriate ways when his or her preferences are not reflected in these decisions. In such cases, noncompliance might be the inevitable re-

Table 7.1. The assessment of social competence (ASC) subscale definitions and examples

Functions	General definition	Sample level definitions	Example items
1. Initiate	Joins an ongoing interaction or starts a new one	Level II: Consistently initiates behavior with other persons	Joins an ongoing activity whether or not participation is wanted
		Level V: Initiates goal-directed social interaction	Finds a store clerk in order to pay for an item
2. Self-regulate	Manages one's own behavior without instruction from others	Level II: Uses specific behavior to gain access to a person or event in order to return to a more comfortable state	Attempts to raise head, orient toward or look at a specific object (may use reflex pattern, abnormal posture, etc.)
		Level V: Generates personal strategies to monitor behavior	Makes lists to remember which tasks to do that day
3. Follow Rules	Follows rules, guidelines, and routines of activities	Level II: Daily activity routines follow those consistent with usual environmental demands, but is inflexible so that a break in routine may result in an effort to follow the usual pattern or even disruptive behavior	Wakes up and demands attention at the same time the family usually gets up in the morning, even on weekends or holidays when others sleep late
		Level V: Follows well-established rules for specific environments and situations, even though the rules are no longer posted or the person who originally provided the instruction is no longer present	Chooses correct line and waits appropriately for service in a store or fast food restaurant
4. Provide Positive Feedback	Provides positive feedback and reinforcement to others	Level II: Positive affect occurs, directed to persons in general	Smiles when someone calls his or her name
		Level V: Positive affect appropriately varied for different persons and the environment or situation	Behaves differently in a classroom than in the hall or outside the building (e.g., may shout outside, but would be quieter inside)

(continued)

Table 7.1. (*continued*)

Functions	General definition	Sample level definitions	Example items
5. Provide Negative Feedback	Provides negative feedback and communicates disapproval to others	Level II: Negative affect occurs, directed toward persons in general	When approached, turns or moves away as if to avoid contact
		Level V: Waits until a more appropriate, future time to provide negative feedback	In a group situation, does not immediately tell a friend that he or she does not want to do something but will wait until later when alone with that friend
6. Obtain Cues	Obtains and responds to relevant situational cues	Level II: Orients directly toward a stimulus in order to better receive information	Turns and faces someone who begins to talk to him or her
		Level V: Seeks out and responds appropriately to signs and other information sources that are not immediately obvious	Checks temperature of water with finger before stepping under shower
7. Offer Assistance	Provides information and offers assistance to others	Level II: Directs attention of another person who is nearby toward an ongoing event that is occurring in the immediate environment	When extremely interested in something on TV, looks to another person while vocalizing and pointing at TV as if to attract their attention to what is occurring on the TV
		Level V: Tailors information and assistance to the comprehension level of a listener; initiates an offer of help or information in familiar situations	Talks differently to a younger child (e.g., using baby talk) than to a peer or adult
8. Accept Assistance	Requests and accepts assistance	Level II: Shows signs of distress, discomfort, and other needs that are directed toward someone who might help; tolerates help from another	When hungry or bothered by something, will tantrum or cry to get help from an adult who is present
		Level V: Directs or makes requests to those persons in the best position to provide the needed help	Asks a store employee rather than another customer for assistance in finding items in the supermarket

(*continued*)

Table 7.1.   (*continued*)

Functions	General definition	Sample level definitions	Example items
9. Indicate Preference	Makes choices from among available and possible alternatives	Level II: Behaves differently depending upon what is presented	Allows people to help with some things but not with others
		Level V: Uses a mediator or symbol to communicate choices to others	Points to a picture of the preferred food item on the display when ordering at a fast food restaurant
10. Cope with Negatives	Exhibits alternative strategies to cope with negative situations	Level II: Persists in continuing behavior that is bothersome to others	Continues to give the same incorrect answer even after being corrected
		Level V: Responds to negative feedback by switching to well-rehearsed, alternative responses in a trial and error fashion until something works	Requests second favorite food when told that first choice is gone
11. Terminate	Terminates or withdraws from an interaction and/or activity	Level II: Uses well-rehearsed and prompted strategies to leave situations	Signals goodbye in appropriate contexts
		Level V: Ceases an activity or interaction appropriately in response to cues that another activity is about to occur	Politely terminates a conversation after noticing that the other person is glancing at his or her watch and otherwise indicating a need to leave

sponse to a series of events in which the client has little say over his or her lifestyle and what happens to him or her on a day-to-day basis.

Table 7.2 provides three examples of problem behaviors that might be serving a social function for the client. In each case, a disruptive behavior, tantruming, appears to be utilized by the client for a purpose or the possible function listed in the second column of the table. Note the suggestions of some alternative adaptive skills that might be needed in each instance, along with ecological modifications that might be effected particularly in the early stages before the new skills have been mastered.

In each case, the assessment has identified the possible social function of the problem behavior. (See the rationale presented for the targeted skill objective for each of the three examples.)

As seen in Table 7.1, several of the ASC functions deal directly with issues of choice and control for the individual. It is difficult to imagine developing someone's abilities to self-regulate, for example, without first dealing with the issue of control. In general, persons with developmental disabilities have very little control over what happens to them. Consider the following 13 choices that most typical adults take for granted:

Table 7.2. Excess Function and Intervention Plan Worksheet: *A sample for tantrumming with social/communicative intent*

Description of excess form	Possible function[a]	Curricular objective	Rationale for objective	Ecological modifications and instructional strategies
1. Becomes irritable, cries, tantrums when shopping in grocery store	Cope with Negatives: Attempts to terminate aversive stimuli with avoidance and protest behavior	Accompany staff to grocery, shop for up to six items, pushing cart through aisles and placing items in cart as staff selects them	Rather than allowing client to avoid situation, it is reasonable to train adaptive behavior in successive approximations of grocery shopping. Ultimate objective would be that client not only accompany staff, but take active role in shopping	1.1. Initial training with one staff person, in criterion grocery store (one close to group home) 1.2. Training with staff after client reaches criterion with three other adults (trainers, peers) 1.3. Initial trips for 1–2 items only, time in store limited to 5 minutes, at least one client-preferred item 1.4. Access to preferred activity after shopping on continuous, then variably intermittent schedule 1.5. Six items always to include one client-preferred item
2. Cries, yells, and may hit peer who consistently tries to steal food at table	Provide Negative Feedback: Escalates negative affect to stop a disapproved behavior by peer	Avoid situations likely to result in conflict by: 1) sitting further away from that peer, and 2) moving food away if/when peer approaches	Client should be able to eat without unnecessary intrusions; objectives are feasible for client's existing social skill level. Ultimate objectives would be that client provide verbal correction (vocal/signed "Stop that.") to peer for intrusions, and follow up by moving to another seat if necessary	1.1. Client prompted with verbal cue and visual (food) when peer is not present, fading to verbal only, during meal time 1.2. Client prompted to find empty chair far from peer at mealtimes 1.3. Client prompted to move food away and, if necessary, change chairs when sitting next to peer 1.4. Client prompted to provide verbal correction and follow up by moving if necessary
3. After approximately 15 minutes of work, tantrums—including yelling, throwing objects, and leaving work area and disrupting others	Leave-taking/Exit: Engages in avoidance and protest behavior to stop trainer demands and performance requirements	After 10–15 minutes of working, will sign request to stop (i.e., "Need a break."), and will return for 10 more minutes of work after 2-minute break	Client has no socially acceptable strategy to signal need for a workbreak. Ultimate objective would be to normalize patterns of work-leisure to those typical of vocational, home, and other settings and to incorporate normalized degrees of choice in existing task demands, postponing work until later, and so forth	1.1. Work sessions initially restricted to 8 minutes, after which prompted to sign "Need a break," and given 1–2 minutes respite prior to no more than 5 additional minutes of working 1.2. Prompting withheld until after 10 minutes or until pretantrum signals occur, at which point client prompted to sign "Need a break," and so forth 1.3. If tantrum occurs, trainer ignores outburst and resumes task demands when tantrum subsides, prompting "Need a break" sign after 2 additional minutes of work

[a]From The Assessment of Social Competence, by Meyer, Reichle, et al, 1985. Reprinted with permission, with some adaptations, from Evans and Meyer (1985).

1. What to eat for a meal or snack
2. What to wear
3. What to do on a Saturday off or after dinner during an evening
4. What television show to watch
5. How to spend money that is not committed for expenses
6. Deciding whether or not to agree to participate in a family activity
7. Being able to telephone a friend or family member
8. What time to go to bed at night or get up in the morning on a Saturday or Sunday
9. Whom one wants for a friend, roommate/housemate, and so forth
10. What job one wants to do
11. Whether to entertain others at home or visit family/friends
12. What sexual lifestyle to adopt
13. Whether to drink, smoke, and/or engage in other "bad habits"

Most of these are fairly ordinary daily decisions that other people take for granted. Three of them, however, are fairly important decisions that most other people expect to have at least some (perhaps major) role in making (items 9, 10, and 12). Kishi, Teelucksingh, Zollers, Park-Lee, and Meyer (1988) did indeed find that nondisabled adults reported that they made such decisions, while adults with developmental disabilities ranging from mild to profound mental retardation and living in community-based group homes apparently are not typically making such decisions. What are the consequences of being forced to live with housemates whom one dislikes? Surely, being able to choose not to live with certain people and, alternatively, living with a person whom one likes has a great impact on one's behavior. In the authors' experience, conflict between housemates, co-workers, and roommates with disabilities who clearly do not like one another and yet are required by the system to be together is not uncommon. If persons with disabilities could provide input, if not actually make the decision, regarding with whom they live and where they work at a level similar to that allowed for nondisabled people, many conflicts at home and work could be alleviated and even eliminated. And many incidents of noncompliance are provoked by requiring clients to retire at a certain agency-prescribed bedtime and to get up on a Saturday in time for cafeteria-style breakfast in an institution, and not allowing clients to call in sick on a bad day, and so forth.

Most of these choices could reasonably be made by persons with developmental disabilities. First of all, of course, the individual has to know how to make a choice, and it has been assumed that persons with severe retardation are not able to make such choices. The authors disagree and can point to dozens of examples of clients with severe to profound retardation who were successfully taught to make choices reliably and meaningfully. Following is a listing of possible opportunities and initial strategies for teaching choice making. (See Wuerch & Voeltz [1982] for more detail.)

Choice Training Procedures

Target objective:

Increase person's ability to make choices that reflect his or her preferences and to select alternatives

Instructional format:

Skill cluster

Prompt procedures:

Individualized form with time delay fading procedures

General instructions:

A total of nine choice sessions should be conducted weekly, three each during dinner, during household jobs, and during leisure time activity, as below.

Activity: Dinner (three sessions weekly)

Natural cue	Instructional cue	Target skill
Offered a choice of a second helping of two food items	Model a point to randomly selected choice with verbal, "Do you want the _____?"	Learner will spontaneously point to preferred item within 5 seconds after offer of second helping choice

Activity: Household jobs (three sessions weekly)

Natural cue	Instructional cue	Target skill
Choice of beginning job of sweeping floor or dusting cupboards	Offer the broom and dust cloth and physically prompt a random choice after verbal, "Time to clean your room. Do you want to dust or sweep first?"	Client will start job by selecting either dust cloth or broom in response to natural cue, "Time to clean your room."

Activity: Leisure (three sessions weekly)

Natural cue	Instructional cue	Target skill
Offered a choice between a preferred and a less preferred activity	Verbal cue, "Freetime: Do you want _____ or _____?" along with model point to randomly selected activity item	Student will point to preferred toy when offered choice between two toys and given cue, "Free time"

Instructional procedures:

During each activity, allow the natural cues to occur (i.e., the choice of foods, household tasks, and activities), then immediately prompt the learner to point toward a choice that is selected randomly. Use the time delay procedure to fade the use of physical prompts. Do not deliver any artificial verbal instructional cues. The verbal offer should be one that would be typically used (e.g., "Would you like more potatoes?") and should vary naturally with the situation.

Time delay procedures:

Time delay—no delay to 1-second delay

Present five training trials for each activity, providing the physical prompt immediately after the natural cue. On the sixth training trial for each activity, allow the natural cue to occur and delay presentation of the physical prompt for 1 second:

1. If the learner does not make an error for 3 consecutive trials before receiving the prompt and after the natural cue occurs, move on to the 2-second delay procedure
2. If the learner makes an error during the time delay trial, return to the no delay procedure and deliver five more pairing trials. On the sixth trial, repeat the 1-second delay procedure as above.

Time delay—2-second delay

Allow the natural cue to occur, and delay presentation of the physical prompt 2 seconds.

1. If the learner does not make an error on three consecutive trials before receiving the prompt and after the natural cue occurs, move on to the 3-second delay procedure.
2. If the learner makes an error during the 2-second time delay trial, return to the 1-second delay procedure.

Time delay—3 seconds

Allow the natural cue to occur and delay presentation of the physical prompt 3 seconds.

1. If the learner does not make an error on three consecutive trials before receiving the prompt and after the natural cue occurs, move on to the 4-second delay procedure.
2. If the learner makes an error during the 3 second time delay trial, return to the 2 second delay procedure.

Time delay—4 seconds

Allow the natural cue to occur and delay presentation of the physical prompt 4 seconds.

1. If the learner does not make an error on three consecutive trials before receiving the prompt and after the natural cue occurs, repeat the 4-second time delay trials until performance on the task is consistently correct.
2. If the learner makes an error during the 4-second time delay trial, return to the 3-second delay procedure.

Choice making may be taught systematically, but can also be actively promoted through more informal incidental teaching techniques such as those listed in the sample Choice Training Procedures. The basic principle is simply to identify opportunities throughout the client's day and schedule that could become trials for choice making. Rather than simply offering the client what he or she obviously wants or prefers, or requiring that he or she do something that is perhaps not really important anyway, the situation should be utilized as a chance to practice making a choice. If the client does not respond, then prompt a choice, sometimes giving the client a nonpreferred and other times a preferred item, so that he or she will learn that the object given will be the object that was chosen. Particularly when choices involve items and activities that represent a range of preferences for the client, he or she will become motivated quite rapidly to initiate choice making to obtain those items that truly are preferred. Note that time delay prompt fading strategies are included for use in choice training. Time delay prompt fading introduces a learning situation that is virtually error-free for the client while also allowing the client to take the initia-

tive when he or she is ready to do so. The authors have found that these time delay prompt fading strategies are particularly helpful for use with individuals who have behavior problems, possibly because they do prevent errors and thus reduce stressful and difficult situations for both the client and the trainer. Most people are more willing to participate more cheerfully when they are having success, and individuals with developmental disabilities and behavior problems are no exception.

FUNCTIONAL COMMUNICATION TRAINING

Every individual should have a functional communication system that he or she can use to communicate with others. This system may be quite conventional, as with standard spoken language. Or, the system that the client learns could be an adapted or alternative system individually prescribed based on his or her needs.

Forms of Communication Alternative to Speech

Signing Exact English (SEE) and *American Sign Language*, for example, are visual communication systems using arm and hand motions (along with facial expression) to represent the content and form of language. While these communication systems were originally developed for persons with hearing impairments that precluded use of spoken language, they have proved quite successful as well for persons with other disabilities such as autism or severe mental retardation. Occasionally, where there is no apparent hearing impairment, Signing Exact English is used in combination with spoken language in the hope that the individual will one day master speech; this is referred to as Simultaneous Communication.

Communication boards or booklets can be extremely useful as formats for the client's communication strategies. A communication board system can be based on any one of several different symbol systems (e.g., Blissymbolics) or simply constructed for someone using actual photographs of vocabulary items. Sometimes the printed word is combined with pictures, particularly where reading might be an eventual goal and/or the printed word might help others in the community who are not disabled to communicate with the client. Such symbols or pictures may be organized on a communication board that the client could have arranged for him on a wheelchair tray or a lapboard. Alternatively, they might be organized in a wallet or three-ring binder that the individual could carry around. Picture systems can be particularly useful because matched pictures also could be organized into a schedule for the student, by using a series of vertically arranged photo display pockets in which the activities pictured are organized in the order in which they will take place. The client would be shown this picture schedule at the beginning of the day, and as each new activity began, the picture of the activity just completed would be turned over in its slot. Eventually, clients would develop an understanding of the day's events, and the system can then be used to show and explain to the client any changes that might occur on any particular day. Clients could also learn to select certain activities during free time periods, or perform certain tasks in an order of their own choosing. Transitions and changes can be particularly difficult times for clients, and it may well be that some of these difficulties are due to confusion and even panic about unexplained variations in familiar routines.

Selecting the Communicative Form for the Client

Communication training is essential whenever the assessment procedure determines that the individual seems to be using a behavior problem to communicate something to others. Suppose, for example, the assessment information suggests that a behavior problem is being maintained because it enables the individual to avoid or even escape what are clearly nonpreferred activities or situations. Step one is to identify the communicative form to teach the learner that will accomplish the same function for him or her as the priority excess behavior. If the individual in question does not have a formal communication system, read his or her files and organize the staff and the client's family to reach some decision regarding what general strategy to use. If a speech therapist has never been involved in planning for this individual, now is the time to involve someone with expertise in this area without further delay. Even if this professional is not available for ongoing training and/or consultation, some initial assistance with these important early decisions is invaluable and should be arranged.

Durand and Kishi (1987) have listed five questions that staff should ask in selecting a particular communicative form to teach someone as a replacement for a behavior problem. The questions they pose are important because the answers determine whether or not the new communicative behavior is likely to be as powerful for the client as the problem behavior it is intended to replace. The answer should be yes for each of the following questions about the communicative form selected:

1. Is this response one that can be easily taught to the individual (i.e., within a few days or weeks)?
2. Is this response one that could be understood by someone not familiar with the individual?
3. Is this response appropriate for those situations in which most problem behaviors seem to occur?
4. Is this response one that will be responded to appropriately by other people?
5. If used appropriately, would other people not find this response annoying?

If the answer is no to any of these questions, then identify a different communicative response form to teach the student that does generate all yes answers. Otherwise, the program is less likely to be successful, because each of these questions addresses an issue that will affect the power of the new form to replace the old behavior problem. For example, if the individual has learned to use the sign for "Help me" whenever having difficulty on a task, but persons who have a great deal of contact with him or her, such as a job coach, do not learn what this sign means, it will not be very powerful for the person. And if it does not work, the person is obviously at risk for reverting to using the behavior that worked in the past at least some of the time.

Teaching the Communicative Form

Following is a sample communication program for a man whose behavior problems seemed to be motivated by task avoidance:

PROMPT FADING STEPS FOR TEACHING REQUESTS FOR A BREAK FROM WORK

Phase	Setting	Prompts	Student Response	Adult Response
1.	Work	Level 1: Task is presented	Points to picture for "break"	Allows employee to spend time away from work in break room
		Level 2: Touch picture to finger	Same as above	Same as above
		Level 3: Hand-over-hand help to point to picture	Same as above	Same as above

At this phase, employee may be prompted to request a break as often as needed to avoid a behavioral incident. Time delay procedures should be incorporated into delivery of prompts.

2.	Work	Level 1: Task is presented	Points to picture for break	Allows employee to spend time away from work in break room
		Level 2: Touch picture to finger	Same as above	Same as above

At this phase, employee may be prompted to request a break on a preliminary schedule (e.g., every 10–15 minutes) or as often as needed to avoid a behavioral incident. Time delay procedures should be incorporated into delivery of prompts.

PROMPT FADING STEPS FOR TEACHING REQUESTS FOR A BREAK FROM WORK

Phase	Setting	Prompts	Student Response	Adult Response
3.	Work	Level 1: Task is ongoing	Points to picture for break	Allows employee to spend time away from work in break room

At this phase, employee may be allowed to obtain a break on a reasonable break schedule (e.g., every ½ hour) and, in addition, may be prompted when needed to avoid a behavioral incident. (Use a Level 2 prompt.)

Phase	Setting	Prompts	Student Response	Adult Response
4.	Work	Initiated by client on reasonable schedule	Points to picture for break	Allows employee to spend time away from work

At this Phase, employee should be working according to the expected work schedule, requesting breaks at a rate that is acceptable to current and immediate future environments. However, staff must also honor occasional requests for breaks over and above this typical rate on a permanent basis to ensure that the employee has a functional communication form (adapted from Durand & Kishi 1987).

This individual was described as being nonverbal but frequently hit himself on the head during various activities on the job. Various tasks at work have been determined as appropriate for him and, in fact, he even seems to enjoy work for at least a few minutes. Thus, the analysis of the various ecological issues that might need to be addressed (see Chapter 6) indicates that the tasks and environment are appropriate, and what he needs is to acquire alternative communication strategies to replace his self-injurious behavior. The assessment results suggest that the learner either tires easily or becomes frustrated with some aspect of the task. Perhaps it is too difficult for him, even though it is something he could in fact learn to do, and he engages in self-injury as a fairly successful strategy to ensure that the task is interrupted for at least a brief period of time.

Because this man has, until now, had little communication training, the team decision is to teach him to use a picture of the break room to ask for a break from work. This particular client also generally requires full physical prompts, hand-over-hand assistance, when he is given a new task to learn, rather than responding to a demonstration or model. Later, he responds well to a partial physical assist. Thus three different levels of prompts are designated. Level 1 represents the natural cue. This situational cue should be all that is necessary to prompt the behavior naturally, without trainer assistance, and the goal is to have the client respond to this level when mastery has been attained. Level 2 is the partial help described. In this case, the trainer would gently touch the client's finger with the picture, but not actually physically prompt him to point. The full physical prompt, Level 3, is hand-over-hand assistance by the trainer to help client point to the break picture.

Notice also that the sample program includes four phases of instruction. Later this chapter returns to the issue of why it is so important to give in to the client at the beginning of a program to teach an alternative skill to replace a problem behavior. That is, even though it would not be appropriate for someone to have a break every few minutes, at the beginning of a communication training program it is crucial that he or she have a break as often as desired or needed. THIS IS VERY IMPORTANT! Self-injury will continue to be more effective if it causes an immediate response from staff, and the communication skill—asking for a break by pointing to the picture—will *not* be effective if staff do not honor the employee's request rapidly and consistently. Thus, the sample instructional program indicates that during Phase 1, breaks might be allowed quite frequently, perhaps even every few minutes. During Phase 2, the rate of taking breaks is slowing down a bit, but the employee might still be taking a break every 10–15 minutes (clearly, far more often than would be considered acceptable in a typical work environment). By Phase 3, the goal is not only that the employee respond to the natural cue of the ongoing task (i.e., no longer requiring physical prompting), but also that the rate of taking a break is becoming closer to something that would be more acceptable in the community. And finally, by Phase 4, the employee is expected to work according to a typical schedule. But remember, even at mastery, there may be occasions when someone simply must have a nonscheduled break. Otherwise, again, the communication form is not truly empowering (as the self-injurious behavior would continue to be because it is certain to provoke a response from everyone) but has become yet another means of control over the client by staff. It will help staff to be more accepting of the individual's right to occasionally ask for things like unscheduled breaks if they think of all the times when they simply had to call in sick or make some excuse to leave the room, if only for a few minutes, to avoid a particular meeting or task on a bad day.

Figure 7.1 shows a completed sample Communicative Form Program Summary for the example discussed above. Note that the sample summary includes a brief description of procedures staff should follow

when the learner engages in the desired response (using the break picture) and the undesirable response (head hitting).

One final comment on functional communication training: please do not begin and end functional communication with only an effort to teach one alternative communicative form to replace one particular problem behavior. As indicated above, the selection of a particular communicative form to teach should be made in the context of some general decisions about what communication system is appropriate for the individual. The presence of behavior problems with clear communicative intent provides irrefutable evidence that communication training should be a priority. This particular program should be the first step, and additional communication goals should be incorporated into the habilitation plan, so that the person can communicate with others to do far more than simply ask for a break. There are many invaluable references on how to develop and implement good communication training programs for learners with even the most severe disabilities. Contact the state education agency or a speech therapy or special education program at a university for these resources.

A Caveat on Teaching Alternatives

This section on functional communication training emphasizes the communicative function that excess behavior might have. Because such problem behaviors are not random or bizarre but are intended by the individual to accomplish something, the intervention implication confronting the team is to replace them with the alternative communication skill. The assumption, thus far, has been that staff not only know what the client wants to accomplish, but agree that he or she can have it. But in some situations staff might believe the client should not have it. Once the communicative function of any problem behavior is identified, two things are possible:

Communicative Form Program Summary (Form 4)

Employee's name: *Aaron T.*   Date: *9/15/88*

Communication system (e.g., verbal, sign, communication board):

Combination picture and token symbol system

Target communication goal (describe each of the following objectively):

A. Situation and natural cue(s)

Working on sorting or labeling supplies at jobsite

B. Communicative initiation or response from employee:
1. Present negative behavior in situation:

Aaron hits his face or head with his fist.

2. Target positive communicative behavior for this situation:

Aaron will point to the "Break" picture and then leave the task briefly. (He'll be allowed to sit in the breakroom for 5 minutes.)

C. Expected response by others (e.g., assistance, tangibles): *(see also crisis management procedures.)*
1. Expected response to present negative behavior:

Try to anticipate and distract, then prompt a break. If he hits, interrupt, distract, then prompt a break after 2 minutes.

2. Expected response to target positive communicative behavior:

Immediately say "Yes, take a break," and allow him to have a break.

D. Staff/others expected to respond to employee:

All supervisors, the job coach, the therapists, and direct service staff.

Criteria for mastery:

Aaron will initiate a work break 1-2 times per period, and as needed on "difficult" tasks.

Target date for mastery: *12/15/88*

Person responsible for monitoring this program (must observe employee in situation at least daily):

Mr. James (job Coach)

Team review date (no later than 1 month after start date noted above):

10/13/88

FIGURE 7.1. Communicative Form Program Summary.

1. Staff know what the client wants and are willing to give it to him or her. This situation is no problem. The alternative positive communication strategy for accomplishing the same function is taught and staff do their best to ensure that whenever the client uses that new skill, the client gets what he or she wants. It may even be that what the client wants is a long-overdue change in schedule or activities that have needed some adjustments. But staff are quite willing to comply with the client's communicative request when he or she makes it.

2. Staff know what the client wants but do not want to give it to him or her. It is possible that what the client wants is not good for him or her, that he or she wants it too often, and so forth. This situation is far more difficult than the first one. Like the first situation, it is still critical that staff teach the client a new, more appropriate communicative form to say that he or she wants something, and that the client use this new form rather than the old problem behavior to make such requests. It is useful to take a serious look at who is right whenever staff disagree that the client's request is reasonable. Staff may well be right but could also be overprotective or denying the client the right to exercise the kind of autonomy that would be appropriate if handled reasonably well. Careful judgment is needed to decide when staff and families need to reconsider their biases that clients may not do or have certain things they want.

But suppose staff are quite correct in the assumption that what the client wants is not appropriate. Suppose, for example, that an employee clearly wants a break from work but wants a 10-minute break every 5 minutes. A real-world work environment would not support this number of breaks. Nevertheless, the hard truth is that to succeed in teaching the client that signing "break" is preferable to throwing objects, hitting others, or head banging as a strategy to obtain a change of pace, staff must respond to his or her requests for breaks as often as necessary in the early stages of the skill training to prevent negative behavior from occurring. That is, staff must give in to his requests, as long as he uses the appropriate communicative form. Later on, once the new skill is firmly established because the client has experienced success in using it, he can be taught to wait longer and longer for his breaks, until staff have succeeded in normalizing the rate of break-taking to a rate that is acceptable to his or her work environment.

It is crucial to discuss these two very different situations with staff whenever beginning a skill training program to replace a problem behavior with an adaptive alternative. The client must be empowered by the new skill. Ignoring it runs the risk of encouraging the learner to try the old behavior again instead. At the same time, mastery involves more than learning only the form of the alternative skill. Learning is not completed until the form has been learned but the rate of using that form is normalized to what typical environments will support and reinforce. Sometimes this learning is best accomplished in stages.

LEISURE EDUCATION

Some excess behaviors seem to be a strategy to entertain oneself when alone and appear to be maintained by their intrinsic reinforcement value for the individual. For example, they may be unaffected by whether other people are in the room and, in fact, the individual may pay no attention to what else is occurring while engaged in certain excess behaviors. Chapter 2 discussed stereotypic behaviors such as hand flapping, rocking, finger flicking, and so forth, that are most likely to occur when the individual is left alone. In some cases, even more serious behaviors such as eye poking or face slapping may commonly occur whenever a particular client is not busy with some other activity. These behaviors might be much more frequent, in fact, during free or down time. They are said to occur most frequently in large-scale institutional settings where residents have a great deal of free time on their hands, where staff–client ratios might be relatively poor so that residents do not receive a great deal of attention from staff, and there may not be much to do because materials are locked away for safekeeping, and the environment generally is quite barren.

Whenever the assessment seems to suggest that excess behavior is most likely to occur under circumstances such as these, the most reasonable hypothesis for their occurrence is that they are analogous to play or leisure time activities. Most people learn to entertain themselves fairly constructively when they have time on their hands, and various environments are even arranged to help with this process, such as the doctor's office with magazines. People even learn to pretend to be busy under such conditions (e.g., reading magazines in that office that are months old). For persons with developmental disabilities, however, both opportunities to develop age-appropriate leisure time repertoires and access to the needed materials are restricted. Nondisabled children and youth can choose to participate in many leisure and recreation activities as they mature, including various school-sponsored and neighborhood-focused programs designed specifically for extracurricular and community recreation purposes. Children and youth with severe mental retardation, autism, dual sensory impairments, and so forth, are not given access to similar experiences. Thus, lack of opportunity added to learning disabilities further reduces the possibility that a constructive, adaptive leisure repertoire will develop by adulthood.

There is considerable evidence that stereotypic behaviors in particular are maintained by the sensory feedback they provide the individual. A behavior such as finger flicking or eye poking serves a function for the individual that is quite similar to solitary play. In 1973, Favell showed that excess behaviors of this type could be reduced by providing encouragement to engage in toy play instead, which presumably offers similar personally enjoyable sensory feedback. Unfortunately, not all of the subjects in Favell's study continued to engage in toy play without systematic intervention to reinforce them to do so. It appeared that these individuals lacked a sufficiently rich leisure repertoire to offer reinforcement that equaled that available from their stereotypic behaviors. What they might have needed was, quite simply, training in how to play with the kinds of more novel and reinforcing materials that would have been sufficiently self-reinforcing to result in more lasting and generalizable changes.

In investigating this issue, the authors taught several teenagers who had severe to profound mental retardation and other disabilities, such as autism, to play independently using age-appropriate leisure time activities, such as play with video games, pinball, and electronic keyboard toys. The authors then monitored their behavior during free time as a function of the toy play skill instruction and were able to show a relationship between their use of the new leisure activity skills and a corresponding reduction in stereotypic behaviors (Meyer et al., 1985). Whenever the assessment information suggests that a problem behavior is being maintained by its intrinsic feedback rather than by social variables, leisure activity training or therapeutic recreation should be a priority. Just as individuals with severe disabilities may require instruction to learn communication and self-regulation skills, systematic intervention may be needed to ensure that every person has a constructive leisure repertoire. Wuerch and Voeltz (1982) have developed and validated a comprehensive curriculum for teaching self-initiated, age-appropriate leisure activities to teenagers with very severe disabilities; their curriculum includes detailed instructional programs for 10 leisure activities that can be used by the individual during free time in typical home and neighborhood settings, either alone or with a friend.

Leisure education also can provide alternatives to engaging in less desirable disruptive behaviors that are motivated by a desire for social attention. Suppose a young adult has few social and leisure skills, but likes someone else in his or her group home. What appears to be harassment of another client might actually represent efforts to initiate a positive social interaction, but the efforts become negative behaviors because of a lack of skill. The major stimulus for the leisure curriculum development effort by Wuerch and Voeltz described above was concern from parents about their children's use of leisure time. Parents said that they were unable to leave their children alone for even a few minutes before dinner, and that their children basically required constant supervision. The intervention reasoning was that these children needed to learn some enjoyable, appropriate, constructive leisure activities to occupy their down time, either alone or with a sibling or friend. Teaching children such activities should greatly reduce the need for supervision and, consequently, also reduce the stress on the family entailed by the child's need.

To initiate a leisure activities program, the authors recommend that a recreation therapist or physical education instructor be located to conduct a thorough analysis of the opportunities that could be provided as well as assess the capabilities of the client to take advantage of those opportunities. For individuals with significant motoric impairment and/or sensory impairments, an occupational or physical therapist and a mobility specialist might also be needed. Listed below are the various steps that should be followed to design a specific leisure activity instructional program for a client.

Identifying Reinforcers

First identify the types of objects and/or activities that appear to motivate the client. Look closely at the nature of the individual's stereotypic behavior, for example. Does it appear that he or she enjoys the visual stimuli, auditory stimuli, vibration, or other stimuli? Does the client prefer playing alone or with another person? Make a list of the kinds of feedback that seem to be motivating the individual's engagement in the behavior.

Evaluating Available Leisure Activity Options

Now, identify some age-appropriate materials and activities that match the kinds of personal preferences identified for the individual. Select items and activities that are motivating because they seem to represent similar stimuli, but apply some additional criteria to ensure that the new behaviors taught will be more positive than the excess behaviors they were designed to replace. Thus, a teenager would not be taught to play with a toddler's toy, regardless of how interesting that toy might be for him or her. Playing with an age-inappropriate toy is simply going to introduce another stigma into the client's life and further highlight the discrepancies between that individual and nondisabled peers. There are, however, many alternative leisure materials that reproduce similar stimuli that also are age-appropriate, so identify one of these for the client. For example, experiment with electronic games such as pinball or with video games; play training programs for these kinds of activities are included in the Wuerch and Voeltz (1982) text. It is useful to visit a large toy store and to interview the client's peers to discover new possibilities and determine which of these might be appropriate. Once there is a list of possibilities, the Leisure Activity Selection Inventory can be used to narrow it down on behalf of a specific client (see Figure 7.2). The checklist considers features of the activity that relate to normalization (e.g., whether the activity is age-appropriate), individualization (e.g., whether it can be adapted easily for various multiple disabilities), and environmental (e.g., whether it is expensive and/or likely to continue to be available) considerations.

Assessing Individual Client Interest

Next, make some final decisions about which particular materials and activities are going to be the best match for the person's interests. For some individuals, it may be very difficult to determine in advance what kinds of materials and activities would be preferred. Thus, the authors recommend use of Wuerch and Voeltz's (1982) Student Interest Inventory (see Figure 7.3) to identify good first choices for a training program. The inventory requires only a few minutes to conduct. The individual is given the item; someone models play with the item very briefly, and then moves away to record how the client reacts by completing the inventory. After 2 or 3 minutes the first item is removed, and a second item is presented following the same procedures. After doing this for three or four activities, the inventory scores can be compared to estimate which activities seem to be most interesting for the client. Wuerch and Voeltz (1982) also pointed out that even if the interaction with the materials is inappropriate (e.g., tapping on the toy or tossing it into the air repetitively), such interaction is a good indication of interest in learning to play with those materials. However, stereotypic behavior that does not involve the materials

(e.g., rocking back and forth without even glancing at them) strongly suggests no interest.

Teaching Leisure Skills that Are Preferred

Now that the materials that are presumably most interesting to the client have been identified, begin systematic training. Short time periods such as two 15-minute periods each week on each of two separate leisure activities has been found to be effective in establishing an initial leisure repertoire for teenagers and young adults with moderate to profound disabilities and multiple disabilities. A great deal of time is not required. However, it is crucial that any activity intended to occupy leisure time be personally rewarding to the individual. If the person does not like the activity, it will have almost no use as a free time activity. The choice training procedure introduced earlier in this chapter (described in more detail in Wuerch and Voeltz, 1982, as part of a leisure education program) will help to ensure that choices are considered throughout any such curricular effort designed to increase leisure time skills.

SUMMARY

This chapter ends with the habilitation plan that was developed for an individual who exhibited many very serious problem behaviors and whose previous lifestyle had become extremely restrictive, partly as a function of those behaviors. In this case, implementing major changes in that lifestyle in a manner that continuously involved the client in each decision was a major theme of the intervention. Procedures were specified to respond to the behavior when and if it did occur, but the intervention was to both replace it with more constructive alternatives as well as make it less necessary from the client's perspective.

Leisure Activity Selection Inventory (Form 5)

Student: _____ Date: _____ Completed by: _____

	Activity	Activity	Activity
Normalization: A concern for selecting activities that have social validity and that will facilitate normalized play and leisure behaviors, as well as provide opportunities for movement toward increasingly complex interactions.			
1. *Age Appropriateness.* Is this activity something a nonhandicapped peer would enjoy during free time?	yes no	yes no	yes no
2. *Attraction.* Is this activity likely to promote interest of others who frequently are found in the youth's leisure time settings?	yes no	yes no	yes no
3. *Environmental Flexibility.* Can this activity be used in a variety of potential leisure time situations on an individual and group basis?	yes no	yes no	yes no
4. *Degree of Supervision.* Can the activity be used under varying degrees of caregiver supervision without major modifications?	yes no	yes no	yes no
5. *Longitudinal Application.* Is use of the activity appropriate for both an adolescent and an adult?	yes no	yes no	yes no
Individualization: Concerns related to meeting the unique and ever-changing needs and skills of handicapped youth.			
1. *Skill Level Flexibility.* Can the activity be adapted for low to high entry skill levels without major modifications?	yes no	yes no	yes no
2. *Prosthetic Capabilities.* Can the activity be adapted to varying handicapping conditions (sensory, motor, behavior)?	yes no	yes no	yes no
3. *Reinforcement Power.* Is the activity sufficiently novel or stimulating to maintain interest?	yes no	yes no	yes no
Environmental: Concerns related to logistical and physical demands of leisure activities on current and future environments and free time situations.			
1. *Availability.* Is the activity available (or can it easily be made so) across the youth's leisure environments?	yes no	yes no	yes no
2. *Durability.* Is the activity likely to last without need for major repair or replacement of parts for at least a year?	yes no	yes no	yes no
3. *Safety.* Is the activity safe, i.e., would not pose a serious threat to or harm the handicapped youth, others, or the environment if abused or used inappropriately?	yes no	yes no	yes no
4. *Noxiousness.* Is the activity not likely to be overly noxious (noisy, space consuming, distracting) to others in the youth's leisure environments?	yes no	yes no	yes no
5. *Expense.* Is the cost of the activity reasonable? That is, is it likely to be used for multiple purposes?	yes no	yes no	yes no
Area of Concern Scores 1. Normalization 2. Individualization 3. Environmental	_____ _____ _____	_____ _____ _____	_____ _____ _____
Total Activity Score	_____	_____	_____

FIGURE 7.2. Leisure Activity Selection Inventory. (From Wuerch & Voeltz, 1982, p. 181; reprinted by permission.)

Student Interest Inventory (Form 6)

Student: _____

	Activity						
Instructions: *For each activity, answer each of the questions below by placing the number of the description that best matches the child's behavior in the appropriate box for that activity.*	Date						
	Rater						
A. For this child's usual level of interest in play materials, he or she is: 1. Not as interested as usual 2. About as interested as usual 3. More interested than usual							
B. For this child's usual level of physical interaction with materials (pushing control buttons, turning knobs, putting things together, etc.), he or she is: 1. Not as busy as usual 2. About as busy as usual 3. Busier than usual							
C. For this child's usual "affective" behaviors (smiling, signs of enjoyment, etc.), he or she seems to be: 1. Enjoying this less than usual 2. Showing about the same amount of enjoyment as usual 3. Enjoying this more than usual							
D. For this child's usual level of "looking" or "visual regard" of an activity, object, or person, he or she is: 1. Not looking as much as usual 2. Looking as much as usual 3. Looking more often or longer than usual							
E. Compared to this child's usual behavior during a short period of time with minimal supervision, he or she is: 1. Engaging in more negative behavior than usual 2. Engaging in about the same amount of negative behavior as usual 3. Engaging in less negative (or off-task) behavior than usual							
Activity Interest Scores: *Total the numbers in each column*		___	___		___	___	___

FIGURE 7.3.   Student Interest Inventory. (From Wuerch & Voeltz, 1982, p. 182; reprinted by permission.)

A HABILITATION PLAN FOR EMPHASIZING ADAPTIVE ALTERNATIVES

Client: Mr. Jordan, age 43

Referral behaviors:

Head hitting, head banging, scratching and picking skin, picking and tearing off fingernails and toenails, body slapping, eye and ear poking, placing sharp objects in his shoes and walking on them, body banging, operant vomiting, rumination, spitting on others, hitting and kicking others, crying and yelling (Note: Most of these behaviors were recorded in written records through institutional records beginning at age 6.)

Assessment data:

Self-injurious behaviors associated with task and situation/environment avoidance

Intervention:

1. Short-term prevention: Drastically changing the stimulus conditions associated with self-injury
2. Immediate consequences: Normalized consequences (i.e., verbal reprimand) for self-injury, with crisis management backup procedures if necessary (i.e., personal restraint until calm)
3. Adaptive alternatives: Instruction and opportunities in functional, community-based activities and social-communication system
4. Long-term prevention: Self-regulation and active decision-making by Mr. Jordan

Habilitation plan goals:

1.0 Decision-making: To provide Mr. Jordan with the power to make decisions to lessen the likelihood of self-injury as noncompliance.
    1.1. Opportunity to make choices about where he goes during free time at home and in the community
    1.2. During meal times, use of picture communication system to indicate food choices
    1.3. Before any new activity is started, options discussed with Mr. Jordan and encouragement to indicate his preferences
2.0. Home management: Increase independence in home domain (Note: Mr. Jordan has moved to a supported apartment in the community, for which these goals were written.)
    2.1. Given a choice of responsibility for one of three domestic chores (vacuuming, dishes, taking out the garbage), Mr. Jordan will select one chore each week as his responsibility, mark the planned chore date and time on his weekly calendar, and initiate the chore as scheduled
    2.2. After completing a meal, take his own dishes to the sink, rinse them, wash and dry them, and replace them in the cupboard
    2.3. Independently awaken to clock radio, shower and dress, groom self, and replace pajamas in bureau drawer with no verbal reminders
    2.4. Before retiring to bed, change into pajamas, place dirty clothes in hamper, and replace clean clothes in closet or drawers as appropriate
3.0. Self-management
    3.1. Review newspaper movie and entertainment section each evening to identify possible interest for that week/evening, including requesting activities
    3.2. Review daily picture schedule of activities and review calendar weekly, marking appointments, planned activities, jobs, staff vacations/absences, and other events. After breakfast each day, participate in brief discussion of day's planned activities
    3.3. Actively participate in planning the menu for two meals each week, indicating preferred main courses from four choices
    3.4. Actively participate in using local bank account for personal funds, including salary from work and spending money
    3.5 Use a picture listing to independently select food items from grocery store on weekly shopping trips: Mr. Jordan will select items and place them into his cart independently

4.0. Employment training
    4.1.   Observe employees working at three different job sites, with staff observing Mr. Jordan from a different area, one 15-minute period daily at each site for one week each
    4.2.   Perform selected job tasks at these three different job sites for 1-hour period daily at each site for 1 week each, with staff observing Mr. Jordan at the job site and providing assistance as needed
    4.3.   Complete a 6-hour work day, 5 days per week with minimal supervision (staff present within view) for 1 month
    4.4.   Complete a 6-hour work day, 5 days per week with no immediate supervision (staff in building) at job placement
5.0. Leisure/Recreation
    5.1.   Walk with direct service staff member for one-half hour daily in his immediate community area to become familiar with the neighborhood
    5.2.   Choose to visit someone, using his picture album, twice weekly, with one reminder
    5.3.   Independently initiate one leisure activity per day, including watching television, listening to the stereo, seeing a movie, going for a walk, watching a sporting event, eating out with a friend, visiting friends/family. (This plan is based on the actual program developed for the client described in Berkman & Meyer [1988].)

chapter

8

Strategies To
Support Behavior Change

OVERVIEW

This chapter describes various strategies that can be used to support behavior change. These include strategies to change the client's emotional state or mood, as well as procedures to change the general social climate or social interaction pattern in an environment or program.

The authors also suggest adaptations that can be made to techniques that have become widely available for nondisabled clients (e.g., systematic desensitization) so that they are suitable for clients who have significant cognitive and/or language disabilities.

The purpose of the chapter is to display a wide range of general ways that might be creatively refashioned to facilitate overall improvements in behavior and the maintenance of behavior change. It is not expected that direct service staff be responsible for designing formal treatments based on these behavior therapy procedures. The details and further references provided are really more suitable for professionals with direct clinical responsibili-

ties. However broad concepts like gradually exposing someone to feared situations, encouraging self-control, understanding client's feelings, and deciding where and when an excess behavior might be appropriate should help all staff design successful environments.

TRAINEE OBJECTIVES

At the completion of this unit, participant trainees will be able to:

1. Recognize examples of emotional states or moods in individuals that make them more likely to exhibit problem behavior.
2. Give an example of typical schedule or activity changes and how to explain these to a client who may be having difficulty with such changes.
3. Describe a warm-up social interaction exchange, and give an example for a specific client.
4. Give an example of adaptations for each of the five steps of Anger Control

Training for someone with developmental disabilities.

5. Adapt systematic desensitization procedures for an individual who is nonverbal.

6. Recognize the circumstances that must be altered to help a client change a habit that is problematic.

7. Be able to encourage self-regulation in a client rather than relying on social or other external control.

8. Give an example of a behavior that varies in acceptability based on circumstances, and suggest the zone discrimination that needs to be learned.

INTRODUCTION

Chapters 6 and 7 detailed strategies for the four major components that make up any comprehensive treatment plan. Chapter 5 also emphasized that interventions for problem behavior should not be thought of as extras—procedures added to the individual client's overall plan. The total plan itself must meet the criteria for an effective set of living arrangements, and the more specific interventions (arranging antecedents or consequences and planning methods for teaching new skills) should be blended into the grand design. This ideal obviously is difficult to achieve whenever clients come into new situations—such as a well-designed program in a community residence—with a certain amount of extra baggage. Examples of this include inappropriate behaviors learned in a less desirable program, emotional problems rooted in the past, or new difficulties arising from such factors as medical problems and developmental changes.

Many of the behavior change needs for clients with disabilities may closely parallel those of nondisabled clients experiencing difficulties in adjustment. Certain treatment strategies developed for very similar problems in nondisabled people can very usefully be modified to assist individuals

who have severe disabilities. This chapter reviews some of these very specific techniques, relates them to the basic methods already described, and suggests how they can be adapted for the clients who are the focus of this manual. There are many valuable therapies developed for specific psychological problems that can be utilized to promote personal growth.

It might be helpful to give one or two examples of what the authors mean at this point. The authors know an older woman, Clara, who had recently been transferred to a group home from a large institution. The staff in the group home were very concerned because she stole food from the refrigerator and the cupboards and hoarded some of it in her bedroom. They decided that since the house really was her home, she should be allowed access to the refrigerator any time, much like any teenager or adult in a regular family. Thus the only rule was that if she took some food, she should eat it then and there as a snack and not hoard it. Unfortunately, but perhaps predictably, three negative consequences occurred. She started to eat large amounts of junk food between meals, she started to gain significant amounts of weight, and she helped herself to food that had been bought or prepared by the other five residents for themselves. The third problem was tackled by a discrimination training program that taught her not to take things that belonged to others. However, the other two aspects of the problem were really what in nondisabled persons would be considered eating disorders. Thus an additional plan to reduce binge eating and weight gain had to be devised.

A second example is Heather, who, at age 19, had lived at home all her life and was making the transition to a supervised apartment. Part of her program involved using the local bus to get to her vocational training program run by Goodwill Industries. However, she refused to go to work, tantrummed when the staff tried to teach her to use the bus system, and her behavior in the apartment deteriorated. It was discovered that Heather's parents, who were extremely wealthy, had never allowed her to take the bus and had driven her everywhere. In an attempt to protect her from strangers, they also had told her many times that it was dangerous to go places alone or use public transportation. She was therefore quite frightened to go anywhere by bus but did not know how to explain this. The authors developed a simple procedure to desensitize her (the details are explained later) by explaining in very simple terms that riding a bus was safe and by arranging for a close friend to accompany her on the initial journeys, while her rehabilitation counselor sat a few seats behind.

In both examples, general learning principles from behavior therapy were included as important parts of the overall treatment. And in both cases the intervention supported or permitted other interventions which were more directly focused on the problem behaviors.

MODIFYING EMOTIONAL STATES

Chapter 2 argued that one of the most important concepts to recognize is that maladaptive or undesirable behavior rarely if ever occurs in isolation from all the other behaviors in a person's repertoire. These behaviors include thoughts and feelings as well as other overt actions. Thus, actions identified as inappropriate often are really part of a more general pattern of behavior, patterns that generally are called moods or emotional states. It is obvious from studies of emotional expression that moods such as sadness, depression, irritation, or happiness are accompanied by characteristic behaviors, such as low activity levels, noncompliance, aggression, and so forth.

If the concept of mood or emotional state indicates only that certain behaviors co-occur in a regular way, the concept

would be of interest descriptively but not much use in explaining or functionally analyzing behavior. After all, perceiving a client as aggressive because he or she was in an aggressive mood would not provide a very insightful or helpful explanation of the behavior. But the idea of an emotional state does have very interesting implications for two reasons. One is that the mood or state can be caused (i.e., be a function of) some event quite unrelated to the person's current behavior. Thus a client who is in a depressed mood because of an event that happened on a home visit might be very noncompliant with direct service staff 3 days later. And second, the notion of mood is important because emotional states influence the way individuals respond to situations. For example, if a person is in an irritable mood, an order or mild reprimand from a supervisor at work might elicit a hostile, aggressive response, when normally the person might just proceed calmly without incident. There are two possible reasons for this very obvious phenomenon. The simplest is that moods change emotional thresholds, making people less tolerant. This results in situations where milder, less significant stimuli produce reactions like much more serious or dramatic events would. Examples are yelling at the cat or dog for some minor event after having been frustrated or angered at work or by traffic on the way home. A more complex process is that moods can change cognitive processes, so that interpretations and memories of events are changed and perhaps distorted. Thus, in a mood state like depression, a request from a work supervisor such as, "Please don't use furniture polish on this type of wood," might be interpreted as a criticism, whereas in a positive mood it would be interpreted as a simple directive.

There is a great deal of formal research on these issues, but the average person realizes intuitively that people have an everyday understanding and knowledge of such behavioral phenomena. Moods caused by physical effects such as headache, menstrual period, allergy, or lack of sleep are commonly used to explain negative behavior. Similarly, people understand very well that moods can be caused by experiences like making a bad grade, having an argument with a friend, being criticized at work, and so forth.

These are important issues, but they are almost totally neglected in traditional behavior modification, probably because of a narrow Skinnerian or operant orientation that still dominates so much of the field. Thus, important concepts from behavioral research in personality, for example, are ignored, and treatments for persons with severe disabilities are limited to simple contingency principles derived from animal operant conditioning, instead of being drawn from the latest developments in all of behavior therapy. Obviously, with people who have severe cognitive or intellectual impairments and who might have limited or no verbal skills, it is more difficult to define mood and design its modification. Generally, interpretation of a person's mood is based on self-report, and these individuals do not say in the usual ways that something is bothering them. But assuming the person's emotional state can be judged from the pattern of behavior and the dominant affect (e.g., smiling, crying, irritability, sadness), why would the treatment implications be any different from those for nondisabled persons with emotional problems? As explained in the following synopsis, the authors think the strategies for changing mood that have been developed in other contexts can be translated for adults with developmental disabilities.

The major approaches used to alter mood or emotional state have been cognitive interventions. The original procedure popularized by Beck (1976) assumes that negative self-statements (e.g., "I'm a worthless person.") elicit negative emotional responses, such as feelings of depression. The client is therefore trained to reduce the frequency of these cognitions in his or her daily thoughts, and to replace these thoughts with more upbeat, positive thoughts ("People do like me."), regardless of whether the person initially believes the content of the cognition or not. In Ellis's (1971) technique, the influence of thoughts on mood is attributed to irrational cognitions, that is, errors of inference based on limited evidence. An example might be interpreting criticism from one person as a sign that one is disliked by everyone. Treatment involves teaching people to recognize these irrational thoughts and understand why they are not logical, and encouraging the client to replace them with constructive beliefs (e.g., "He criticized me because of what I did. He'll still like me if I stop doing that.").

Neither of these approaches can be thought of as directly applicable to people who have very limited cognition to begin with. Yet it would seem that such individuals may be very susceptible to cognitive distortion. While cognitive errors and distortions do not seem to be related to verbal intelligence, the fact is that persons with severe intellectual disabilities do have limited access to information. Thus, for example, a person who is told that his or her job training program is coming to an end might not have the cognitive ability to understand that withdrawal of federal funding is the reason. Instead, the person might interpret the situation as being fired and take on blame, thus eliciting a depressed mood.

This general principle shows that a task for direct service personnel is to provide clients with as much information as possible about causes for events in their lives and things that happen to them. Explanations of why circumstances have to be arranged the way they are would be crucial for helping clients understand their worlds. Even if there is a lack of certainty that the client understands the explanation, give it anyway and do so in the way that would seem to be best. This begins with very simple changes—such as telling someone in a wheelchair that he or she is about to be pushed somewhere—to the more complex issues described next.

Interrupting a goal-directed activity or changing a well-established routine is anxiety-producing for most people. Systematic and predictable household or work routines provide clients with feelings of security that can easily be disrupted by sudden changes. And yet staff may not always help clients anticipate such changes. Staff might reason that the client would not understand that everyone has to leave the group home for a day because exterminators are coming in, or that a promised outing was cancelled because the tickets were sold out, or that a relative is not coming to visit because of an unexpected work commitment. The task is to find some method whereby changes and their causes can be communicated, using pictures, calendars, careful prior discussions, and so forth. For example, the authors knew a client living in a nursing home after being severely disabled by a traumatic head injury. His excess behavior was to tantrum—shouting and swearing—when being told it was not time for lunch, for coffee, for his cigarette, and so forth. Staff usually simply said no to these requests. The authors asked them instead to explain to the client that, for example, lunch was not until 12 noon, or that he had just had his coffee. This required development of a daily schedule because his immediate memory of events had been affected by the brain damage.

The authors have tried to point out the close connection between these general strategies for ensuring positive mood and the broader strategies discussed earlier concerning proper scheduling, futures planning, and the whole objective of ensuring that there is meaning and purpose to the lives of people with severe disabilities by helping them look forward to future events and desired accomplishments. Following are some additional examples that may be used as a training exercise.

EXAMPLES OF MOODS AND VERBAL INFLUENCE STRATEGIES

The following are examples of a variety of different moods with suggestions regarding their common causes and what might constitute a reasonable verbal influence strategy. These examples can be used as a training activity by giving the trainees the initial situation and asking them to generate the type of mood likely to result and what they could do or say that would reduce the mood. Note that the terms given to emotions are often ambiguous and complex. The words given here are not the only possible ones, so if the trainees come up with others, that is acceptable. Use individual judgment as to whether or not they are on the right track.

Eliciting situation: A promised camping trip has to be cancelled because the staff member who was going to lead it is sick.

Possible cognitive distortion/error: "I won't ever get to go camping."

Mood: Client is disappointed.

Negative collateral behavior: Client is noncompliant, talks back to staff, destroys property.

Cognitive intervention: "When John gets better, we will plan our trip." "Help me make a list of things we'll need for next week when John will be better." "I know it's disappointing; I'm disappointed too, but let's try to look on the bright side. Think of one advantage of going a couple of weeks later."

Eliciting situation: Mary, a popular staff member, is sitting talking to Clayton, one of the clients. Another client, Bobby, who likes Mary a lot, sees the two of them talking.

Possible cognitive distortion: "Clayton gets all the attention; I don't get any."

Mood: Bobby is jealous.

Negative collateral behavior: Bobby is aggressive toward Clayton. He is disruptive to attract Mary's attention.

Cognitive intervention: "Mary likes you too." "Clayton needs his share of attention too. Everyone is going to get a fair share."

Obviously one could arrange things so that Mary spends more time with Bobby and less with Clayton, however, that does not help Bobby cope with his feelings. Thus, if Bobby is nonverbal, a cognitive strategy might be to take some pictures of Bobby and Mary together on outings or around the house and put them up on Bobby's bulletin board. Then, if Bobby seems to be feeling jealous, one can point to the pictures and remind him that he is special too.

Eliciting situation: Ellie's sister is getting married, but Ellie was not invited to the wedding.

Possible cognitive distortion: "My family doesn't love me."

Mood: Ellie feels rejected.

Negative collateral behavior: Ellie self inflicts injury and runs away.

Cognitive intervention: Contact the family and ask them to explain to Ellie that they cannot afford the airfare, and make sure that they include Ellie in the planning. Find a few activities that Ellie does well and emphasize them; make her feel special.

Eliciting situation: A client in a job program cannot learn to use the industrial dishwasher and is having a hard time getting his wheelchair around the work-site.

Possible cognitive distortion: "I can't do anything; I can't get things right."

Mood: Client feels depressed.

Negative collateral behavior: Client becomes noncompliant; he refuses to carry out simple requests.

Cognitive intervention: Give him examples of people who have overcome difficulties, and have him verbalize, "I can do it if I try." Modify task demands so that there is guaranteed success after some initial effort. Provide more opportunities for him to control his environment, and, instead of providing simple social reinforcement like praise, have him verbalize or sign statements such as, "I did it on my own!"

Eliciting situation: The staff have reprimanded Ray repeatedly for not keeping his room cleaner; he says it is his roommate who is at fault.

Possible cognitive distortion: "The staff are unfair; they don't like me here; my roommate is trying to get me into trouble."

Mood: Ray is angry.

Negative collateral behavior: Ray is aggressive. He yells at and punches his roommate, slams doors, and is rough with equipment.

Cognitive intervention: Let Ray explain by signing that he is angry; express concern over need to solve the problem fairly. Talk it out with both Ray and roommate together. It is important to change the perception that people are unfair to him.

Specific Mood Induction Strategies

The previous discussion emphasized the importance of including clients in the process of decision-making and the importance of explanation, which give them some degree of control over events in their lives. There are, however, a few specific strategies that can be attempted to change mood.

Verbal Induction Words, whether in thoughts or spoken language, have powerful conditioning histories that allow them to control feelings. (See Staats [1975] for a detailed technical discussion.) Sports coaches are well aware of the value of words during a pregame pep session to enhance motivation and create a positive upbeat feeling. Before an outing or event that a client might be anxious about or has been negative about in the past, take time to motivate the client with remarks such as, "We're all going to have fun today, aren't we?"; "I want to hear everyone tell me how happy they are!"; "OK, everybody tell me one thing they are going to buy for themselves on this trip." In the authors' experience, effective caregivers spontaneously engage in these kinds of everyday, family types of encouragement and ways of creating positive mood. They may not even realize they are engaging in skillful behavior modification, which always seems to be described professionally as contingency management, token economy, planned ignoring, and so forth. Note that it is important for mood induction to make sure that clients have these positive emotional words in their repertoires and that they themselves use the words to cope with negative feelings that lead to undesirable behaviors.

Picture Stimuli Words are not the only stimuli that can induce positive moods. Pictures, familiar objects, the long-anticipated completion of a task, completing a project, and doing something meaningful for others are all examples of circumstances that make people feel good. Adult clients need their own individual security blankets. Staff can translate from their own experiences to find something that is effective for the client. An example is looking at a picture of the family when feeling a bit lonely on a trip. Encourage the client to create a small photo album of pictures of friends, family members, or himself or herself in fun situations. At times when the client seems to be in a negative mood, he or she then can be asked to sit down with the photo album and look through it, perhaps in the company of the staff person.

Warm-Ups Another method for altering moods emphasizes that possibly the most powerful induction of a positive mood comes from positive social interactions. When the client seems to be having a bad day, or some specific event has occurred to upset the client, the authors feel it is very constructive to arrange for a relatively brief social interaction with another adult. This might involve a few minutes of quiet counseling with one of the professional staff, or just a positive conversation with anyone who has a few minutes of time to spare. Obviously, following the general principle, these conversations should revolve around themes such as anticipating a positive event, looking forward to the accomplishments for the end of the day, talking about something pleasant that just occurred, and so forth. The authors have referred to these kinds of planned interactions as *warm-ups*, because this term helps convey the intent of the strategy. In other

words, these brief social interactions would not be times for giving little lectures, questioning the client as to why she or he is in a bad mood, or any other more didactic, directive, or formal kind of interaction. They should be purely social conversation, involving a positive topic of interest to the client.

Recently, Singer, Singer, and Horner (1987) reported a procedure they called *pretask requesting* as a way of increasing compliance with instructors' requests. The procedure simply involves delivering requests that have a high probability for compliance immediately before requests that have a lower probability of being complied with. Requests the students were likely to be agreeable to were such things as "Give me five," or "Shake hands." The authors of this report suggest that the strategy is effective because it consists of trials in which some high probability members of a given response class (compliance) have been reinforced, thus increasing the likelihood of other target responses from the same class being performed. This is consistent with some useful nonaversive strategies that have emerged in the 1980s in which clients have been taught a generalized response class called compliance (e.g., Neef, Shafer, Egel, Cataldo, & Parrish, 1983). While this kind of phenomenon is always valuable to consider—reinforcing some behaviors in a class will increase the probability for other behaviors in that same class—the authors tend to think that the warm-up effect might be an equally viable explanation for the positive results. In fact, the authors feel that positive social interactions between a client and instructor, caregiver, or other professional create a more natural motivational repertoire in which the client wants to please and cooperate with others, rather than being reinforced for obeying commands and directives as a general class. The latter tendency may not always be an adaptive behavior for adult clients in more normalized and community settings. Also, staff should not always approach clients as people who need to comply and be told what to do at all times. Any strategy to help staff engage in the more natural social interactions with clients that would be typical of exchanges between adults should support a more positive treatment of clients in general.

Another variant of warm-up procedures is to arrange tasks so that the person initially experiences a few minutes of an enjoyable activity that elicits a positive mood for further work of a less enjoyable nature. Of course, this has to be done sensibly, as the individual might resent suddenly having to stop a fun activity and start something less desirable. But one way of arranging the sequence is to ensure that before a new task is introduced the person has a few success experiences with identical but much easier tasks. This would appear to be the exact opposite of the Premack principle that often is recommended in behavior modification textbooks. According to this principle, a behavior will be reinforced if it leads to or gains access to a higher probability behavior. In clinical practice this is usually translated as making sure that a less pleasant activity (washing dishes) is followed by a more desired activity (e.g., playing a card game). As explained earlier in connection with planning schedules and natural routines, such arrangements of activities are good common sense and fit the Premack principles quite well. However, there are other factors to consider in motivation. One is that the person must have some expectation that the given task will result in reward (achieving the desired outcome). These motivational aspects of cognition (expectancy, belief in one's own ability) seem to come from subtle arrangements whereby the person has a number of early success experiences and a number of experiences in which effort and persistence are rewarded. Thus, enjoyable, high success activities can logically precede more difficult and onerous activities.

These can in turn lead to the opportunity to engage in more preferred activities.

Relaxation Training

Because activities determine mood states, there are other ways that scheduling can be arranged to create a positive climate. A good example is the use of a procedure for relaxation. It is fairly easy to teach people with severe disabilities to be able to relax motorically. A brief period of relaxation can then be used to calm someone who is upset and agitated. Following is a description of some methods for teaching relaxation.

METHODS FOR TEACHING RELAXATION SKILLS TO PEOPLE WITH DEVELOPMENTAL DISABILITIES

Instruction should take place in a natural situation or context, such as sitting outside in the sun, as part of a group yoga class taught by the physical therapist. Since modeling is a basic instructional technique, it is best if the instructor does all the relaxation procedures along with the client.

Always use a consistent cue—a word or sign that will be associated with the relaxed state—since that cue will be used to help the person calm down later on. "Now we're going to relax," or, "Let's get calm," are good ways to begin the instruction. It is also useful to ask the client to start off with a deep breath (it is easy to model this), to hold it for a moment, and then to let it out very slowly, saying "Calm," or "Relax," at the same time.

Begin the training by asking the client to imitate certain body movements, such as closing eyes, lifting up an arm and letting it flop back down again, settling into the chair in a wriggling, getting-comfortable motion. When the client has the general idea, concentrate on imitating floppy relaxed extremities. It is sometimes helpful to use the traditional relaxation method of having the client first tense a muscle (e.g., tighten a fist, scrunch up face, grit teeth), hold the tension for a moment, and then let go. However, this is not always easy to explain to a nonverbal client, and the major thing is to have the person imitate floppy, loose muscles.

Check how the client is doing by lifting up an arm and shaking it gently. Is it loose, or does the client resist this passive movement? Let the client lift up your arm to feel what a relaxed body part is like.

For some clients with more verbal skill, it is useful, and fun, to think up images for them to use to enhance the state of relaxation. A game for a child might be: "Pretend you are fast asleep; that's right, lie very still, eyes closed. Hmm, I wonder if Jane is really fast asleep? Let's pick up her hand, oh wow! She's really floppy and relaxed; she must be asleep," and so forth. One could have a teenager imagine being like a pot on the stove, ready to boil over. Ask her, "Turn down the heat; get that pot off the stove; don't let those bubbles make the pot boil over." Another example involves a client who lived in Hawaii and was very fascinated by volcanoes because he had seen an eruption on the Big Island. He was asked, "Imagine being like a volcano; stay calm; don't let the lava come bubbling up from inside; I don't want to see any steam coming out of there! Better cool down that fire deep inside."

The relaxation exercises can be practiced for a few minutes every so often, perhaps when waiting for a TV program to start, riding on the bus, during the coffee break at work. Ideally, the client should be able to learn to relax himself or herself; relaxation then becomes a self-control strategy, as explained later in this chapter.

Physical exercise also has a calming affect for most people. The literature shows that a number of programs have been devised involving some kind of physical exercise, especially following an excess behavior. For example, a learner might be made to run in place or do push-ups (e.g., Borreson, 1980). These programs, sometimes referred to as a variant of overcorrection, are very clearly aversive in intent and almost certainly have their effect on the client because they are punishments (Luce, Delquadri, & Hall, 1980). But exercise per se can be a very positive activity; it is *forced* exercise that is so undesirable to impose on persons with disabilities. People often use some kind of exercise regimen to influence their moods. For example, when feeling disgruntled and out of sorts, one might decide to go for a run, swim a few laps, or work strenuously in the backyard. Thus, the authors recommend that staff help a client exhibiting undesirable behavior to find some appropriate physical activity that he or she enjoys doing, such as jogging or working out. This activity would be planned for whenever the client seemed to be in a negative mood. Thus it would not be contingent upon undesirable behavior, like some kind of punishment, but would be used to change a mood state. Similarly, exercise such as a period of therapeutic recreation or a gymnastics class can be planned to occur before some activity likely to elicit the excess behavior, since even if the activity does not put the person in a good mood, it might at least tire out the person. Again, such a regimen should not be punitive, and the exercise would have to be something normalized and functional for the client as well as something he or she were quite willing to do.

Anger Control Training

Chapter 2 suggested that aggressive behavior is sometimes a learned coercive strategy to obtain what one wants, but more often it is motivated by feelings of anger; thus, methods of dealing with anger are especially noteworthy. Arnold Goldstein and his colleagues have developed numerous interventions for use with nondisabled adolescents who are assaultive, disruptive, and generally hostile in their interactions with others (Goldstein, 1981). Many of their procedures were developed and validated with institutionalized young people serving sentences for criminal activities. Aggression Replacement Training (ART), for example, is described as "a multimodal, psychoeducational intervention" relevant for programs in institutions, schools, mental health clinics, and prisons (Glick & Goldstein, 1987).

ART includes three major components. *Structured Learning Training* involves a 50-skill curriculum of prosocial behaviors. It is based on the assumption that delinquent teenagers get into trouble at least in part because they actually lack a sufficiently rich repertoire of prosocial skills to solve problems. This component is quite similar to the authors' educative approach (Evans & Meyer, 1985), and it involves teaching the kinds of skills described in Chapter 7 of this manual. *Moral education* is a set of procedures designed to raise someone's level of fairness, justice, and concern with the needs and rights of others, and is based on Kohlberg's work on exposing children to a series of moral dilemmas (Kohlberg, 1973). The authors know of no parallel at this writing in work focused on persons with developmental disabilities, with the possible exception of the interest in religious instruction that is somewhat similar in purpose if not in form.

The last component of ART that the authors have adapted clinically for use with young adults with moderate to severe handicaps is *Anger Control Training*. The goal of this component is to teach people to identify situations that typically make them angry, to recognize their own signs that they are becoming angry, and to use strategies to remove themselves from the situation and/or calm down (Glick & Goldstein, 1987). Following is a list of the steps of Anger Control Training and an example of how the techniques have been adapted for clients who are at risk for becoming angry and attacking others.

AN ANGER CONTROL TRAINING EXAMPLE

		Definition	*Example*
Step 1:	Identify triggers	External events and internal self-statements that provoke anger and aggression	Being close to a particular co-worker or having one's space suddenly invaded by anyone
Step 2:	Identify cues	Individual physical events such as clenched fists, raised hand, flushed face, particular vocal sounds, and so forth, that let someone know he or she is angry	Becoming red in the face and starting to vocalize loudly
Step 3:	Using reminders	Self-statements such as "Calm down" or "Relax" or nonhostile explanations of others' behaviors	Saying to oneself, "Take a break," or "Talk quiet," (using a trained sign, symbol, or vocalization)
Step 4:	Using reducers	Techniques designed to lower the individual's level of anger, such as deep breathing, counting backward, imagining a peaceful scene, or thinking about the long-term consequences of one's behavior	Walk to a designated quiet area in the room and listen to music using headphones and a portable tape deck Taking out a wallet and looking at pictures of 3–4 favorite scenes or activities that took place that week
Step 5:	Using self-education	Reflecting on how well the situation was handled	Initially, being told by a favorite staff person that he or she did very well and later, saying to self, "Good job"

SYSTEMATIC DESENSITIZATION

In some ways the various methods suggested in this chapter for changing mood are similar to the ecological manipulations discussed in Chapter 6. This is because they mostly involve environmental modifications that have a temporary effect on a person's emotional state. Many excess behavior problems, however, occur because of a maladaptive emotional response pattern, so that it might be advantageous to try to permanently change or treat that emotional response. Systematic desensitization was designed for just that purpose. It is one of the oldest and best established treatment strategies in clinical behavior therapy. It was first developed by Wolpe (1952) and is based on the principle of extinction. In order for an inappropriate emotional response to be extinguished, the individual is exposed to the stimuli or cues that elicit the emotional reaction, but in a safe situation where the emotional response is least likely to occur. Cues that elicit the least anxiety (or anger, fear, etc.) are presented first, and the exposure to these cues continues until there is no observable or subjective response to the cue. Additional cues are then presented, in a hierarchical fashion, so that the individual is gradually exposed to more and more emotion-arousing material, and the emotional response is eventually extinguished. Numerous studies have demonstrated that systematic desensitization is an extremely effective technique for reducing maladaptive emotional responses. (For a very detailed coverage of techniques for reducing children's fears, see Morris and Kratochwill, 1983.)

One reason that the method may not have been used very extensively with persons with mental retardation is that the procedure typically involves a variety of verbal strategies along with a certain amount of cooperation and comprehension on the part of the client. For example,

the context created to minimize anxiety is typically that of progressive muscle relaxation, and although a suitable modification of the clinic method has been described here, relaxation usually is taught by means of a verbal training procedure. Similarly, the exposure to the hierarchy of cues generally is done through imagination. The situations are described to the client, and he or she is asked to imagine the anxiety evoking situations as vividly as possible. However, it is quite clear from the available research that these aspects of the method are not intrinsically necessary. What is needed is that the client be systematically exposed to the relevant cues in a manner that does not produce a desire to escape or avoid the situation. Thus there have been many successful demonstrations of systematic desensitization *in vivo*; that is, the client is exposed to the actual situation rather than being asked to imagine the cues. A good example of this would be to take someone who is afraid of heights to a tall building and ask him or her to look out initially from windows on the first floor and then the second, and then the third, and so forth. Similarly, the context in which the exposure takes place does not need to be that of deep muscle relaxation. For example, if the client is anxious in open and unfamiliar places, but is much less anxious when accompanied by a trusted friend, then exposure to a busy public area would take place in the company of such an individual. In the example that began this chapter, Heather's program involved riding the bus in the company of her good friend who was not at all afraid of public transport.

In other words, therefore, the general method can be readily extended to working with adults with severe intellectual disabilities who exhibit maladaptive emotional responses. Such problems are not uncommon when working with adult clients, particularly when people are being moved to community environments after long periods in institutional settings. Unfamiliarity with normal, everyday surroundings obviously is one source of emotional arousal. However, it is equally possible that a client might have developed an unreasonable or excessive emotional response as a result of abuse or trauma of some kind in the less protected setting of a large institution. Persons with disabilities who exhibit these phobic reactions will not necessarily be able to explain verbally that they are anxious or afraid; instead the manifestation of the emotional response may take the form of tantrumming, self-injury, attempts to get away, or aggression. (It is well established that aggression can follow fear as well as anger.) Naturally, one has to make a rather complex judgment as to whether the emotional reaction is indeed a maladaptive response that should be treated, or a legitimate expression of the client's dislike of a situation. The authors emphasize that, in the latter case, the individual should be allowed to exercise his or her right to choose not to be part of that situation. However, in cases where the individual's emotional response does not seem to be rational, the following criteria can be used to support the decision to implement a systematic desensitization program:

1. The undesirable behavior (e.g., bolting, aggression, self-injury) clearly is accompanied by related emotional expression (e.g., crying, trembling, looking frightened).
2. This pattern is elicited or triggered by predictable stimuli.
3. These stimuli would not normally cause anxiety (i.e., are not intrinsically frightening, like the sight of a person being injured) but are the sort of things that a nondisabled person might be phobic about (e.g., crowds, high places, dogs, the dark, hypodermic needles).
4. The emotion-arousing situations are not those being imposed by an authority figure (e.g., being directed to stay in one place, work on this job, eat this food).

5. Although the effect of the behavior is to communicate fear or some other emotion, this is not its intent or purpose.

Assuming that the decision to intervene has been carefully made, and it seems desirable to proceed with some sort of systematic desensitization, the following general principles should be adhered to. First, it is necessary to develop the hierarchy. With nondisabled clients, this is achieved through a detailed interview, but with individuals with severe disabilities the hierarchy must be developed on the basis of careful observation. Note all the situations that elicit the emotion and try to discern their common elements. If the person avoids elevators and cars, the stimulus event might be enclosed spaces. If the person avoids elevators and vacuum cleaners, high-pitched sounds might be the eliciting cue. Careful reports from those who know the client best usually will reveal what the critical element of the feared situation is to the person. The hierarchy can then be constructed in terms of varying dimensions away from the critical stimulus elements. Useful dimensions to vary are physical characteristics such as size, number, or distance. Following is an example of setting up a hierarchy:

EXAMPLE OF HIERARCHY FOR IN VIVO SYSTEMATIC DESENSITIZATION

Donna, who is 18, exhibits a considerable fear of men. Her foster mother thinks she may have been sexually abused or otherwise traumatized, but no one really knows exactly why she is so scared. She has become very dysfunctional because there are male staff members in her new group home, and she tantrums whenever they approach her, sometimes grabbing objects and throwing them. Recently she needed her eyes tested again and she refused to go into the optometrist's office because he was a man. There have been many other similar incidents. During a staff meeting, based on a number of people's knowledge of her reactions and a little creative guesswork, the following dimensions were established:

a. A few men she knew extremely well did not elicit any fear at all (e.g., her brother, her foster father).

b. Men she had never seen before did not really bother her that much, unless they came physically close.

c. Men she recognized as being around in some official capacity (e.g., mailman, bus driver) made her quite fearful.

d. Men approaching her to talk to her, or interact with her in a personal way, produced much fear (e.g., store assistant, staff).

e. Any man resembling a doctor (e.g., someone in a white coat, orderly at the hospital) made her especially anxious.

This was then translated into the following hierarchy of opportunities for direct exposure. Only when she seemed really comfortable with one item was the next higher item introduced:

1. On outings into the community, such as to a fast food restaurant, staff will try to select a table near a group of men. Donna can sit in the middle of her own group.

2. On similar occasions it will again be arranged to be near men, and Donna will sit on the outside.

3. When the opportunity arises to interact with a male in an official role (e.g., delivery person, store assistant), Donna is to make eye contact and smile.

4. Staff will try to select stores, banks, and so forth, that have male service personnel; Donna has to approach a man, with one of her friends, and ask for something.

5. Male staff in the home will sit on the other side of the room from her and talk to other female clients, not Donna.

6. Male staff will interact with Donna from a distance, talking quietly and pleasantly to her but not trying to approach directly.

7. On outings, Donna is encouraged to approach men (e.g., waiters, ushers at the movies, store clerks) and ask for something, without her friends right next to her.

8. Donna is asked by trusting female staff member to get something from one of the male staff members, initially some treat that she really likes.

9. Donna is taken to optometrist's office,

but no actual exam is scheduled; she just talks to him. Staff remind her to keep calm.

10. Donna goes for eye test with a male staff member and a trusted female friend. There should be a lot of discussion beforehand about the kind of smart new glasses she is going to have.

It can be seen that, although Donna was trained in relaxation, most of the time it was the way the situation was structured that made it safe or pleasant for her. Of great importance is the problem of protecting her from further abuse, if that indeed had taken place. Some wariness and caution around strange men is a necessary survival skill. Donna was taught not to talk to strange men unless they are in an official role and there are other people around. She was also counseled on the danger of sex abuse, following the preventive programs designed for elementary school children: "Your body is private; it is not right for me to be physically intimate; never go anywhere with a stranger; keep close to your friends; tell the staff if anyone does anything to you you don't like." Desensitization is not supposed to make a person blasé about realistic dangers!

Second, once a hierarchy has been constructed, it should be written down as a list of the situations to which the client will be exposed. The context under which exposure should take place must then be determined, possibly through a process of trial and error. Remember that these situations will contain some of the stimuli that elicit the emotional response but must also be safe in some way. Thus, activities, places, or things that compete with the fearful emotion must be identified for the individual client. Perhaps another person whom the client knows well and likes could be present, or a positive or neutral activity (e.g., relaxation, eating a meal, playing a game, or some other activity with which the client is very comfortable and familiar) that is likely to counteract emotional arousal could be ongoing.

In summary, in order to carry out systematic desensitization with persons with severe disabilities, two sets of conditions are necessary. First, a hierarchy must be identified that includes cues and situations varying from those in which the client is least likely to exhibit the emotional response (or show only a very small reaction) to those in which the client is most likely to exhibit the response (or show the largest reaction). Second, one must find some set of safe circumstances in which the person is least likely to exhibit the emotional response, such as when with a trusted person, eating a meal, feeling relaxed, and so forth. Situations can also be used that elicit an incompatible emotional response, for example, happiness while engaged in a game. Note that these incompatible situations or responses are not used because one wishes to teach the client these particular responses, as in other strategies where one teaches an incompatible, positive alternative behavior to the undesirable behavior. Instead, the situations are presented to inhibit the undesirable behavior while presenting the cues likely to elicit that behavior. This therefore aids in the extinction of the emotional response as the cues are presented up the hierarchy in a systematic fashion.

HABIT BREAKING

Habit breaking strategies are similar to systematic desensitization since both involve the principle of extinction. The idea is to have the client practice a behavior incompatible with the undesirable habit in the presence of the stimuli likely to elicit that habit. For example, one might decide that a client's tendency to pick at his or her skin is more of a habit than a functional behavior. It tends to occur most often in situations where he or she has to stand around and wait for something to happen, as when in a bus line or in the lunch room. A reasonably appropriate behavior that would be

physically incompatible with this habit would be putting his or her hands in pockets. The client might be taught to do this on command, so that instead of giving the reprimand, "Don't pick," one could give the cue, "Relax." If the client has been taught to look relaxed and put his or her hands in pockets on this command, then the cue elicits physically incompatible behavior in a situation normally eliciting skin picking. The cue can be eventually faded and the client will have a new, but more desirable habit to exhibit while waiting for something.

Habit breaking strategies were one of the first approaches to be developed in behavior therapy. They are based on principles of extinction as described by Guthrie (1935). The central idea is that habits can be characterized as behaviors under strong stimulus control, as a result of being practiced hundreds of times. Generally the stimuli that are the eliciting cues are the proprioceptive cues or internal cues produced by behavior itself. This is why in normal habit breaking methods, the client is asked to voluntarily interrupt the habit, and to perform another response in the presence of the stimuli usually controlling the habit, and to do this repeatedly until the old stimulus–response chains are broken (or, more technically, extinguished). When the client is someone with a severe disability and an undesirable habit, such verbal control over behavior may be limited. However, as the authors have tried to show, the general principle still can be put into effect if instruction is utilized to elicit a strong competing response (that is socially appropriate) under some stimulus control, and then to elicit that response in the presence of the cues for the undesirable habit. It should be remembered that the key feature of a behavior that can be conceptualized as a habit (e.g., nail biting and thumb sucking) is that it is not generally under reinforcement control, nor does it have any special function for the person. Generally, a habit is a stereotypic behavior, performed topographically very much the same way every single time. It is not under a great deal of voluntary control and is often performed automatically by the individual. This suggests that the cue complex eliciting the habit usually includes internal proprioceptive stimuli as well as external stimuli.

An illustration of a habit breaking strategy can be provided here. It refers to pica, which can be quite a difficult behavior to modify since the major adaptive alternative is learning to discriminate which objects (e.g., food, gum) *may* be put in one's mouth. What often happens is that staff try to keep the client away from likely objects that the client may mouth, and when catching the client with an object in his or her mouth, they ask him or her to spit it out and throw it away. But as Guthrie pointed out many years ago, that type of correction does nothing to weaken the overlearned behavior of putting things into the mouth in the first place. Thus a habit-breaking strategy is to let the client hold and handle objects he or she often mouths, even raising them to his or her lips (thus producing the powerful cue that usually elicits the behavior), but then, instead of placing them in the mouth, slowly and carefully putting them back where they belong. Someone doing this procedure has to be quite vigilant, and ready to use brief interruption if it looks as if the object is going in the mouth. In any event, the client is then rehearsing the opposite behavior to the habit, thus breaking the stimulus–response chain. Note that this is somewhat similar to some of the early versions of overcorrection; unfortunately, however, that method has become predominantly punitive and nonfunctional. Any method that encourages the client to voluntarily interrupt the habit and produce another, opposite behavior requires some degree of coopera-

tion, and that leads to the topic of self-modification.

SELF-REGULATION

In behavior therapy a number of clinical treatments have been devised that are really educational and essentially involve teaching clients new skills to replace maladaptive behaviors or to rectify deficits in individual repertoires. Two good examples of these techniques are social skill training, such as assertiveness training, and teaching self-control skills. Obviously, from the educative perspective, one would not try to teach these skills in isolation from the many other skills that the person with severe disabilities might need to learn. However, occasions may arise when a particular behavior problem seems to need a rather specific alternative—being able to regulate one's own maladaptive behavior.

This need arises most obviously when the person seems to understand that the excess behavior is undesirable and wrong and the person is motivated (whether to please, to conform, or to obtain a programmed reward) to reduce its occurrence. If the behavior is a well-ingrained habit, or triggered by specific stimuli, as might be the case for aggressive behaviors set off by anger, it might be difficult for the individual to inhibit the action when the controlling stimuli occur full strength. An example of this is a client who has an inappropriate sexual behavior such as exhibitionism outside in the yard of the group home. A self-regulation strategy for a behavior such as this would involve reduction of internal and external cues, and voluntarily inhibiting the behavior.

Reduction of internal and external cues, the first stage of self-regulation, is roughly equivalent to a prevention strategy. In the case of the adult client in the example, internal cues for exhibitionism might be those of sexual arousal which he or she could reduce by having an alternative behavior, such as masturbating in the privacy of his or her own room. External cues could be that if alone outside, not engaged in some other activity, a male client saw a woman walking past, then that would represent a powerful cue complex likely to elicit the behavior. Self-control in this case involves engaging in some other behavior that takes one away from a tempting situation before the stimuli come together in a way that would be difficult to resist. (An example in the behavior therapy literature is that for someone who is trying to lose weight, it is helpful to move fattening foods away from sight or easy access at a time when one is not feeling hungry or predisposed to eat.) The client could learn that if he is outside, alone, and he sees a woman in the distance, he should go inside and find some other activity. Obviously this suggestion is not a real treatment or a very satisfactory outcome; verbal inhibition through a self-talk routine in which he says to himself, "I must not expose myself; it is wrong; I could be arrested," is a more typical strategy. With very severely disabled clients, teaching this kind of verbalization is not possible, but there are close approximations to the strategy. For example, clients who have learned a manual sign for "wrong" can use that sign to give themselves a cue that will inhibit the occurrence of a socially undesirable behavior.

The second stage of self-regulation is learning to *self-monitor.* In their interesting discussion of teaching self-monitoring procedures to school-age children, Mace and Kratochwill (1988) point out that "self-monitoring is consistent with a trend in behavior therapy away from external control of behavior toward greater participation of the client in managing his or her own therapeutic program" (p. 489). The authors want to see this trend more strongly in evidence in treatment design for persons with severe disabilities. Although there are convincing

data for the value of self-control strategies (see the excellent review by Shapiro, 1986), they remain one of the best kept secrets in coping with excess behavior. The authors are confident from clinical experience that all clients, regardless of severity of disability, can and should participate in the design of their own intervention programs. In fact, one of the most interesting requirements of self-regulation is that it is necessary to obtain some sort of *prior commitment to change behavior* from the client. In the case of Clara, mentioned at the beginning of the chapter, the need to lose weight and stop binging was carefully explained to her, using concepts she seemed to understand, such as getting sick, looking bad, not fitting into her clothes, and the binging being viewed negatively by others. Clara readily agreed to a simple contract for her to try to change her behavior.

A wide variety of self-monitoring methods have been taught to people with mental retardation (see Litrownik, 1982), and it is commonly observed that if an undesirable excess behavior is self-monitored, it has a reactive effect and the behavior decreases. As the opposite effect happens with positive behavior, self-monitoring is a valuable procedure for use in job-training and work settings. Clara could not easily comprehend the idea of a hand-held counter or a mark on a chart, so she was taught to save the wrappers of the junk food she binged on during the day, pinning them up on a cork board in her room. For monitoring her weight, it was found that talking scales gave her a great deal of amusement; although she really did not understand large numbers, this particular scale could be set to provide positive or negative feedback.

The third stage of self-regulation is the *setting of specific goals and performance standards* and learning to judge whether one has met them or not. Clara could not do this entirely on her own and so the staff, with help from a nutritionist, set a reasonable goal for weight loss. She could understand fitting into clothes, so every so often the staff asked her to do the jeans test—pulling on a pair of tight fitting jeans that she used to be able to fit into quite easily. The goal for the daily collection of food wrappers on her bulletin board was very simple—having none to collect. The fourth stage of self-regulation is *self-reinforcement* based on meeting one's own internal performance standards. Since it was hard to teach Clara to say things to herself like, "Good job, you lost a pound," or "I'm great, there are no wrappers on the board," a modified plan was devised in which she was taught to come and tell the staff that she had done well. They then gave her social praise and encouragement and told her how well she was doing with her own health plan, as the original commitment had been called.

Learning self-control may not deal directly with the function of the excess behavior. Learning to control binge eating when it is really evoked by feelings of rejection, or learning to relax one's facial muscles to reduce headaches that are really caused by stress at work do not represent satisfactory therapies for complex problems. Simple self-control strategies for persons with disabilities are similar to ecological interventions in that they are stopgap or temporary strategies in most cases. Using the four-stage model, self-regulation training generally is going to be a combination of short-term prevention (self-regulation of external cues is essentially a self-imposed ecological intervention) and the learning of alternatives. Ultimately, for example, a client who has excess sexual behaviors has to be considered from the life span perspective. What opportunities does the person have for normal sexual activity and sexual relationships, and how can these be fostered and encouraged over time? The next section deals with some of these issues.

ZONE DISCRIMINATION

Behaviors can have totally different meanings depending on the situation or context. The very same behavior can be acceptable under certain circumstances and be completely inappropriate at other times and in other places. People learn, for example, to control their voice volume depending on where they are. A conversation between friends that would be regarded as perfectly normal on a public bus or while sharing lunch in a fast food restaurant would be likely to provoke disapproving looks in church. People are accustomed to greeting family members or close friends with a hug and kiss after a short absence, but it would be regarded as quite odd to give a stranger or even a casual acquaintance who provided a ride from the airport the same greeting. Masturbation and sexual intercourse are generally regarded as not just appropriate but positive activities for adults under a set of well-specified conditions, including elements of privacy, responsibility, consent, and relationships. However, in this culture, though these activities are intrinsically harmless (provided that participation is voluntary), few other behaviors are as likely to provoke strong reactions of disapproval as public masturbation or intercourse. In fact, such public displays are illegal and highly likely to result in an arrest.

Finally, most people pursue overt conversations with a spouse or close friend, while some private (i.e., covert) thoughts are never intended for others to hear. People learn to control what they say as well as what they do depending on who is present, their relationship to others, and so forth.

These variations in behavior can be conceptualized as *zone discriminations*. People learn complex rules and become fairly sophisticated in the mastery of changing behavior depending on where they are, what time it is, who is present, what just occurred, the mood of the other person, and so forth. Sometimes, the behavior problems of persons with developmental disabilities can be viewed as failures to learn to make the appropriate zone discriminations. There is a failure to identify (discriminate) which behaviors are appropriate depending on circumstances (the zone). It is possible that the actual behavior is fine, but the person needs to learn when and where and how it is appropriate to do it. Consequently, rather than trying to eliminate a behavior, it might be both more correct and more effective to instead teach the person to make the necessary zone discriminations.

A few examples should help, starting with the obvious one of masturbation. It not only seems futile to try to extinguish masturbation once a healthy adult has discovered this activity, it also does not seem fair. Why should adult or even adolescent clients not be able to masturbate if they wish? This culture has not become as accepting of certain sexual activities as some other cultures, and sex therapy is almost never provided for persons with disabilities who also have mental retardation and therefore might literally need some instruction in order to engage in sex safely and responsibly.

The authors feel that this is one area where some important decisions about rights and responsibilities will have to be made very soon. They have been asked for advice about clients who, for example, masturbate in public and/or by using odd or inappropriate materials, in certain instances actually causing physical injury. As they believe these individuals do have a right to the activity, the authors advocate teaching more appropriate and safer behavior rather than attempting to completely prevent the behavior from occurring or punishing it. An essential need is, first of all, for the client to learn the appropriate zone discriminations. Masturbation is something that is done only in privacy, perhaps in one's bedroom. In other cases, the discrimination that must be learned might involve which materials may be used and which may not. One of the authors was asked about a client who stole plastic salt and catsup containers from the institution dining room or dolls made of rubber (he would remove the doll's head and use the resultant cavity) for his masturbatory activities. Using such materials occasionally resulted in injury, and, as they were readily available and he had become quite adept at stealing and hiding them, the behavior seemed almost impossible to control. For such a client, why not order from the appropriate devices catalogue to find something more pleasurable that is, at the same time, so different from a catsup container that the client simply would no longer be motivated to use anything else? Why not order this device by medical prescription if necessary? Sexual behaviors are not atypically under strong stimulus control, so that teaching the appropriate zone discriminations could also, by definition, assist in ensuring that the individual is self-motivated to be safe, private, and also responsible as a function of circumstances.

Zone discrimination training also can be quite helpful to deal with problem verbal behavior or vocal noises. The authors knew a client who often engaged in conversation with an imaginary companion. Within minutes, the initially harmless bizarre conversation would escalate into angry yelling and then physically attacking any other person close by. This adolescent was taught that he could only talk to his companion at a certain table located in an area of the classroom some distance from the other students. If he started a conversation in any other location in the school, he was simply reminded to go to the table (if close by) or that he had to wait until he could go to the table (if in another part of the school). For some reason, he seldom became agitated when conversing at the table and even if he did, there was no one close enough to attack. He quickly acquired the discrimination, and even though the behavior did not completely cease, it did decrease in frequency and become more manageable so that it no longer interfered with his participation in other activities.

Another student, Steven, who had autism, had a very irritating habit of loud moaning, which he did quite often and which, ironically, seemed to be a technique he used to cope with stressful situations. The team decided, therefore, that it might be a behavior that Steven needed, so rather than forbid him to do it, he was told, "Do that quietly." Steven would then literally either whisper his moaning or seem to be moaning silently. And rather than becoming more upset, which likely would have occurred had he been told to stop, when told to do it quietly he did not react negatively. The authors think this is another example of learning a useful and reasonable zone discrimination.

SUMMARY

The variety of procedures for treating excess behavior that are described in this chapter were developed in behavior therapy during the 1970s and 1980s. They have been somewhat overlooked in the literature on developmental disabilities. This is perhaps because of the exclusive focus on contingency management in behavior modification for persons with severe disabilities and a de-emphasis on cognitive factors. The use of language to mediate behavior has been a major feature of most of the procedures described in the chapter, but this is not an essential ingredient. The authors are trying to show that the principles described are helpful ones, and the task of the professional designing an intervention is to translate the procedures into methods that can be used with clients who may have very limited verbal or cognitive skills.

Clients with severe intellectual disabilities may not have elaborate verbal repertoires but do still have thoughts and feelings that must be considered just as important as overt behaviors. Also, all clients, no matter how severely disabled, process information from their physical and social environments, and this emphasis on information processing underscores the importance of creating an environment that supports the adaptation of the individual to the requirements and demands of that environment. This is why the strategies proposed here are so closely related to the general themes of this manual, which are that interventions must be carefully planned and also implemented in such a way that they blend into the creation of an environment whose physical and social characteristics are supportive of effective functioning and adaptation by clients. The key to the treatment of excess behavior is always to have an effective, habilitative program, one that respects the psychological needs of clients and recognizes that they have much in common with those of all other persons. (Following is a trainee activity on how to help clients learn self-regulation.)

ACTIVITY: HOW TO HELP CLIENTS LEARN SELF-REGULATION

As already mentioned, direct service personnel are not encouraged to design specific treatment plans using any of these behavior therapy techniques. However, when thinking about the day-to day interactions between staff and clients, it does seem that, if staff understand some of these principles, they will be able to respond in a more constructive way to clients having behavior problems. Helping people acquire self-regulatory skills is a particularly valuable way of emphasizing—for the staff—the importance of not over controlling the clients. Even positive reinforcement techniques can be overused, if the emphasis is always on external control.

The following activity is therefore designed as one that can be used with trainees so that they can begin to recognize the value in everyday activities that might foster self-regulation. The activity involves relating the principles of self-regulation to the trainee's own behavior and experiences.

Begin by briefly discussing the general advantages of self-regulation, and then illustrate each of the four main components as follows:

Making a Commitment

Ask the trainees to list two or three things that they have decided to change in themselves. Common personal goals are:

a. To quit smoking
b. To lose weight
c. To exercise more
d. To write more letters home
e. To stop yelling at the kids

Then ask them to circle which ones they have been completely successful in changing. This leads to a discussion of making commitments.

Switch from here to thinking about clients with excess behavior. Remind the trainees that clients want to change for the same reasons they do—to feel better, to look better, to be more acceptable to others, to feel better about themselves. Ask the trainees to think of an individual client's behavior problem and write down the kinds of reasons they could give that client for him or her to change behavior. Emphasis should first be on making changes for oneself, only secondarily for others. Common scenarios might be:

a. "Would you like to work on not picking your skin? Think how much better you'll feel when you look in the mirror."
b. "Do you think more people would talk to you at work if you didn't shout and yell so much when you get angry on the job?"
c. "Let's make a deal: you agree to work on losing weight; I'll take you shopping for some new clothes."

A client with very limited or no verbal skills may not make an actual agreement, but the principle is that the client should still be explained the given program. Let the staff be inventive. They may come up with a drawing, a photo, a picture of what the program will be, a handshake, and a nodded confirmation that the agreement has been made. And remember, the best commitment is one whereby one says what one will *do*, rather than what one will *try to stop* doing!

Self-Monitoring

Return to the trainees' own efforts. How did they or could they have monitored their own performance? Common strategies are:

a. Weighing oneself every day and keeping the data on a chart when trying to lose weight
b. Wearing a golf counter and recording on a daily basis the number of occurrences of a habit one wants to break
c. Noting on a calendar each cup of coffee drunk per day when trying to stop drinking coffee

Then switch again to the clients, and ask the trainees to suggest ways that clients can self-monitor. Remember, the method should be private. (This is *self*-control.)

a. Moving colored thumb tacks from one side of a bulletin board to the other
b. Making a mark in a notebook each day one spends at work with no angry outbursts

Setting Standards

Discuss with the trainees how they set internal goals both for the long term (e.g., lose 15 pounds) and for the short term (e.g., eating vegetables and avoiding cookies). Where do their standards come from; do they tend to be realistic? Clients may need help in setting standards for their own performance. Sometimes before enthusiastically praising a client, stop and ask what the client thinks. Did the client really do the job the way he or she was taught? Does he or she have good comparison points; is the client comparing himself or herself with peers, or with nondisabled individuals? In a very formal self-modification program, the standard to be achieved will be clearly designated on whatever recording system is used for the self-monitoring.

Self-Reinforcement

Trainees will describe many different ways they reinforce themselves for meeting their goals. Some people go somewhere special; others tell their friends; some feel more personal satisfaction and pride. But some people are never satisfied with their performance and tell themselves they could have done better. The discussion will yield interesting insights into the importance of self-reward. Then ask if their clients have similar opportunities. Can they verbalize, "I did a fine job;" can they feel pride when their personal goals are met; can they excitedly tell a staff member when their self-monitoring chart reaches the predetermined level? To assist the clients in developing these skills, have the trainees give examples of:

a. Helping clients to verbalize their own self-reinforcement strategies
b. Encouraging a client to reward himself or herself when the client thinks he or she has done a good job, instead of just automatically praising the client when he or she seeks approval or praise

chapter

9

Evaluating Outcomes

OVERVIEW

This chapter provides a summary of evaluation criteria and procedures that should be applied to judge meaningful outcomes. Such outcomes include not only immediate improvements in priority excess behaviors, but also long-term behavioral changes that are documented by full participation in a productive daily lifestyle.

TRAINEE OBJECTIVES

At the completion of this unit, participant trainees will be able to:

1. Specify outcome criteria for remediation of behavior problems that reflect behavior change rather than behavioral control.
2. Analyze the information collected in incident records to identify possible problems in treatment integrity and to document changes in client behavior.
3. Evaluate client participation in meaningful activities in each of the four life domains: home, recreation/leisure, work, and community.
4. Identify the need for additional team problems solving and/or consultation

based on information that the treatment plan is not working.
5. Give an example for each of the eight possible intervention outcomes and suggest a useful strategy for evaluation of the outcome.

INTRODUCTION

Objective evaluation of treatment effectiveness has always been one of the hallmarks of the behavioral perspective. For a detailed account of how the related systematic data gathering principles can be used in settings serving people with severe disabilities, the authors strongly recommend consulting Browder (1987). Not only have outcome data allowed us to perpetuate treatments that work, but also, in routine practice, objective data can be used to guide treatment decisions, suggesting when to change the intervention, whether assessment hypotheses are correct, and so forth. This latter emphasis on formative evaluation has been argued most eloquently by Barlow, Hayes, and Nelson (1984). In practice, however, in natural settings, if there is a very close relationship between the exact conditions of the intervention and the frequency of some excess behavior, then more likely behavioral *control* has occurred, rather than significant and lasting behavior *change*. This is most obvious when an intervention must remain in place indefinitely; under these conditions it would seem to be controlling the person artificially.

Changes in the frequency of a target behavior, then, even if the behavior apparently is reduced to zero levels, does not represent an adequate criterion for a successful intervention. A truly effective treatment procedure is one that has ended, so that when the person is in a typical environment and involved in everyday activities, each of the following is true:

1. The problem behavior no longer occurs in an environment that is appropriate and situations or circumstances that are normalized.
2. When the kinds of situations or circumstances take place that once predicted the behavior, the person now uses some alternative, more appropriate, and positive strategy to deal with the situation.
3. The consequences that occur for the behavior are natural ones, that is, the kinds of things that would happen to anyone in such situations if their behaviors were inappropriate.
4. All these improvements continue over time and in various settings and circumstances, regardless of the presence of the direct service worker or any person who was once responsible for the intervention.

In order to demonstrate experimental control, it has become widely accepted in behavior modification research methodology that the targeted behavior *should* revert to pretreatment levels when the intervention is withdrawn. Realizing that this is not a very satisfactory outcome, applied researchers have tried to demonstrate that the short-term behavior change has shown *maintenance*, that is, evidence that the behavior change has continued perhaps 6 months to a year later. Additionally, evidence of *generalization* might be collected to show that the improvements have been consistent in different locations or with different people.

Such maintenance and generalization data are not very impressive, however, if the reality is that the client still is under fairly tight control in what is basically a highly restrictive environment. If the individual remains in settings that are artificial and highly supervised, there is no way of knowing whether he or she has genuinely abandoned maladaptive behavior. Neither is it evident that the person has mastered alternative, positive behaviors that will be used reliably in everyday situations and to solve new problems when they occur. Significant behavior change must involve more than simple frequency counts or duration measures of targeted behavior problems. Unless the excess behaviors have been replaced by substitute, prosocial alternatives, *and* these improvements are supported by evidence that the person is participating fully in integrated community environments, it would be precipitous to conclude that an intervention is a success.

Thus, more meaningful outcome criteria to support the effectiveness of an intervention must address each of the following: 1) the intervention is associated with a reduction in the problem behavior(s), 2) the individual has acquired new alternative skills that he or she now uses in place of the problem behavior(s), 3) the individual has acquired new strategies to prevent the occurrence of future behavior problems in similar risk situations, 4) the person has socially adapted to integrated community environments and engages in positive social interactions with others. The authors have referred to positive social interactions with others as representing *educational validity* (Voeltz & Evans, 1983). The process and procedures described in this chapter are designed to address all of these issues.

DESIGNING AN EVALUATION

Figure 9.1 lists various possible outcomes that can be used to support the success of an intervention, and examples are provided for each. In addition, a strategy to document evidence for such outcomes is suggested. Some of these are typical data collection procedures, most involve verifiable records that agencies already are required to keep, and others are highly subjective and, quite simply, will be difficult to verify objectively. However, even these can be at least indirectly supported through certain objective signs. For example, perceptions of improvement by family and significant others could be supported by an increase in visits from the family with a client, along with fewer complaints and concerns following such visits.

Evaluation Design

In the traditional research literature there is a great deal of discussion of different single-case experimental designs (Barlow & Hersen, 1984). It has sometimes been suggested that it would be ideal if practicing professionals within agencies would use similar designs in evaluating their everyday programs. But this is not always possible or desirable. Consider, for example, the classic single-subject design, a reversal design, sometimes referred to as an ABAB design. In this design the intervention phase, B, is withdrawn for a period of time and experimental control is demonstrated if the behavior reverts more or less to its previous level seen in the baseline phase, phase A. Obviously, for applied settings, if the treatment seems to be working, the last thing staff want to do is allow the behavior to revert to previously high levels. Furthermore, if the intervention procedure is something that is rather artificial, staff will

want to be able to eliminate it as soon as possible and not have the excess behavior increase again. In other words, if the behavior simply fluctuates with the treatment's presence or absence, this is fine for demonstrating that the treatment truly causes the behavior change, but it does not indicate a very effective or valuable treatment. Again, the desired outcome is behavior change, not behavioral control.

Fortunately, however, for most practical situations a simple AB design is more than sufficient. If the behavior problem is a longstanding one and it begins to show improvement with the implementation of the plan, it is usually reasonable to attribute the improvement to the intervention. This position can be supported even for formal research studies. However, one is not usually trying to do formal research studies. The purpose is not to prove unequivocally that it is one's own intervention and that alone which is resulting in the client's gains. For each outcome, the authors suggest a straightforward A-B-C system of data collection. This means simply that at baseline A, before the new intervention plan is in place, some relevant information is collected on each possible outcome according to an agreed-upon plan. For some of these variables, data will continue to be collected in a time series fashion throughout the intervention phase and perhaps indefinitely. This is true for incident records, for example. For all variables, at least a B phase—information collected after the intervention has been in effect for a few weeks—and a C phase—information collected at least 6 months after the intervention has been faded—*must* be represented by evidence regarding the status of that outcome. And for certain variables, somewhat more precise measures need to be developed, with training and supervision provided to ensure that these measures are taken accurately and reliably.

The authors do not agree that it is neces-

Possible Outcomes

Outcome	Examples	How measured/documented
1. Improvement in target behavior (reduction of excess)	Decrease in frequency of head banging to near zero levels	Frequency counts of hits collected in Daily Logs Incident Records
	Decrease in operant vomiting behavior	Frequency counts of vomiting incidents Quantity measures Weight gain
2. Acquisition of alternative skills and positive behaviors	Asking for a break rather than hitting others or throwing objects	Frequency count of number of breaks requested related to incident frequency
	Playing video games rather than engaging in rocking	Time spent in arcade; tokens used; time clocked on microcomputer on site
3. Positive collateral effects and absence of side effects	Increased peer interactions as aggression declines	Participation in small group activities that were previously impossible
	Decrease in skin irritations as hand mouthing decreases	Red and flaky skin becomes more normal in appearance
4. Reduced need for and use of medical and crisis management services for client and/or others	Decrease in cuts due to head banging that require sutures	Medical/hospital records
	Decrease in staff injuries due to aggression	Workers' compensation and health insurance records and claims
	Decrease in medication prescribed for behavioral control	Reductions and elimination of dosages
	Decrease in emergency and respite hospitalizations	Hospital/respite center records (also Incident Records)
5. Less restrictive placements and greater participation in integrated community experiences	Home: lives in supported apartment, not institution	Placement records
	Work: supported work with pay, not day treatment or sheltered workshop	Placement records and salary amount
	Leisure/recreation: normalized leisure time repertoire, not Special Olympics or barren day room	Schedule of activities
	Community: participation in community experiences, not restriction to home/work settings	Schedule of activities

(continued)

FIGURE 9.1. Possible outcomes of a successful intervention.

FIGURE 9.1.   *(continued)*

Outcome	Examples	How measured/documented
6. Subjective quality-of-life improvement: happiness, satisfaction, choices for client	More smiling and general positive affect	Observation and reports
	More choices	Rating scale (see Chapter 7 for choice listing) and record of opportunities
	General motivation to participate in daily activities	Incident Record
7. Perceptions of improvement by family/ significant other	Family is pleased with behavior change	Increased contact with family documented by visit and phone records
	Staff is pleased with behavior change	Fewer complaints, requests for time off, assignment elsewhere, and so forth
	Client problems disappear	Agency records of actions involving client problems: need for plans, meetings, and so forth
8. Expanded social relationships and informal support networks	Increased community participation with peers	Agency records and activity schedule
	Fading of once-necessary one-to-one staff assignment to client	Staffing changes: reduced need for staff
	Friendships	Whether client has friends; number of friends
	Social dating	Whether client has girlfriend or boyfriend

sary to demonstrate *experimental control* in the traditional sense over serious and long-standing problem behaviors. Traditionally, a treatment would be judged as being responsible for behavior change only if it could be shown that when the intervention was in place, the behavior did not occur, and, alternatively, when the treatment was removed, the behavior reappeared— the reversal design. We have questioned the validity of treatments that can so easily be manipulated and have argued elsewhere that the treatment cannot be regarded as effective if, in fact, its removal (during a reversal phase) or absence (in another situation or environment) results in the reappearance of the behavior problem (Evans & Meyer, 1987; Voeltz & Evans, 1983). For long-standing, chronic, and serious behav-

ior problems, evidence of significant reductions in such behavior that: 1) correspond to the implementation of the treatment, and 2) do not revert to the original levels when that treatment is faded, is the crucial information. If there is such evidence, one can be reasonably confident that the intervention was responsible. (See Berkman & Meyer, 1988, for an example of an intervention study following this logic.)

Treatment Integrity

The major reason for needing to know something about the relationship between the treatment plan and the outcome is decision-making. Does the procedure need to be changed? What could be done to make it still more effective? What should be done if the treatment plan does not seem to be working? Does it just need more time; does it need to be fine-tuned in some way; or should it be replaced with another approach? In order to be able to answer these questions realistically, it is important to have some concept of what sort of change the treatment is expected to produce, given the nature of the problem behavior and the complexity of the treatment.

For example, if a systematic desensitization procedure is being used to reduce anxious behavior, progress should be expected to be slow and steady. But if using an ecological intervention that dramatically alters the person's environment, one should expect an immediate and equally dramatic change in behavior, though it might be of a more temporary nature. It is from these expected changes that one can decide very early on whether the treatment plan is working along the right lines. Similarly, in accordance with the principles advocated throughout this manual, one way of knowing whether a treatment plan seems to have a good chance of succeeding is to see if the client responds well to it. This may mean either that the client has given consent, has agreed to the contract and likes the general plan, or through his or her behavior communicates some sort of pleasure or satisfaction with the treatment arrangements being made. The authors have seen professionals design technically excellent plans, but from the moment they were introduced, the client resisted them. For example, a client might become more aggressive, physically, when being taken to a time-out room because of his or her verbal aggression and shouting. A treatment so obviously unacceptable to a client does not have much future.

Clearly there must be some process in place to evaluate systematically the degree to which the treatment plan is being reliably and accurately implemented. This is called treatment integrity. Is the treatment really being carried out the way it was designed or carried out at all? One most ob-

vious reason why some treatments fail is that they were never used in the first place! Evaluation of treatment integrity can be very formal, with a program supervisor or designated co-worker actually collecting objective data on staff behavior by means of direct observation. The authors hesitate to recommend such formal procedures, however, because generally it is not realistic for a typical agency to use them. Instead, two processes that can be extremely relevant and helpful in ensuring treatment integrity are *ecological validity* and *informal observation and problem solving*.

Ecological Validity If the various procedures advocated throughout this manual are followed, the treatment plan should have good ecological validity. This means that it is possible or realistic to carry out the planned intervention, given the way things really are. Ideally, the Wish List in Chapter 5 should be implemented, and all professionals should try to accomplish such goals and lifestyles for their clients. But by requiring staff to identify a Now List and make a commitment to doing the things that can be done now, using available staff and resources, a positive step is taken toward guaranteeing that these things will be done. Elaborate treatments developed in laboratories or designed as if the client will be on a one-to-one basis with a staff person all day and every day will not be easily transferred or implemented in actual homes and workplaces. If staff are given a serious opportunity to tell supervisors and funding sources what they can and truly will be able to do with current resources, they should be more motivated to follow through with those activities. Furthermore, addressing the issues of ecological validity should force attention on the design of interventions that work in systems and in the real world, rather than in theory or in highly idealized treatment dyads between therapist and client in isolation.

Informal Observation and Problem-Solving As emphasized in Chapter 5, the case manager for each client's plan must be someone who has frequent contact with that client and, therefore, the various other individuals with whom he or she interacts, including other staff. Obviously, the case manager is responsible for monitoring the data being collected for the outcomes listed in Figure 9.1. In fact, the case manager must establish this evaluation system and make sure that the information is collected. In addition, the authors recommend that the case manager observe each of the key elements of the treatment plan (observe the activities themselves and how the procedures are being done by staff) at least once every other week, and meet with key staff members on alternate weeks to discuss how things are going, offer suggestions, problem-solve, and so forth.

Whenever it becomes clear that procedures are not being done correctly, or even at all, this should be the signal for an immediate revision of the treatment plan, to reach clear agreement among staff about what should and will be done. If staff are simply failing to implement reasonable procedures (or using unacceptable ones not specified in the plan or by agency policies), this is grounds for administrative action. It should be evident to everyone that the plan is developed with full participation of those expected to carry it out, so that the time for disagreement or airing difficulties regarding implementation is at the planning and problem-solving meetings. And, if the case manager is doing a responsible job of regularly observing and assisting everyone involved with implementation, misunderstanding about procedures or lack of skill to carry them out should be easily and promptly remediated.

POSSIBLE OUTCOMES: WHAT IS EFFECTIVE?

This section considers each of the possible outcomes listed in Figure 9.1 and describes some alternatives for measurement and documentation. The authors are only making suggestions that should not be seen as formal instruments but still could be used. The purpose here is to try to give an idea of what is useful, rather than specify every possible measurement procedure and strategy.

Improvement in Target Behavior

Some behaviors lend themselves quite well to traditional counting methods, and behavioral events that are not of very high frequency can be recorded in incident reports, on counters, or on specially designed charts (as long as these are natural and do not stigmatize the client in any way). It is always best, if possible, to record examples of the nonoccurrence of the behavior as well. Most problem behaviors leave some sort of product—binge eating results in weight gain, mouthing fingers produces sore and calloused patches, head hitting produces bruises, and so forth. Sometimes it is simplest to record the consequences of the excess behavior, based on what it produces.

Acquisition of Alternative Skills

If the alternative skill program is a rather formal one that is being taught in an educational context such as a classroom, then it is likely that there will be some form of data sheet that permits recording of steps achieved with limited prompting and so forth. But for all other situations the authors recommend developing some clear outcome criteria and waiting for the client to match them. For example, if staff are teaching an alternative communication skill, the desired outcome is for the client to quite spontaneously say or sign, "Please come and help me," with someone who has never been a part of the training program. Enormous excitement is generated among staff when someone reports, "She did it, all by herself, just like we were teaching her!" It is more viable an outcome than watching some graph inch its way toward a supposed criterion that may or may not reflect a really functional skill.

Positive Collateral Effects and Absence of Side Effects

Once again it is recommended that for each intervention plan, a possible collateral effect be identified. It then becomes almost a game for the trainers to look for this effect and be able to be the first to report it to the team. Thus, if another desirable collateral effect is identified first, the staff's ability to predict ripple effects of a good intervention plan will be enhanced.

Reduced Need for Medical or Crisis Intervention

There are typically a number of natural places where such data must be recorded. Figure 9.2 shows a reproduction of a useful monitoring form for keeping track of medication range.

Less Restrictive Placement and Integrated Community Involvement

It should be clear that an actual move to a new more normalized living environment represents real proof that an intervention has worked. It is ironic that for none of the classic cases in the literature on excess behaviors being treated with aversives is there information on where those clients involved are now living and whether it would represent an improvement in quality-of-life. In the absence of specific placement changes, approximations toward progress in living environment, work rating, and community opportunities can be assessed using the following three forms: a) Table 9.1, Community Living Evaluation; b) Table 9.2, Employment Evaluation; and c) Figure 9.3, Community Participation and Leisure/ Recreation Involvement Rating.

Subjective Quality-of-Life

In the treatment design, try to specify the signs to look for in the client that would indicate real improvement in happiness and other affective signs. This would include improved appetite, better sleeping habits, more cheerful disposition, signs of liking oneself (putting up pictures of self on a bulletin board). For the areas of work motivation and available choices see the sample checklists that can be used to estimate changes in these outcomes: the Work Motivation Rating (Table 9.3) and the Individual Decision-Making Evaluation Checklist (Figure 9.4).

Perceptions of Improvement

Typically these will emerge spontaneously. However, the Client Outcome Rating (see Figure 9.5) reflects the subjective judgments of those who know the client well.

Expanded Social Relationships

It is often helpful to draw a sociogram, that is, a diagram of the client's social network. Usually, in research, this is formally based on direct observation or based on peer nominations of who is liked or who their friends are. However, it is perfectly possible to draw such a diagram based on one's knowledge of the person. Start by drawing the client in the middle and connect him or her to everyone with whom he or she has contact. Social networks are complex and no various clear levels need to be established, such as friend, acquaintance, work associate, professional relationship. If the relationship is equal and clearly reciprocal, draw an extra connecting arrow. This sociogram will give a good picture of the nature of the client's social support network. Relationships are the key to successful outcomes, and following is the final section, which returns to the issue of professional interaction as outcomes.

PERSONNEL INVOLVEMENT: A SPECIAL FORM OF TREATMENT INTEGRITY

When behavior modification principles first began to be used with clients who were developmentally disabled, direct ser-

Medication Data Collection/Communication (Form 7)

Patient Information   Name: _____ Birth Date: _____ C.A.: _____ School: _____

Case Manager/Teacher: _____ Physician: _____   DATA COLLECTION MODE

MEDICATION: _____ DATE INITIATED: _____   F = Frequency recording

DOSAGE: (a) _____ (b) _____ (c) _____   D = Duration recording

ADMIN. INTERVAL: (a) _____ (b) _____ (c) _____   M = Momentary time sampling

Date of Observation																			
Time of Observation	Start																		
	Finish																		
Admin. Interval																			
Dosage																			
Time most recent admin.																			
BEHAVIORS	1.																		
	2.																		
	3.																		
	4.																		

Description of Target Behaviors   *Physician Comments:*

1.

2.
                                           Observer Comments:
3.

4.

FIGURE 9.2.   Medication data collection/communication form. (From Evans & Meyer, 1985, p. 157; reprinted by permission.)

Table 9.1. Community living evaluation

Dimension	Most restrictive option	Restrictive option	Appropriate community living
A. Present home environment: Where is this person living now?			
1. Children/youth (under 21)	Hospital or institutional placement with other persons with disabilities Large-scale congregate facility (e.g., ICF or residential center) for persons with disabilities Group home or apartment in the community with more than four unrelated children/youth with disabilities living together	Group home or apartment in the community with four or fewer unrelated children/youth with disabilities living together	Biological/adoptive family[a] with support Foster-care family with support Shared-care[b] families with support
2. Adults (21 and over)	Hospital or institutional placement with other persons with disabilities Large-scale congregate facility (e.g., ICF or residential center) for persons with disabilities	At home with biological/adoptive parents or family members (e.g., sister's family) Adult foster care[c] Home or apartment in cluster of two or more such homes in the community, where each home is family-scale or larger scale	Home or apartment in the community, family-scale (generally no more than four adult clients living together) with support Living alone in house/apartment in the community with support[c]
B. Future/projected home environment: If all goes well and reasonable resources are available, where do you anticipate that this person will be living 5 years from now?			
1. Children/youth (under 21)	Any of the options listed above, regardless of level of supervision and support	Any of the options listed above, regardless of level of supervision and support	Any of the options listed above, with supervision and support needed by that individual
2. Adults (21 and over)	See above	See above	See above

(continued)

vice staff were conceptualized as behavioral engineers. Their task was defined as implementing formal intervention plans and ensuring that their interpersonal and social interactions with clients adhered to basic contingency management concepts,

that is, ignoring negative behavior, reinforcing positive behavior, and so forth. Staff training was thus geared to making direct service personnel into mini behavior modifiers; in-service training often included coverage of such technical issues as

Table 9.1. *(continued)*

Dimension	Most restrictive option	Restrictive option	Appropriate community living
C. Choices: With whom does this person live?			
1. Children/youth (under 21)	Unrelated persons with disabilities, regardless of facility, home, or placement type		Biological/adoptive family Foster-care family Shared-care families
2. Adults (21 and over)	Unrelated persons without disabilities, not chosen by person with a disability (generally agency decision) Unrelated persons with disabilities, not preferred or chosen as roommates by person with a disability (generally agency decision)	Relatives, where decision was made by them and not by the person with a disability Unrelated person/s with disabilities, who may be preferred but were not chosen as roommates by person with a disability (i.e., original decision made by agency) Alone, but not by choice, with support (generally agency decision)	Alone by choice with support Unrelated person(s) with disabilities who are preferred and were chosen as roommates by person with a disability Relatives, where decision was made by person with a disability to live with them, with support

[a]Biological/adoptive family arrangements may include child living with biological/adoptive parents or another relative, such as an adult sister and her family.

[b]Shared-care refers to a formal arrangement between two families (one of which is typically the biological or adoptive family) who share parenting, with the child spending agreed-upon periods of time living with each family. This system is well-developed in England and New Zealand, for example, and is supported by formal agency-negotiated agreements and financial remuneration to the second, shared-care family.

[c]In some cultures, these options might actually be considered more or less restrictive, dependent upon cultural norms. For example, it might be very appropriate for a person with a disability who is older to live with a family in an aunt or grandparent type role.

charting and graphing of behavior or single-subject research designs. (See Evans [in press] for a detailed critique of such an approach.) Obviously the authors' view of the role of direct care staff is rather different. Chapter 3 described the natural social context within which sound behavioral principles are embedded. The success of the educative approach depends on the degree to which the staff, the people in most direct contact with the clients, can implement a prescribed plan and, at the same time, maintain effective, positive social relationships with their clients.

Because of this perspective, the authors feel that some of the attitudes and values emphasized throughout this manual might be more important for dealing with serious excess behavior than knowing every detail about schedules of reinforcement. When evaluating the success of the training using this manual it is recommended that attention be given to the degree to which the staff participants have internalized the major ideas. When discussing problem behavior, for example, do they recognize that there are problem settings, not just problem clients? Or if they are thinking of

Table 9.2. Employment evaluation

Dimension	Most restrictive	Restrictive	Appropriate employment
1. Secondary/ post secondary school age (14–21)	Person is not employed, and there are no plans for employment training for this person.	Person is not employed but is attending a vocational program to prepare for sheltered work.	Person is over 16, no longer attending school, and has chosen one of the options listed below for adult employment.
	Person is not employed but does have a prevocational component in his or her program.	Person is not employed, but there are plans to implement a work experience program for him or her before graduation.	Person is not employed but receives systematic employment training several times weekly at actual job sites as part of his or her high school program, and will be employed with support after graduation.
	Person is not employed but attends school during the day. However, there is no vocational component in his or her program.		Person is not employed but is attending community college as part of his or her preparation for one of the options listed below for adults.
2. Adults (21 and over)	Person is not employed, and employment is not a goal for this person at present.	Person is not employed, but employment is a goal for this person, and he or she is receiving job training.	Person is not a wage-earner but has chosen alternative work such as volunteer work or being a primary housekeeper in a household.
	Person is not employed, but job training is planned for the future to determine positive employment options.	Person is employed in a sheltered workshop (regardless of wage).	Person is employed part-time by choice, at minimum wage or higher, with job support.[a]
		Person is employed, but part-time because full-time is not available and/or staff have decided person is not yet ready for full-time.	Person is employed full-time by choice, at minimum wage or higher, with job support.[a]
		Person is temporarily unemployed but is trained and actively seeking employment.	Person is past retirement age and has chosen not to work.

[a]Job support would generally be provided by a supported work arrangement, ranging from part-time supervision and support by agency staff to full-time job coach arrangements as individually appropriate.

Community and Leisure Involvement (Form 8)

For the activities listed below, please fill in the requested information *to the best of your knowledge.*

Activity	Use: Estimate no. of times last month	Access (check one): Accessible — Walking distance	Access: Accessible — Easy public transportation	Access: Restrictive — Inconvenient or too far to use often without staff help	Access: Most restrictive — Virtually no access unless staff arranges	Level of independence/supervision: Does without staff help (alone or with friends)	Level of independence/supervision: Needs some help from staff	Level of independence/supervision: Needs much help/supervision from staff	Do you see this as a goal for this person? Yes	No	Not sure
1. General shopping (not groceries)											
2. Grocery shopping											
3. Using public transportation											
4. Banking											
5. Visiting fast food restaurant											
6. Visiting sit-down restaurant											
7. Attending community gym, swimming pool, fitness facility											

FIGURE 9.3. Community participation and leisure/recreation involvement rating.

(continued)

FIGURE 9.3. (continued)

Activity	Use: Estimate no. of times last month	Access (check one)					Level of independence/supervision			Do you see this as a goal for this person?		
		Accessible		Restrictive	Most restrictive		Does without staff help (alone or with friends)	Needs some help from staff	Needs much help/supervision from staff	Yes	No	Not sure
		Walking distance	Easy public transportation	Inconvenient or too far to use often without staff help	Virtually no access unless staff arranges							
8. Attending community college or adult education classes or programs												
9. Visiting post office												
10. Attending house of worship												
11. Attending concert, play, movie												
12. Attending sporting events (as spectator)												
13. Visiting bowling alley, skating rink, video arcade												

164

14. Touring museum, art gallery, or other tourist attraction									
15. Walking in the neighborhood									
16. Visiting friend's house									
17. Visiting with family									
18. Talking on the telephone									
19. Visiting dentist/doctor (health care)									
20. Having hair cut and/or styled at hair salon or barbershop									
21. Using community library									
22. Attending dances (non-alcoholic setting)									
23. Attending bar or discotheque (alcohol served)									
24. Having picnic or camping									
25. Visiting park or zoo									

(continued)

FIGURE 9.3. (continued)

Activity	Use: Estimate no. of times last month	Access (check one)				Level of independence/supervision			Do you see this as a goal for this person?		
		Accessible		Restrictive	Most restrictive	Does without staff help (alone or with friends)	Needs some help from staff	Needs much help/supervision from staff	Yes	No	Not sure
		Walking distance	Easy public transportation	Inconvenient or too far to use often without staff help	Virtually no access unless staff arranges						
26. Entertaining guests											
27. Dating											
28. Keeping social service/welfare appointment											
29. Going to laundromat or dry cleaner											
30. Involvement in organized special activity or club (e.g., Toastmasters)											
31. Attending community education programs, hobby classes, private lessons, and so forth.											

Table 9.3. Work motivation rating

		MOTIVATION			
	Low		Medium		High
1. Desire to continue present job	1	2	3	4	5
2. Enjoyment of present job	1	2	3	4	5
3. Enjoyment of social interactions at present job	1	2	3	4	5
4. Desire to do better work, continue learning new skills, and so forth, at present job	1	2	3	4	5
5. Desire to be more independent at present job	1	2	3	4	5
6. Satisfaction with present wages	1	2	3	4	5

Total motivation rating: _____
(Range 6–30)[a]

[a]Any score less than 3 on an individual item should be cause for concern. Moderate to high job satisfaction would be supported by a total score ranging from 18–30, with no individual item scored below 3.

teaching social skills, do they think of their relationships with the client, not just social praise or planned ignoring? These ideas have very practical implications for the likely integrity of treatment implementation. Staff should behave naturally, but not too naturally, particularly where problem behavior is concerned, because it can be extremely frustrating and limiting to staff. It is natural to give the client clear feedback that his or her behavior is unacceptable, but it might be even more natural to lose one's temper and yell at the client.

This concern is nicely illustrated by a manual on behavior modification that is used by one state's developmental disability services to certify its direct service personnel. One of the test questions asks how one would react if a client with the habit of grabbing shoelaces started to untie one's own. Think about that for a moment. The correct answer provided in the training manual is to ignore the client, supposedly revealing the trainee's knowledge of extinction. But how many people actually could ignore someone doing this to them, and how many people normally would? Only an unusual staff member would be capable of the degree of self-control necessary. Obviously not many had it because presumably the client had plenty of reinforcement in developing this unacceptable form of social interaction. But, by the same token, it might require considerable skill

not to overreact and yell or otherwise punish the client. It does take special training and restraint to be able to respond assertively, but not aggressively, and give clear, firm verbal feedback that this behavior is unacceptable. It is also important to learn to restructure social interactions with the client so that there are more opportunities for him or her to initiate normal social contact. Direct service staff, therefore, should not be left to their own natural devices; professional skills require careful training.

There are a number of ways that one can monitor staff agreement with the spirit of a formal intervention plan. When there is real adherence to the concepts outlined here, direct service staff often come up with extensions of the original plan. Someone who has internalized the idea that a client should exercise preferences, otherwise his or her motivation will be weak, will go beyond the suggestion for a meaningful leisure skill and perhaps comment, "You know, I've often seen this person staring at people with fancy jewelry; I wonder if I could get this person interested in some costume jewelry?" That is a much more satisfying response from staff than a repeated remark like, "Oh, she's not interested in anything but chewing on her fingers." Another comment sometimes heard in planning meetings is, "We tried that before and it didn't work." A person with this

Individual Decision-Making Evaluation Checklist (Form 9)

For each item, check only the one response that best matches the present choice options available to this client.

Does he or she choose:	Most restrictive: No choices		Restrictive choices	Appropriate choices
	No opportunity to observe	Decision does not seem appropriate for this person	Needs help with this decision or will do this inappropriately	Yes, does make this decision reasonably, appropriately
1. What to wear				
2. How to comb/style hair				
3. Activities on a day off (e.g., Saturday or vacation day)				
4. To occasionally sleep in on day off				
5. What T.V. show to watch				
6. What radio station/type of music to listen to				
7. What chores he or she is assigned at home				
8. Whether to do a chore right away or do it later (e.g., dishes)				
9. To invite a friend to do something together				
10. To invite a friend to visit				
11. What to eat for a meal or snack				
12. How to spend money that is not allocated for expenses				
13. To exercise				
14. To diet for weight control				
15. To have a drink (e.g., beer, wine)				
16. To smoke				
17. To have a friendship				
18. To have a girlfriend or boyfriend				
19. To have sexual relations				
20. To masturbate in privacy				
21. What form of birth control to use				

Figure 9.4. Individual decision-making evaluation checklist: The kinds of choices and decisions this individual makes.

FIGURE 9.4. (*continued*)

Does he or she choose:	Most restrictive: No choices		Restrictive choices	Appropriate choices
	No opportunity to observe	Decision does not seem appropriate for this person	Needs help with this decision or will do this inappropriately	Yes, does make this decision reasonably, appropriately
22. Whether to agree to or say no to participation in a group activity				
23. What clothes to buy				
24. Whom he or she wants to live with				
25. When to visit family				
26. To make a phone call to a friend or family member				
27. Whether to stay up later than or go to bed earlier than the usual time				
28. What job he or she wants to have or what work he or she wants to do				
29. To ask permission to take a sick day (stay home from work) when not feeling well				
30. What to do/where to go on vacation				
31. Whether or not he or she can own a pet				
32. His or her own dentist/ physician				
33. Whether or not he or she receives therapy services (e.g., speech, occupational therapy, etc.)				
34. What type/style of adaptive equipment or prosthetic devices he or she utilizes (e.g., wheelchair, braces, etc.)				
35. What form of augmentative communication system or devices he or she utilizes (e.g., signing, electronic board, etc.)				

Total Number of Most Restrictive Choices (cols. 1–2): _____

Total Number of Restricted Choices (col. 3): _____

Total Number of Appropriate Choices (col. 4): _____

Client Outcome Rating (Form 10)

Instructions: Complete this section by referring to the *most integrated* domain that this person experiences. For example, if the individual lives in a large ICF/MR but works at a fast food restaurant, think about his or her performance at the restaurant when you fill in ratings.

1. How do you rate this person's *overall performance on tasks* he or she is expected to do (on the job, around the house, etc.)?

1	2	3	4	5	6	7
Totally inadequate			It varies— about half and half			Exceptionally good performance

2. How do you rate this person's *general behavior* (adjustment, work habits, etc.)?

1	2	3	4	5	6	7
Totally dissatisfied with his or her behavior			It varies— about half and half			Completely satisfied with his or her behavior

3. Are this person's *social interactions with co-workers and peers* positive and appropriate?

1	2	3	4	5	6	7
Almost never			It varies— about half and half			Almost always

4. Are this person's *social interactions with supervisors* positive and appropriate?

1	2	3	4	5	6	7
Almost never			It varies— about half and half			Almost always

5. Are this person's *social interactions with persons in the general community* positive and appropriate?

1	2	3	4	5	6	7
Almost never			It varies— about half and half			Almost always

6. In comparison to other persons with similar disabilities whom you know, how well is this person doing overall?

1	2	3	4	5	6	7
Not nearly as well as others with similar disabilities			It varies— about half and half			Much better than others with similar disabilities

FIGURE 9.5. Client outcome rating.

(*continued*)

FIGURE 9.5. (*continued*)

7. Does this person seem to like the work and/or activities he or she does during the day?

   | 1 | 2 | 3 | 4 | 5 | 6 | 7 |

   Not at all   It varies—   Very much
   about half
   and half

8. Does this person seem to like being in the community, around persons who are not disabled?

   | 1 | 2 | 3 | 4 | 5 | 6 | 7 |

   Not at all   It varies—   Very much
   about half
   and half

9. Does this person seem to like the people at his or her job site or day activity?

   | 1 | 2 | 3 | 4 | 5 | 6 | 7 |

   Not at all   It varies—   Very much
   about half
   and half

10. Does this person seem to be motivated to do his or her share?

    | 1 | 2 | 3 | 4 | 5 | 6 | 7 |

    Not at all   It varies—   Very much
    about half
    and half

11. When things do go wrong, does this person manage to recover within a reasonable period of time and go back to work or join the activities again in a positive way?

    | 1 | 2 | 3 | 4 | 5 | 6 | 7 |

    Almost never   It varies—   Almost always
    about half
    and half

The environment that I used as a referent to complete this section for this person was:

Total score: _____

High score:	55–77
Moderate score:	33–54
Low score:	11–32

attitude is not participating as a problem-solver in treatment planning but expects to be supplied with solutions, or has become external in locus of control, no longer believing in the power of a direct service person to make a difference.

Direct service staff are not necessarily used to being treated as the central figures in intervention designed to help another individual make a successful and enjoyable accommodation for the demands of the natural community. However, this manual attempts to reveal clearly our respect for the unique interpersonal demands of the caregiver role. With professional respect comes professional responsibilities. Knoll and Ford (1987) have suggested that the role of the service provider needs to be reconceptualized. They list 10 criteria that would serve as sign posts if the desired degree of the community integration goal is being realized. The authors use these criteria to suggest evaluation standards whereby trainees learning from this manual can judge the kinds of intervention programs they are designing. The following activity could serve as a final overview activity for participants in a training workshop.

ACTIVITY

List the basic description of the proposed or ongoing treatment plan and then list the way in which the plan addresses the following standards (critiques are derived from Knoll & Ford, 1987):

1. *Does the plan ensure the building of further relationships and natural supports?*
   Will the client be able to develop new, nonprofessional relationships? Is there anything in the plan that might interfere with interactions among family and friends?

2. *Does the plan foster involvement with the community beyond the confines of the setting (workplace, group home)?*
   There should be identifiable elements in the staff's plan that will increase visibility and participation in the community.

3. *If the client were in the company of people who knew nothing about the treatment plan, would any of its elements be detectable?*
   This is the interpretation of active participation. In an ideal program the client would be able to self-initiate at least some features of the plan.

4. *Are the features of the treatment program sufficiently nonintrusive that an outside observer would have difficulty recognizing that a treatment is in place?*
   Even positive intervention can be intrusive and serve to identify the client as a problem. The authors have advocated that well-designed programs blend into the natural social ecology.

5. *Does the plan respect the client's right to privacy and personal space?*
   Is the intervention taking place within a structure that permits the usual cultural expectation for periods of privacy or solitude?

6. *Is there a provision in the plan to avoid or deal with periods of dead time?*
   Opportunities for being left alone should not be confused with periods in which a person with limited ability or opportunity to initiate his or her own activities is obliged to spend unconstructive, unengaged time.

7. *Does the formal intervention plan also permit the client to follow the typical routines of a person's home life?*
   The intervention implemented by direct service staff should not require special regimentation or unusual schedules and timing.

8. *Are the elements of the treatment plan all age-appropriate—with respect to both materials and activities?*

Have the staff considered that the client is an adult with adult responsibilities and freedoms? Consideration of this criterion will almost always lead to an intervention that emphasizes self-regulation as one element.

9. *Is there provision in the plan for real choices?*
    Staff should show their sensitivity to the ease with which many clients will go along with procedures or perhaps try to please those whom they like and respect. If the client was taught to be an effective self-advocate, would the same program have been designed?

10. *If the reader were the client, would the reader want such a treatment plan?*
    Direct service personnel benefit a great deal from thinking of the client's life compared to their own. This is roughly what is meant by empathy.

Obviously the criteria described in this activity are demanding ones. Staff should not feel like failures because the treatment setting is not ideal in every respect. But most of the standards described are not technically difficult to implement. If direct service personnel envisage their ability to create such conditions, the likelihood that treatment plans will show integrity to the principles represented in this manual should be greatly enhanced.

References

Accord reached on autistic schools. (1987, January 10). *New York Times.* p. 50.

Aman, M.G., & Singh, N.N. (1983). Pharmacological intervention. In J. Matson & M. Hersen (Eds.), *Handbook of mental retardation.* Elmsford, NY: Pergamon.

Anderson, L., Dancis, J., & Alpert, M. (1978). Behavioral contingencies and self-mutilation in Lesch-Nyhan disease. *Journal of Consulting and Clinical Psychology, 46,* 529–536.

Barlow, D., Hayes, S., & Nelson, R.O. (1984). *The scientist practitioner.* Elmsford, NY: Pergamon.

Barlow, D.H., & Hersen, M. (1984). *Single case experimental designs.* (2nd ed.). Elmsford, NY: Pergamon.

Barrett, R.P. (Ed.). (1986). *Severe behavior disorders in the mentally retarded: Nondrug approaches to treatment.* New York: Plenum.

Bates, P., Morrow, S.A., Pancsofar, E., & Sedlak, R. (1984). The effect of functional vs. nonfunctional activities on attitudes/expectations of non-handicapped college students: What they see is what we get. *Journal of The Association for Persons with Severe Handicaps, 9,* 73–78.

Baumeister, A.A. (1978). Origins and control of stereotyped movement. In C.E. Meyers (Ed.), *Quality of life in severely and profoundly mentally retarded people: Research foundations for improvement.* Washington, DC: American Association on Mental Deficiency.

Baumeister, A.A., & Rollings, J.P. (1976). Self-injurious behavior. In N.R. Ellis (Ed.), *International review of research in mental retardation* (Vol. 8). New York: Academic Press.

Baumgart, D., Brown, L., Pumpian, I., Nisbet, J., Ford, A., Sweet, M., Messina, R., & Schroeder, J. (1982). Principle of partial participation and individualized adaptations in educational programs for severely handicapped students. *Journal of The Association for the Severely Handicapped, 7,* 17–27.

Beck, A.T. (1976). *Cognitive therapy and the emotional disorders.* Madison, CT: International Universities Press.

Berkman, K.A., & Meyer, L.H. (1988). Alternative strategies and multiple outcomes in the remediation of severe self-injury: Going "all out" nonaversively. *Journal of The Association for Persons with Severe Handicaps, 13,* 76–88.

Berkson, G. (1967). Development of abnormal stereotyped behaviors. *Developmental Psychology, 1,* 118–132.

Blanchard, D.C., & Blanchard, R.J. (1986). Punishment and aggression: A critical reexamination. In R.J. Blanchard & D.C. Blanchard (Eds.), *Advances in the study of aggression,* (Vol. 2). Orlando, FL: Academic Press.

Blatt, B., & Kaplan, F. (1966). *Christmas in purgatory.* Newton, MA: Allyn & Bacon.

Borreson, P.M. (1980). The elimination of a self injury avoidance response through a forced running consequence. *Mental Retardation, 18,* 73–77.

Breuning, S.E., Davis, J.J., & Poling, A.D. (1982). Pharmacotherapy with the mentally retarded: Implications for clinical psychologists. *Clinical Psychology Review, 2,* 39–53.

Browder, D.M. (1987). *Assessment of individuals with severe handicaps: An applied behavior approach to life skills assessment.* Baltimore: Paul H. Brookes Publishing Co.

Carr, E.G. (1977). The motivation of self-injurious behavior: A review of some hypotheses. *Psychological Bulletin, 84,* 800–816.

Carr, E.G., & Durand, V.M. (1985). Reducing behavior problems through functional communication training. *Journal of Applied Behavior Analysis, 18*, 111–126.

Carr, E.G., Newsom, C.D., & Binkoff, J.A. (1980). Escape as a factor in the aggressive behavior of two retarded children. *Journal of Applied Behavior Analysis, 13*, 101–117.

Cataldo, M.F., & Harris, J. (1982). The biological basis for self-injury in the mentally retarded. *Analysis and Intervention in Developmental Disabilities, 2*, 21–39.

Chock, P.N., & Glahn, T.J. (1983). Learning and self-stimulation in mute and echolalic autistic children. *Journal of Autism and Developmental Disorders, 13*, 365–381.

Cole, D.A., & Meyer, L.H. (in press). Impact of family needs and resources on the decision to seek out-of-home placement. *American Journal of Mental Retardation.*

DiLorenzo, T.M., & Ollendick, T.H. (1986). Behavior modification: Punishment. In R.P. Barrett (Ed.), *Severe behavior disorders in the mentally retarded: Nondrug approaches to treatment.* New York: Plenum.

Donnellan, A.M., Mirenda, P.L., Mesaros, R.A., & Fassbender, L.L. (1984). Analyzing the communicative functions of aberrant behavior. *Journal of the Association for Persons with Severe Handicaps, 9*, 201–212.

Duker, P. (1975). Behaviour control of self-biting in a Lesch-Nyhan patient. *Journal of Mental Deficiency Research, 19*, 11–19.

Durand, V.M. (1988). Motivational Assessment Scale. In M. Hersen & A.S. Bellack (Eds.), *Dictionary of behavioral assessment techniques.* New York: Pergamon Press.

Durand, V.M., & Kishi, G. (1987). Reducing severe behavior problems among persons with dual sensory impairments: An evaluation of a technical assistance model. *Journal of The Association for Persons with Severe Handicaps, 12*, 2–10.

Durand, V.M., Meyer, L.H., Janney, R., & Lanci, A. (1988). *New York State Education Department behavioral management guidelines.* Albany: New York State Education Department.

Edgerton, R., Bollinger, M., & Herr, B. (1984). The cloak of competence: After two decades. *American Journal of Mental Deficiency, 88*, 345–351.

Ellis, A. (1971). *Growth through reason.* Palo Alto, CA: Science and Behavior Books.

Evans, I.M. (in press). Training personnel in state-of-the-art nonintrusive interventions. In A. Kaiser & C. McWhorter (Eds.), *Preparing personnel to work with persons who are severely handicapped.* Baltimore: Paul H. Brookes Publishing Co.

Evans, I.M., & Meyer, L.H. (1985). *An educative approach to behavior problems: A practical decision model for interventions with severely handicapped learners.* Baltimore: Paul H. Brookes Publishing Co.

Evans, I.M., & Meyer, L.H. (1987). Moving to educational validity: A reply to Test, Spooner, and Cooke. *Journal of The Association for Persons with Severe Handicaps, 12*, 103–106.

Evans, I.M., Meyer, L.H., Kurkjian, J.A., & Kishi, G.S. (1988). An evaluation of behavioral interrelationships in child behavior therapy. In J.C. Witt, S.N. Elliott, & F.M. Gresham (Eds.), *Handbook of behavior therapy in education.* New York: Plenum.

Evans, I.M., & Scheuer, A.D. (1987). Analyzing response relationships in childhood aggression: The clinical perspective. In D.H. Crowell, I.M. Evans, & C.R. O'Donnell (Eds.), *Childhood aggression and violence: Sources of influence, prevention, and control.* New York: Plenum.

Evans, I.M., & Voeltz, L.M. (1982). *The selection of intervention priorities in educational programming of severely handicapped preschool children with multiple behavioral problems* (Final report, Grant G007901960, U.S. Department of Education). Honolulu: University of Hawaii.

Favell, J.E. (1973). Reduction of stereotypes by reinforcement of toy play. *Mental Retardation, 11*, 21–23.

Forehand, R., & Baumeister, A.A. (1976). Deceleration of aberrant behavior among retarded individuals. In M. Hersen, R.M. Eisler, & P.M. Miller (Eds.), *Progress in behavior modification* (Vol. 2). New York: Academic Press.

Fowler, H. (1971). Suppression and facilitation by response contingent shock. In F.R. Brush (Ed.), *Aversive conditioning and learning.* New York: Academic Press.

Foxx, R.M., Bittle, R.G., Bechtel, D.R., & Livesay, J.R. (1986). Behavioral treatment of the sexually deviant behavior of mentally retarded individuals. In N.R. Ellis & N.W. Bray (Eds.), *International review of research in mental retardation* (Vol. 14). Orlando, FL: Academic Press.

Foxx, R.M., McMarrow, M.J., Storely, K., & Rogers, B.M. (1984). Teaching social/sexual skills to mentally retarded adults. *American Journal of Mental Deficiency, 80*, 9–15.

Frankel, F., Freeman, B.J., Ritvo, E.R., & Pardo, R. (1978). The effect of environmental stimulation upon the stereotyped behavior of autistic children. *Journal of Autism and Childhood Schizophrenia, 8*, 389–394.

Glick, B., & Goldstein, A.P. (1987). Aggression replacement training. *Journal of Counseling and Development, 65*, 356–362.

Goldstein, A.P. (1981). *Psychological skill training.* New York: Pergamon.

Greenspan, S., & Shoultz, B. (1981). Why mentally retarded adults lose their jobs: Social competence as a factor in work adjustment. *Applied Research in Mental Retardation, 2*, 23–28.

Guthrie, E.R. (1935). *The psychology of learning.* New York: Harper.

Hanley-Maxwell, C., Rusch, F.R., Chadsey-Rusch, J., & Renzaglia, A. (1986). Reported factors contributing to job termination of individuals with severe disabilities. *Journal of The Association for Persons with Severe Handicaps, 11*, 45–52.

Harris, S.L., & Romanczyk, R.G. (1976). Treating self-injurious behavior of a retarded child by overcorrection. *Behavior Therapy, 7*, 235–239.

Hill, B.K., & Bruininks, R.H. (1984). Maladaptive behavior of mentally retarded individuals in residential facilities. *American Journal of Mental Deficiency, 88*, 380–387.

Hollis, J.H. (1978). Analysis of rocking behavior. In C.E. Meyers (Ed.), *Quality of life in severely and profoundly mentally retarded people: Research foundations for improvement.* Washington, DC: American Association on Mental Deficiency.

Janney, R., & Meyer, L.H. (1988). *Child-centered consultation to assist schools in serving students with disabilities and severe behavior problems in integrated settings: A module on effective consultation.* Syracuse: Syracuse University Division of Special Education and Rehabilitation.

Jones, M.L., Lattimore, J., Ulicny, G.R., & Risley, T.R. (1986). Ecobehavioral design: Programming for engagement. In R.P. Barrett (Ed.), *Severe behavior disorders in the mentally retarded: Nondrug approaches to treatment.* New York: Plenum.

Kerr, M.M., & Nelson, C.M. (1983). *Strategies for managing behavior problems in the classroom.* Columbus, OH: Charles E. Merrill.

Kishi, G., Teelucksingh, B., Zollers, N., Park-Lee, S., & Meyer, L. (1988). Daily decision-making in community residences: A social comparison of adults with and without mental retardation. *American Journal on Mental Retardation, 92*, 430–435.

Knoll, J., & Ford, A. (1987). Beyond caregiving: A reconceptualization of the role of the residential service provider. In S.J. Taylor, D. Biklen, & J. Knoll (Eds.), *Community integration for people with severe disabilities.* New York: Teachers College Press.

Koegel, R.L., & Covert, A. (1972). The relationship of self-stimulation to learning in autistic children. *Journal of Applied Behavior Analysis, 5*, 381–387.

Koegel, R.L., Firestone, P.B., Kramme, K.W., & Dunlap, G. (1974). Increasing spontaneous play by suppressing self-stimulation in autistic children. *Journal of Applied Behavior Analysis, 7*, 521–528.

Kohlberg, L. (1973). *Collected papers on moral development and moral education.* Cambridge, MA: Harvard University Press.

LaGreca, A.M., Stone, W.L., & Bell, C.R. (1982). Assessing the problematic interpersonal skills of mentally retarded individuals in a vocational setting. *Applied Research in Mental Retardation, 3*, 37–53.

Landesman-Dwyer, S., & Berkson, G. (1984). Friendship and social behavior. In J. Wortis (Ed.), *Mental retardation and developmental disabilities* (Vol. 13). New York: Plenum.

LaVigna, G.W., & Donnellan, A.M. (1986). *Alternatives to punishment: Solving behavior problems with non-aversive strategies.* New York: Irvington.

Lazar, J.B., & Rucker, W.L. (1984, November). *The effectiveness of manipulating setting factors on the ruminative behavior of a boy with profound retardation.* Paper presented at the annual conference of The Association for Persons with Severe Handicaps, Chicago.

Leff, J.P., & Vaughn, C.E. (1976). The influence of family and social factors on the course of the psychiatric illness. *British Journal of Psychiatry, 129*, 125–137.

Litrownik, A.J. (1982). Special considerations in the self-management training of the developmentally disabled. In P. Karoly & F.H. Kanfer (Eds.), *Self-management and behavior change: From theory to practice.* Elmsford, NY: Pergamon.

Luce, S.C., Delquadri, J., & Hall, R.V. (1980). Contingent exercise: A mild but powerful procedure for suppressing inappropriate verbal and aggressive behavior. *Journal of Applied Behavior Analysis, 13*, 583–594.

Mace, F.C., & Kratochwill, T.R. (1988). Self-monitoring. In J.C. Witt, S.N. Elliott, & F.M. Gresham (Eds.), *Handbook of behavior therapy in education.* New York: Plenum.

Maisto, C.R., Baumeister, A.B., & Maisto, A.A.

(1977). An analysis of variables related to self-injurious behavior among institutionalized retarded persons. *Journal of Mental Deficiency Research, 12,* 232–239.

Martin, P.L., & Foxx, R.M. (1973). Victim control of aggression of an institutionalized retardate. *Journal of Behavior Therapy and Experimental Psychiatry, 4,* 161–165.

Matson, J.L. (1985). Punishment. In R.M. Turner & L.M. Ascher (Eds.), *Evaluating behavior therapy outcome.* New York: Springer.

McFall, R.M. (1982). A review and reformulation of the concept of social skills. *Behavioral Assessment, 4,* 1–33.

Meyer, L.H., Cole, D.A., McQuarter, R., & Reichle, J. (1988). *Validation of a measure of social competence in children and young adults with mental retardation and other disabilities.* Unpublished manuscript, Division of Special Education and Rehabilitation, Syracuse University.

Meyer, L.H., & Evans, I.M. (1986). Modification of excess behavior: An adaptive and functional approach for educational and community contexts. In R.H. Horner, L.H. Meyer, & H.D.B. Fredericks (Eds.), *Education of learners with severe handicaps: Exemplary service strategies* (pp. 315–350). Baltimore: Paul H. Brookes Publishing Co.

Meyer, L.H., & Evans, I.M. (1987). *Non-aversive intervention for behavior problems: A manual for community and residential settings.* Syracuse, NY: Division of Special Education and Rehabilitation, Syracuse University.

Meyer, L.H., Evans, I.M., Wuerch, B.B., & Brennan, J.M. (1985). Monitoring the collateral effects of leisure skill instruction: A case study in multiple-baseline methodology. *Behaviour Research and Therapy, 23,* 127–138.

Meyer, L.H., & Janney, R. (in press). Behavioral intervention: Child centered and systems research. In R. Gaylord-Ross (Ed.), *Issues in research in special education* (Vol. 2). New York: Teachers College Press.

Meyer, L.H., Reichle, J., McQuarter, R.J., Cole, D., Vandercook, T., Evans, I.M., Neel, R., & Kishi, G. (1985). *The Assessment of Social Competence (ASC): A scale of social competence functions.* Minneapolis, MN: University of Minnesota Consortium Institute.

Meyer, L.H., St. Peter, S., & Park-Lee, S.H. (1986, November). *The validation of social skills for successful performance in community environments by young adults with moderate to severe/profound disabilities.* Paper presented at the meeting of the Association for Advancement of Behavior Therapy, Chicago.

Morris, R.J., & Kratochwill, T.R. (1983). *Treating children's fears and phobias: A behavioral approach.* Elmsford, NY: Pergamon.

Mulick, J.A., & Schroeder, S.R. (1980). Research relating to management of antisocial behavior in mentally retarded persons. *The Psychological Record, 30,* 397–417.

Neef, N.A., Shafer, M.S., Egel, A.L., Cataldo, M.F., & Parrish, J.M. (1983). The class-specific effects of compliance training with "do" and "don't" requests: Analog analysis and classroom application. *Journal of Applied behavior Analysis, 16,* 81–99.

O'Brien, J. (1987). A guide to life-style planning: Using *The Activities Catalog* to integrate services and natural support systems. In B. Wilcox & G.T. Bellamy, *A comprehensive guide to the Activities Catalog: An alternative curriculum for youth and adults with severe disabilities.* (pp. 175–189). Baltimore: Paul H. Brookes Publishing Co.

Powers, M.D. (1988). A systems approach to serving persons with severe developmental disabilities. In M.D. Powers (Ed.), *Expanding systems of service delivery for persons with developmental disabilities.* (pp. 1–14). Baltimore: Paul H. Brookes Publishing Co.

Reid, D., & Schepis, M.M. (1986). Direct care staff training. In R.P. Barrett (Ed.), *Severe behavior disorders in the mentally retarded: Nondrug approaches to treatment.* New York: Plenum.

Rincover, A., & Devany, J. (1982). The application of sensory extinction procedures to self-injury. *Analysis and Intervention in Developmental Disabilities, 2,* 67–81.

Romanczyk, R.G. (in press). *Self-injurious behavior: Etiology and treatment.* New York: Plenum.

Romanczyk, R.G., Kistner, J.A., & Plienis, A. (1982). Self-stimulatory and self-injurious behavior: Etiology and treatment. In J.J. Steffen & P. Karoly (Eds.), *Advances in child behavior analysis and therapy: Autism and severe psychopathology.* Lexington, MA: D.C. Heath.

Sailor, W., Guess, D., Rutherford, G., & Baer, D.M. (1968). Control of tantrum behavior by operant techniques during experimental verbal training. *Journal of Applied Behavior Analysis, 1,* 237–243.

Salholz, E., & Hutchison, S. (1986, December 1). How to treat autistic kids: Is punishment the way? *Newsweek,* p. 82.

Santarcangelo, S., Dyer, D., & Luce, S.C. (1987). Generalized reduction of disruptive behavior in unsupervised settings through specific toy training. *Journal of The Association for Persons with Severe Handicaps, 12,* 38–44.

Schroeder, S.R., Mulick, J.A., & Rojahn, J. (1980). The definition, taxonomy, epidemiology, and ecology of self-injurious behavior. *Journal of Autism and Developmental Disorders, 10,* 417–432.

Schroeder, S.R., Schroeder, C.S., Smith, B., & Dalldorf, J. (1978). Prevalence of self-injurious behaviors in a large state facility for the retarded: A three-year follow-up. *Journal of Autism and Childhood Schizophrenia, 8,* 261–270.

Shapiro, E.S. (1986). Behavior modification: Self-control and cognitive procedures. In R.P. Barrett (Ed.), *Severe behavior disorders in the mentally retarded: Nondrug approaches to treatment.* New York: Plenum.

Singer, G.H.S., Singer, J., & Horner, R.H. (1987). Using pretask requests to increase the probability of compliance for students with severe disabilities. *Journal of The Association for Persons with Severe Handicaps, 12,* 287–291.

Solnick, J.V., Rincover, A., & Peterson, C.R. (1977). Some determinants of the reinforcing and punishing effects of timeout. *Journal of Applied Behavior Analysis, 10,* 415–424.

Sroufe, L.A., Steucher, H.V., & Stutzer, W. (1973). The functional significance of autistic behaviors for the psychotic child. *Journal of Abnormal Child Psychology, 1,* 225–240.

Staats, A.W. (1975). *Social behaviorism.* Chicago: Dorsey Press.

Tarpley, H.D., & Schroeder, S.R. (1979). Comparison of DRO and DRI on rate of suppression of self-injurious behavior. *American Journal of Mental Deficiency, 84,* 188–194.

Tate, B.G., & Baroff, G.S. (1966). Aversive control of self-injurious behavior in a psychotic boy. *Behaviour Research and Therapy, 4,* 281–287.

Touchette, P.E., MacDonald, R.F., & Langer, S.N. (1985). A scatter plot for identifying stimulus control of problem behavior. *Journal of Applied Behavior Analysis, 18,* 343–351.

Voeltz, L.M. (1984). Program and curriculum innovations to prepare children for integration. In N. Certo, N. Haring, & R. York (Eds.), *Public school integration of severely handicapped students: Rational issues and progressive alternatives* (pp. 155–183). Baltimore: Paul H. Brookes Publishing Co.

Voeltz, L.M., & Evans, I.M. (1982). The assessment of behavioral interrelationships in child behavior therapy. *Behavioral Assessment, 4,* 131–165.

Voeltz, L.M., & Evans, I.M. (1983). Educational validity: Procedures to evaluate outcomes in programs for severely handicapped learners. *Journal of The Association for the Severely Handicapped, 8,* 3–15.

Voeltz, L.M., Evans, I.M., Derer, K.R., & Hanashiro, R. (1983). Targeting excess behavior for change: A clinical decision model for selecting priority goals in educational contexts. *Child and Family Behavior Therapy, 5,* 17–35.

Voeltz, L.M., Wuerch, B.B., & Wilcox, B. (1982). Leisure and recreation: Preparation for independence, integration and self-fulfilment. In B. Wilcox & G.T. Bellamy, *Design of high-school programs for severely handicapped students.* (pp. 175–209). Baltimore: Paul H. Brookes Publishing Co.

Wahler, R.G. (1980). The insular mother: Her problems in parent-child treatment. *Journal of Applied Behavior Analysis, 13,* 207–219.

Walters, B. (1987, January 8). *20/20.* ABC television network.

Weeks, M., & Gaylord-Ross, R. (1981). Task difficulty and aberrant behavior in severely handicapped students *Journal of Applied Behavior Analysis, 14,* 449–463.

Wehman, P., & Hill, J.W. (Eds.). (1985). *Competitive employment for persons with mental retardation.* Richmond: Virginia Commonwealth University.

Whitman, T., Scibak, J., & Reid, D. (1983). *Behavior modification with the severely and profoundly retarded: Research and application.* New York: Academic Press.

Witt, J.C., & Elliott, S.N. (1985). Acceptability of classroom management strategies. In T.R. Kratochwill (Ed.), *Advances in school psychology* (Vol. 4). Hillsdale, NJ: Lawrence Erlbaum.

Wolfensberger, W. (1983). Social role valorization: A proposed new term for the principle of normalization. *Mental Retardation, 21,* 234–239.

Wolpe, J. *Psychotherapy by reciprocal inhibition.* Stanford, CA: Stanford University Press.

Wuerch, B.B., & Voeltz, L.M. (1982). *Longitudinal leisure skills for severely handicapped learners.* Baltimore: Paul H. Brookes Publishing Co.

appendix

Blank Forms

Daily Log (Form 1)

Client name: _____   Date of week/date: _____
Log entry by: _____   Community experience: _____

Comment briefly on the day's events and the student's behavior. Note any incidents that occurred that seem important to you. Give your impressions regarding what the client enjoyed/did not enjoy and tasks on which he worked well.

1. Overall, what kind of day did the client have? (Circle one number only.)

1	2	3	4	5
Very bad day	Not okay	Not sure	Okay	Very good day

2. How well did he do on tasks while at work today? (Circle one number only.)

1	2	3	4	5
Very poor	Not okay	Not sure	Okay	Very good

3. How well did he do on community activities today? (Circle one number only.)

1	2	3	4	5
Very poor	Not okay	Not sure	Okay	Very good

Comment on any behavior that occurred that was positive or negative.

Incident Record (Form 2)

Briefly describe what was happening just before the behavior occurred:

What was the client doing:

Was anything being said to him, was he being prompted, or? (describe what):

Describe in detail what the client did and what happened through the incident:

Briefly describe what happened to the client immediately after the incident (Include any "consequences."):

SUMMARY DATA

Activity:

Location: Date/Day of week: Time:

Staff present when incident occurred:

Nonstaff present when incident occurred:

Why do you think the person behaved as he or she did and the incident occurred? (What do you think set him off?) This hypothesis should be written by the staff person who was most directly involved in the incident:

How do you think the behavior should have been prevented or handled, and how might it be prevented or handled next time? (Again, the person most directly involved in the incident should fill this out.):

Additional space for comments or anything left over from previous questions:

Who completed this record (name): _____

Behavioral Intervention Plan (Form 3)

Name: Date of birth:
Home address: Sex: Male Female
                                           Own guardian: Yes No
Residence phone: If no, name/relationship of guardian:
School/work program:
Address:
                                           Client role:
                                           Supervisor:
Transportation (describe):   Phone:
Client diagnosis/level:
Any medication (type/dosage):
Any restraint used (describe):

PART A: Referral Priorities

1. List problem behaviors, definition, summary of baseline frequency/duration in order of priority, from highest to lowest priority for change:

	BEHAVIOR	DEFINITION[a]	BASELINE DATA[b]	PREVIOUS TREATMENTS
1.				
2.				
3.				
4.				

[a]This definition must be objective and measurable.
[b]This should include information on frequency and duration.

2. Identify intervention target(s) from above list (top priority):

3. Rationale for priority decision:

(continued)

PART A (*continued*)

4. Persons to be involved in the Team Planning Meeting (NOTE: At least one direct service worker who knows the client well and is liked by the client must be present):

WHO	ROLE	RELATIONSHIP TO CLIENT[c]
1.	Case Manager	
2.	Chief Psychologist	
3.	Program Coordinator	
4.	Direct Service Worker	
5.	Speech, OT, PT, etc.	
6.	Job Coach/Supervisor	

[c] Why it is important for this person to participate in the meeting.

PART B: Intervention Design

1.0. *Short-Term Prevention*

    1.1. Environment/schedule/activity changes:

    1.2. Individualized prevention strategies:

    1.3. Specific distraction and interruption strategies:

2.0. *Immediate Consequences*

    2.1. Redirect instructions (behavior about to occur):

(continued)

PART B (*continued*)

    2.2.   Consequences (behavior has occurred):

    2.3.   Crisis management needed: YES   NO
           If YES, attach detailed description of procedures to be followed.

3.0. *Adaptive Alternatives*
    3.1.   Initial target replacement skill goal (instructional level and cue(s) corrections apply):

    3.2.   Long-term outcome replacement skill goal (rate/duration are normalized and natural cues/corrections apply):

4.0. *Long-Term Prevention*
    4.1.   Self-regulation goals:

    4.2.   Community integration goals:

    4.3.   Residential goals:

(*continued*)

PART B (*continued*)

    4.4.   Employment goals:

PART C: Informed Consent and Professional Review

1.   Level of review required:

2.   Consent required/obtained:

WHO?	NEEDED?	HOW OBTAINED?
Parent/Guardian	YES NO	
Self	YES NO	

PART D: Staff Training Needs

WHO	WHAT		BY WHEN
	INTERVENTION	EVALUATION	

PART E: List of Attachments

Always Required: 1.   Instructional program to teach replacement skills
                          2.   General guidelines for prevention
                          3.   Data collection forms/procedures

May be Required: 4.   Crisis management procedures (requires 5–8 also)
                          5.   Incident record form
                          6.   Signed informed consent form
                          7.   Summary of professional review
                          8.   Previous Treatments Summary (must be attached for any behavior that is regarded as Level I or Level II behavior).

Communicative Form Program Summary (Form 4)

Employee's name: Date:

Communication system (e.g., verbal, sign, communication board):

Target communication goal (describe each of the following objectively):
  A. Situation and natural cue(s)

  B. Communicative initiation or response from employee:
      1. Present negative behavior in situation:

      2. Target positive communicative behavior for this situation:

  C. Expected response by others (e.g., assistance, tangibles):
      1. Expected response to present negative behavior:

      2. Expected response to target positive communicative behavior:

  D. Staff/others expected to respond to employee:

Criteria for mastery:

Target date for mastery:

Person responsible for monitoring this program (must observe employee in situation at least daily):

Team review date (no later than 1 month after start date noted above):

Leisure Activity Selection Inventory (Form 5)

Student: _____   Date: _____   Completed by: _____

	Activity	Activity	Activity
Normalization: A concern for selecting activities that have social validity and that will facilitate normalized play and leisure behaviors, as well as provide opportunities for movement toward increasingly complex interactions.			
1. *Age Appropriateness.* Is this activity something a nonhandicapped peer would enjoy during free time?	yes no	yes no	yes
2. *Attraction.* Is this activity likely to promote interest of others who frequently are found in the youth's leisure time settings?	yes no	yes no	yes
3. *Environmental Flexibility.* Can this activity be used in a variety of potential leisure time situations on an individual and group basis?	yes no	yes no	yes
4. *Degree of Supervision.* Can the activity be used under varying degrees of caregiver supervision without major modifications?	yes no	yes no	yes
5. *Longitudinal Application.* Is use of the activity appropriate for both an adolescent and an adult?	yes no	yes no	yes
Individualization: Concerns related to meeting the unique and ever-changing needs and skills of handicapped youth.			
1. *Skill Level Flexibility.* Can the activity be adapted for low to high entry skill levels without major modifications?	yes no	yes no	yes
2. *Prosthetic Capabilities.* Can the activity be adapted to varying handicapping conditions (sensory, motor, behavior)?	yes no	yes no	yes
3. *Reinforcement Power.* Is the activity sufficiently novel or stimulating to maintain interest?	yes no	yes no	yes
Environmental: Concerns related to logistical and physical demands of leisure activities on current and future environments and free time situations.			
1. *Availability.* Is the activity available (or can it easily be made so) across the youth's leisure environments?	yes no	yes no	yes
2. *Durability.* Is the activity likely to last without need for major repair or replacement of parts for at least a year?	yes no	yes no	yes
3. *Safety.* Is the activity safe, i.e., would not pose a serious threat to or harm the handicapped youth, others, or the environment if abused or used inappropriately?	yes no	yes no	yes
4. *Noxiousness.* Is the activity not likely to be overly noxious (noisy, space consuming, distracting) to others in the youth's leisure environments?	yes no	yes no	yes
5. *Expense.* Is the cost of the activity reasonable? That is, is it likely to be used for multiple purposes?	yes no	yes no	yes
Area of Concern Scores 1. Normalization 2. Individualization 3. Environmental	|||	|||	|||
Total Activity Score			

(From Wuerch & Voeltz, 1982, p. 181; reprinted by permission.)

Student: _____

Student Interest Inventory (Form 6)

	Activity							
	Date							
	Rater							

Instructions: *For each activity, answer each of the questions below by placing the number of the description that best matches the child's behavior in the appropriate box for that activity.*

A. For this child's usual level of interest in play materials, he or she is: 1. Not as interested as usual 2. About as interested as usual 3. More interested than usual								
B. For this child's usual level of physical interaction with materials (pushing control buttons, turning knobs, putting things together, etc.), he or she is: 1. Not as busy as usual 2. About as busy as usual 3. Busier than usual								
C. For this child's usual "affective" behaviors (smiling, signs of enjoyment, etc.), he or she seems to be: 1. Enjoying this less than usual 2. Showing about the same amount of enjoyment as usual 3. Enjoying this more than usual								
D. For this child's usual level of "looking" or "visual regard" of an activity, object, or person, he or she is: 1. Not looking as much as usual 2. Looking as much as usual 3. Looking more often or longer than usual								
E. Compared to this child's usual behavior during a short period of time with minimal supervision, he or she is: 1. Engaging in more negative behavior than usual 2. Engaging in about the same amount of negative behavior as usual 3. Engaging in less negative (or off-task) behavior than usual								
Activity Interest Scores: *Total the numbers in each column*								

(From Wuerch & Voeltz, 1982, p. 182; reprinted by permission.)

Medication Data Collection/Communication (Form 7)

Patient Information   Name: _____ Birth Date: _____ C.A.: _____ School: _____

Case Manager/Teacher: _____ Physician: _____   **DATA COLLECTION MODE**

MEDICATION: _____ DATE INITIATED: _____   F = Frequency recording
D = Duration recording
DOSAGE: (a) _____ (b) _____ (c) _____   M = Momentary time sampling

ADMIN. INTERVAL: (a) _____ (b) _____ (c) _____

Date of Observation																					
Time of Observation	Start																				
	Finish																				
Admin. Interval																					
Dosage																					
Time most recent admin.																					
BEHAVIORS 1.																					
2.																					
3.																					
4.																					

Description of Target Behaviors   *Physician Comments:*

1.

2.

3.   *Observer Comments:*

4.

(From Evans & Meyer, 1985, p. 157; reprinted by permission.)

Community and Leisure Involvement (Form 8)

For the activities listed below, please fill in the requested information *to the best of your knowledge.*

Activity	Use	Access (check one)				Level of independence/ supervision			Do you see this as a goal for this person?		
	Estimate no. of times last month	Accessible		Restrictive	Most restrictive						
		Walking distance	Easy public transportation	Inconvenient or too far to use often without staff help	Virtually no access unless staff arranges	Does without staff help (alone or with friends)	Needs some help from staff	Needs much help/ supervision from staff	Yes	No	Not sure
1. General shopping (not groceries)											
2. Grocery shopping											
3. Using public transportation											
4. Banking											
5. Visiting fast food restaurant											
6. Visiting sit-down restaurant											
7. Attending community gym, swimming pool, fitness facility											

(continued)

Activity	Use — Estimate no. of times last month	Access (check one)			Level of independence/supervision			Do you see this as a goal for this person?		
		Accessible — Walking distance	Accessible — Easy public transportation	Restrictive — Inconvenient or too far to use often without staff help	Most restrictive — Virtually no access unless staff arranges	Does without staff help (alone or with friends)	Needs some help from staff	Needs much help/supervision from staff	Yes	No	Not sure
8. Attending community college or adult education classes or programs											
9. Visiting post office											
10. Attending house of worship											
11. Attending concert, play, movie											
12. Attending sporting events (as spectator)											
13. Visiting bowling alley, skating rink, video arcade											

(continued)

14. Touring museum, art gallery, or other tourist attraction							
15. Walking in the neighborhood							
16. Visiting friend's house							
17. Visiting with family							
18. Talking on the telephone							
19. Visiting dentist/ doctor (health care)							
20. Having hair cut and/or styled at hair salon or barbershop							
21. Using community library							
22. Attending dances (non-alcoholic setting)							
23. Attending bar or discotheque (alcohol served)							
24. Having picnic or camping							
25. Visiting park or zoo							

(continued)

Activity	Use: Estimate no. of times last month	Access (check one) — Accessible: Walking distance	Accessible: Easy public transportation	Restrictive: Inconvenient or too far to use often without staff help	Most restrictive: Virtually no access unless staff arranges	Level of independence/supervision: Does without staff help (alone or with friends)	Needs some help from staff	Needs much help/supervision from staff	Do you see this as a goal for this person? Yes	No	Not sure
26. Entertaining guests											
27. Dating											
28. Keeping social service/welfare appointment											
29. Going to laundromat or dry cleaner											
30. Involvement in organized special activity or club (e.g., Toastmasters)											
31. Attending community education programs, hobby classes, private lessons, and so forth.											

Individual Decision-Making Evaluation Checklist (Form 9)

For each item, check only the one response that best matches the present choice options available to this client.

Does he or she choose:	Most restrictive: No choices		Restrictive choices	Appropriate choices
	No opportunity to observe	Decision does not seem appropriate for this person	Needs help with this decision or will do this inappropriately	Yes, does make this decision reasonably, appropriately
1. What to wear				
2. How to comb/style hair				
3. Activities on a day off (e.g., Saturday or vacation day)				
4. To occasionally sleep in on day off				
5. What T.V. show to watch				
6. What radio station/type of music to listen to				
7. What chores he or she is assigned at home				
8. Whether to do a chore right away or do it later (e.g., dishes)				
9. To invite a friend to do something together				
10. To invite a friend to visit				
11. What to eat for a meal or snack				
12. How to spend money that is not allocated for expenses				
13. To exercise				
14. To diet for weight control				
15. To have a drink (e.g., beer, wine)				
16. To smoke				
17. To have a friendship				
18. To have a girlfrield or boyfriend				
19. To have sexual relations				
20. To masturbate in privacy				
21. What form of birth control to use				

(continued)

Does he or she choose:	Most restrictive: No choices		Restrictive choices	Appropriate choices
	No opportunity to observe	Decision does not seem appropriate for this person	Needs help with this decision or will do this inappropriately	Yes, does make this decision reasonably, appropriately
22. Whether to agree to or say no to participation in a group activity				
23. What clothes to buy				
24. Whom he or she wants to live with				
25. When to visit family				
26. To make a phone call to a friend or family member				
27. Whether to stay up later than or go to bed earlier than the usual time				
28. What job he or she wants to have or what work he or she wants to do				
29. To ask permission to take a sick day (stay home from work) when not feeling well				
30. What to do/where to go on vacation				
31. Whether or not he or she can own a pet				
32. His or her own dentist/ physician				
33. Whether or not he or she receives therapy services (e.g., speech, occupational therapy, etc.)				
34. What type/style of adaptive equipment or prosthetic devices he or she utilizes (e.g., wheelchair, braces, etc.)				
35. What form of augmentative communication system or devices he or she utilizes (e.g., signing, electronic board, etc.)				

Total Number of Most Restrictive Choices (cols. 1–2): _____

Total Number of Restricted Choices (col. 3): _____

Total Number of Appropriate Choices (col. 4): _____

Client Outcome Rating (Form 10)

Instructions: Complete this section by referring to the *most integrated* domain that this person experiences. For example, if the individual lives in a large ICF/MR but works at a fast food restaurant, think about his or her performance at the restaurant when you fill in ratings.

1. How do you rate this person's *overall performance on tasks* he or she is expected to do (on the job, around the house, etc.)?

1	2	3	4	5	6	7
Totally inadequate			It varies—about half and half			Exceptionally good performance

2. How do you rate this person's *general behavior* (adjustment, work habits, etc.)?

1	2	3	4	5	6	7
Totally dissatisfied with his or her behavior			It varies—about half and half			Completely satisfied with his or her behavior

3. Are this person's *social interactions with co-workers and peers* positive and appropriate?

1	2	3	4	5	6	7
Almost never			It varies—about half and half			Almost always

4. Are this person's *social interactions with supervisors* positive and appropriate?

1	2	3	4	5	6	7
Almost never			It varies—about half and half			Almost always

5. Are this person's *social interactions with persons in the general community* positive and appropriate?

1	2	3	4	5	6	7
Almost never			It varies—about half and half			Almost always

6. In comparison to other persons with similar disabilities whom you know, how well is this person doing overall?

1	2	3	4	5	6	7
Not nearly as well as others with similar disabilities			It varies—about half and half			Much better than others with similar disabilities

(continued)

7. Does this person seem to like the work and/or activities he or she does during the day?

1	2	3	4	5	6	7
Not at all			It varies—about half and half			Very much

8. Does this person seem to like being in the community, around persons who are not disabled?

1	2	3	4	5	6	7
Not at all			It varies—about half and half			Very much

9. Does this person seem to like the people at his or her job site or day activity?

1	2	3	4	5	6	7
Not at all			It varies—about half and half			Very much

10. Does this person seem to be motivated to do his or her share?

1	2	3	4	5	6	7
Not at all			It varies—about half and half			Very much

11. When things do go wrong, does this person manage to recover within a reasonable period of time and go back to work or join the activities again in a positive way?

1	2	3	4	5	6	7
Almost never			It varies—about half and half			Almost always

The environment that I used as a referent to complete this section for this person was:

Total score: _____

High score:	55–77
Moderate score:	33–54
Low score:	11–32

Index